To Tom,

 – a bit of background
research for your new
job.

   – from Jim, Di &
   Rosie.

      Xmas '95.

LEFT FOOT FORWARD

LEFT FOOT FORWARD

A Year in the Life of a
Journeyman Footballer

Garry Nelson

HEADLINE

First published in 1995
by HEADLINE BOOK PUBLISHING

10 9 8 7 6 5

British Library Cataloguing in Publication Data

Nelson, Garry
    Left Foot Forward: Year in the Life of a
    Journeyman Footballer
    I. Title
    796.334092

    ISBN 0-7472-1575-8

Typeset by Keyboard Services, Luton, Beds

Printed and bound in Great Britain by
Mackays of Chatham PLC, Chatham, Kent

HEADLINE BOOK PUBLISHING
A division of Hodder Headline PLC
338 Euston Road
London NW1 3BH

CONTENTS

INTRODUCTION

When once in a longish while I've managed to have a good moment or two out on the park, the Charlton fans – or, as it used to be, the Plymouth or Brighton fans – will break into the semi-spontaneous, half-orchestrated song: 'One Garry Nelson, there's only one Garry Nelson.'

I'm always grateful. If it happens while we're warming up (and everyone, despite their better judgment, is still expecting the best), I'll always acknowledge the gesture. Even though I know that it's partly a knee-jerk reaction prompting the singing; even though I know that, once the game has started and if I'm having a 'mare, half the choir will be badmouthing me in flat-out derision, I'll take a moment to salute the supporters back. For that moment, while all is still eager anticipation, the compliment is well meant. It's also, finally, wide of the mark on at least two major counts.

At first glance – or, rather, hearing – it works well. The four syllables of my two names have the same even cadence as Kevin Keegan's. They dovetail into the song's rhythm far better than such longer or shorter or more irregularly sprung names as Andrei Kanchelskis, Ian Rush, Roberto Baggio, Ally McCoist or Marco Van Basten.

But, when you're talking pure football, the only advantage Garry Nelson has over players of such calibre is this nominal one. These players, all forwards like myself, are possessed of technical skills and achievement that I have long since given up any pretence of matching. They and many, many who play alongside and against them are literally out of my league. They have spent the bulk of their careers playing at levels that I can no longer aspire to. I am no Kevin Keegan. I've never imagined that I was.

So let me issue an immediate warning. This book won't give you any indication of what it's like to be a superstar. It won't convey to you what it's like to power-steer your Lamborghini down the fast lane of the Auto del Sol. It won't give you the vicarious kick of knowing what it feels like to brief a top jockey on what sort of a race you want him to give the horse you've bred and trained yourself. It won't serve as a blueprint on orchestrating a board-room coup at the famous club for whom you once scored goal after goal. I'm not a star and this isn't that kind of read.

If you're looking for a book that will give you the (cheap) thrill of brushing shoulders with soccer's famous and high and mighty, then do yourself an instant favour. Lay this one aside.

It simply isn't true, you see, that there is only one Garry Nelson. Currently there are hundreds in the English game. There always have been. Over the years there have been tens of thousands. No, of course they haven't all had those four syllables as their identifying label. Nor have they all been forwards or left-sided midfielders. They've played in every position. But goalkeeper, centre-back or striker, every one has got so far and no further. Every one has reached levels of skill and competency lifting him into the ranks of the good, competent pro footballer. Sometimes with just one club, more usually through a series of up, down and sideways transfers, countless have clocked up their 400, their 600 league appearances. As have I. I sometimes feel that I've played against them all. I've left so many of them for dead at this moment; been left floundering in the wake of so many the next.

Let me not fall into the sin of mock-modesty; of that low-profile 'I could have been a contender' romanticism. Put a ball at my feet and I'm no mug. I've come to regret the reputation I've built up for being a '110 per cent, run 'til his legs turn to water' merchant. I think it's tended to camouflage the fact that I can play a bit. Put me on in a Sunday league game and, as would any full-time pro, I'll make the other twenty-one look like waxworks on the point of melting.

With my 700th first-class appearance coming over the horizon

2

I'm a member of quite a select club – irrespective of whose books I'm currently on. OK – I'm somewhere in the middle of the violin section and not the virtuoso out there in the spotlight, but I'm playing to standards millions envy and not so many achieve. And I think that among my rank-and-file team-mates, and with our counterparts in all the other sides we play against, there's a common, unspoken bond that derives from the satisfaction of knowing this. We're all members of this club and, yes, the qualification requirements are pretty strict.

At the Valley these days the teams take the field to a rather tacky, pop version of Copeland's 'Fanfare For The Common Man'. Tacky but, by and large, apt. Not too many superstars run out there these days. One of the motives behind my writing this book has been to try to offer a grateful tip of my hand to my fellow professionals; to offer a salute of sorts to the everyday player. I've tried, to coin a cliché, to tell it like it was – or, at any rate, how it seemed to me at the time.

Necessarily, I've had to do this looking outward from my own career. It is the one uncontaminated source of data at my disposal. But I've tried to make a virtue of this necessity; tried to convey the typical and general through my own personal experience. In this respect it's an advantage not to have been a superstar – whatever the fans might sing.

On which unharmonious notes there's another way – the profoundest of all – in which their 'One Garry Nelson' is untrue. The person singled out there is a footballer the fans see, on average, a couple of hours a week three or four times a month. A footballer. Not a person. A few public hours a month don't go far towards defining the private individual. The fans applauding the neat one-two, the snap shot going close from twenty-odd yards, don't stop to consider the man who on a bad night, thinking his first-class career is almost at its end, lies awake at night worrying about his mortgage. But I'm inside him and I do. I know how he cares about his family; I know about his determination to protect and cherish them, to see his daughter and son growing up fulfilled, their own potential realised in ways *they* would like it to be realised. Yes, I know. These are universal feelings. My having

3

them puts me in the same bracket as millions. But what about the Garry Nelson, the Essex man proud of his Merseyside roots? The Garry Nelson who's a partner in a modestly successful cottage industry? The Garry Nelson interested in local education? The Garry Nelson with a growing interest in raising camellias; in bettering the way football is marketed in the UK?

One Garry Nelson? Rubbish. Inside me there are dozens of Garry Nelsons. Most of them, beyond the odd nod or two in their direction, I haven't really met up with yet. It may be that the early retirement all footballers experience will prove a (well enough disguised) blessing. It may oblige me to explore some of those so far neglected sides of my nature and get to know myself better. I certainly intend to try.

This is another reason why I've written all these pages. As the gates start to close on my playing career, it's a good time to take stock. It may seem an indulgence that I've pushed the exercise so far forward as to publish the end result. But you are under no obligation to buy or go on reading. If you do, though, and you're a fan, I'm pretty sure I can give you some backstage insights into the running of the game and draw back a curtain or two on some of its less often scrutinised corners.

I would hope that these insights will add to your appreciation of what you see out there on the park. Which would certainly be to my advantage. There are days when if you're not a Shearer or Simone, a Sosa or Signori, you need all the understanding you can get.

JUNE

Sunday 5 June

Sixty seconds into the second half of Charlton's March 1994 sixth round FA Cup tie at Old Trafford, goalkeeper John Vaughan made a reflex save that, in itself, might have won him the 'Man of the Match' award. Sixty-three seconds into the half he was turning to pick the ball out of the net. Reacting quicker than anyone else, Mark Hughes had latched on to the rebound his close-range thunderbolt had produced and, with typically ferocious control, bludgeoned the ball back from close to the by-line through the narrowest of gaps.

The inch-perfect finish put United one up. It also, the hard truth is, pulled the plug on Charlton's entire season.

Minutes earlier in the half-time changing room we had all but been hugging ourselves with glee. Outplayed though we'd clearly been, we had never quite lost our shape. We'd hung on to keep the game goalless. Then had come what we'd thought was the turning point.

A speculative boot of a clearance had found Kim Grant unmarked just inside a deserted United half. He'd turned for goal. Kim's outstanding asset is speed. Surely there was every chance that ... Thunk! Out of nowhere, certainly out of his tree and nearer the halfway than his own goal line, Peter Schmeichel had launched himself at Kim like a feet-first human cannon-ball. Upshot was the entire catalogue of keeper's fouls rolled into one. As Kim, alive at the last instant to the airborne threat to his life, fired off a long-range shot, Schmeichel beat it down with his hands. All Charlton fans swear the shot was goalward bound but no one will ever be sure – least of all Kim. His follow-through was not yet completed when the impact of Schmeichel's long-jumper's landing sent him disorientatedly somersaulting through the air. The keeper's protests to the referee were token and academic. Panic rather than malice had jet-propelled him but, as the half-time whistle blew, United were down to ten men.

Hence our guarded euphoria. All season we had been sitting comfortably in a play-off spot in the First Division. With the advantage of an extra man, surely we could force a draw. A replay at the Valley would be a money-spinner and all things were possible: we'd already done for Blackburn in an earlier round – with ground advantage we might even . . .

Peter Schmeichel's sending off was not the turning point. Mark Hughes' goal was. It galvanised United's ten into what may have been their finest performance of the season. With Andrei Kanchelskis outstanding – he twice scorched through our defence to extend their lead; his work-rate in covering back was prodigious – United produced a masterly display of counter-attacking football as we tried to chase the game. We never totally fell apart. We even got a goal back. But there could be no question as to who were grown-ups and who also-rans.

On the coach back south we were held up by a fatal accident on the motorway. It seemed a fitting part and parcel to our day. By now we all felt like victims ourselves. Mark Hughes' strike had gone to our hearts and reminded us we were vulnerable.

And so it proved. Overnight our league form deserted us. We plummeted down the table as we recorded eleven losses out of thirteen starts.

It wasn't random, I knew very well, that the memory of that goal had come back to me so vividly at this precise moment. I might be sitting 30,000 feet above the Atlantic, one of umpteen passengers crammed aboard a west-bound holiday charter flight, but that was precisely why. I was off duty. The season disastrously concluded, I could finally afford to confront the significance of that hinge moment. Previously, while, on paper anyway, all was still to play for, I'd made a conscious effort to wipe the moment from my memory. Unsuccessfully. Even though I refused to allow it full focus, it was constantly registering somewhere on the edge of my mind's eye. I tried to suppress it by telling myself it was just one of the many downs you're bound to experience in a see-saw season. And I reckon I wasn't the only one. I suspect from the way none of the other lads referred to it during training, on the away coach trips, warming up, they, too, were pretending to themselves it was just a routine goal against.

But now, the flight droning on, the cabin's unnatural air pressure making me feel slightly uncomfortable, Carole and the kids with headsets on watching the formula movie I'd given up on, there was no point in denying what Mark Hughes' flash of brilliance had meant for us all long-term. And for me especially.

Southend, Swindon, Plymouth, Brighton, Charlton – all those clubs, all those years, and, First or Premiership, I had never played in the top division. If Charlton *had* managed promotion, then the coming season I might finally have been running out at Anfield and Villa Park and White Hart Lane ... If! The most commonly used word in football.

Well, not to grieve. I reached for my own headset. Second-hand though the silent movie might be, watching it was a better option than sitting feeling sorry for myself. Yes, always look on the bright side. At bottom you could only have boundless admiration for Mark Hughes' talent and I had shared a pitch with him. And back home was a programme on which my name was printed alongside Ryan Giggs'. That was something to show the grandchildren. I put the headphones on. I was on holiday now. I'd maybe start a little holiday diary so we'd have a record of our break in years to come. One thing was for sure. I was going to forget all about football for the next two weeks. Fat chance!

Wednesday 8 June

A couple of days into our Great American Adventure now and getting over the culture shock – not very great actually – of being first-time visitors to the States. Or, more precisely, Orlando in Florida.

At ten and seven, Carly and Christopher are the perfect age to exploit and be exploited by this 'Can I?' capital of the world. In a few years' time they'll be in 'Don't want to go there with you' mode and everything Disney will well and truly have lost its synthetically magic appeal. But right now their eyes are out on stalks and the thing for Carole and me to do is go with their flow and see it all through those same awe-struck eyes.

To that end we've already negotiated our passes for Sea-World, Universal Studios and a five-day 'see everything, do everything' Disney pass. The family Nelson left the hugely impressive Florida Mall over $1,000 lighter. At an average of around $300 a pass per person, the star Orlando attractions must generate nearly as much revenue as your average Blackburn Rover. The kids are under orders to get every cent of my money's worth out of it all.

As I'm sure, once entered into the local spirit of things, will we. There's no question, after all, that the workmanship and ingenuity that've gone into projects like the Magic Kingdom and Typhoon Lagoon are pretty impressive. And every now and then they throw in a bit of tongue-in-cheek wit that's a genuine laugh. Wish Charlton's set pieces had been half as good last season.

Thursday 9 June

After Sea-World it's a case of the small world. Who should we run into slap bang in the middle of the Florida Mall but Charlton skipper Alan McLeary and his family. Distinct embarrassment from the two soccer-playing macho men to come across each other not on the high board at the pool or way out on our surf boards but meekly bringing up the rear on family shopping expeditions. What's more, neither of us had any idea we'd both be out here at the same time. So much for changing-room communication. We didn't extend the post-mortem on the gut-wrenching collapse of Charlton's past season – done all that already through an alcoholic haze (and at the club's expense) in Tenerife. We did discuss the mind-blowing Orlando humidity – the one thing down here I don't think I'd ever get used to. Any Irish player able to give a sample after the Italy game should be put on the first plane back home for not trying.

Snap! Today in Fievel's Playground I bumped into another

central defender, Dave Higgins of Tranmere. Not literally, for once. Made a nice change to stand chatting without him trying to kick lumps out of me. He seemed reasonably philosophic about Tranmere missing out on promotion after making it into the play-offs as the in-form team. Both of us were sorry it's Leicester who are going up. They're not exactly a flair team who are a delight to watch. But – eat your heart out, Swindon – at least they've got a bit of money to buy in the talent that, as they'll hope, will provide anti-relegation insurance.

Saturday 11 June

Meeting today not by chance but prior arrangement. Chris Carter, Swindon heating oil entrepreneur extraordinaire and a good mate, arrived. He's actually my real live lucky charm. We met first in my Swindon days when I was a customer and he was not only a flat-out Swindon fan but a dedicated follower of football generally. After I moved on he more than kept in touch. He was there both times when I played in promotion-clinching games for Plymouth and Brighton and I always seem to have one of my good days when he's in the crowd.

Chris is full of news right now. First was his up-to-the-minute account of the penalties the FA have socked Tottenham with.

As a Swindon fan, Chris is seething underneath his normal good spirits. He reckons Spurs should have got what Swindon got – out-and-out relegation. But would we have a Football League if that principle was consistently applied? The World Cup will be kicking off in a week's time and you can bet your bottom dollar – which I seem to be fast approaching – that naive will be the 'in' word again. It's hard to think of Alan Sugar as naive but perhaps he is. Or was it a pre-emptive confession? Certainly it's only the tip of the iceberg. In football it's not only the Nelsons who have learned the virtues of turning a blind eye at the right time. Me, though, as much as anyone probably.

As a PFA rep as well as an individual player, I've had more than my share of insights into the bungs and backhanders that go along with the backheels. It's not always been to my advantage when it's come to the team sheet.

9

In which regard, Chris's other news was a bit closer to home and, being honest, a lot more food for thought. Charlton are on the point of selling Scott Minto (a full England cap for Scott is only a matter of time) and Darren Pitcher. Between the two the club should cop well over a million. A good half of that will go on paying the electricity bill and further ground improvements, but there'll be money besides to spend on the squad-strengthening players they didn't buy six months ago to help clinch promotion. Chris rolled out a list of names as long as one of Carl Leaburn's legs – every one rumoured to be in negotiation with Charlton: Nicky Banger, Tony Adcock, Paul Williams, Tony Cascarino, David Whyte, Steve Claridge, John Kerr, Tom Cobbley ... A real holiday pick-me-up. All of them are strikers. OK, it's rumour rather than fact and you can probably divide the list by two. But the truth is that ever since I joined Charlton in August '91 I've had talk of needing/buying a thirty-goal-a-season, go-for-it striker hanging over me.

'Look on the bright side, Garry,' Chris said. 'You and Maradona are exactly the same age.'

'Yeah,' I said. 'We've got one thing in common – and it's not the same chemist.'

Sunday 12 June

As hard to come by as food with a bit of character is anything resembling native wit. I've been gobsmacked by how Americans seem completely unable to pick up on flip, off-the-wall, throw-away jokes. I thought this was the land of city-slicker one-liners, but it's as if they can't be sure it's OK to laugh unless one of those awful canned laugh-tracks gives them the go-ahead. Take Mary-Beth for instance. Thirty-something trying too hard to play twenty-three, Mary-Beth is one of the waitresses who works the tables and recliners around the Delta-Orlando's pool. She weaves in and out like a mobile, silicate-valleyed, Statue of Liberty carrying a tray the size of a centre circle, and even more stacked than she is, up on one shoulder. As she came past our table I couldn't resist it. I asked her the time. She stopped and with great effort put the tray down.

'Twenty after one,' she said.

'Thanks, love,' I said. 'That's what I make it too.'

'You're welcome,' she said and levered the tray back up past her overhang. Dedicated? Oblivious? Strike one.

Monday 13 June

What with the family and footballing Brits, I've not chatted to as many Americans as I would have liked but I had an interesting encounter today. Chris included, we were all sitting around the pool talking when a middle-aged American intervened with a 'Pardon my interrupting, but I just find your accents fascinating – where are you folks all from' line. We went through the bit about not being Australian and exchanged friendly enough small talk and then Chris let out that I was a professional soccer player.

Something came into the American's eyes and he seemed to take on some kind of wary respect for me.

'Say, then, you must be seriously rich,' he said. I pointed out that this wasn't exactly the case. I was thinking, in fact, we might well not be able to afford a holiday like this ever again. He didn't, I think, believe me. I think it upset him I was being mock-modest. And I came to understand it, actually.

The newspapers and TV here have been carrying the story of a Chicago Cubs baseball star, Ryne Sandberg, a nine-time Golden Gloves winner who has just announced his premature retirement as a player. It's been calculated he's turning his back on about $13,000,000 in wages and sponsorship deals. Sandberg's stated reason for quitting is that his heart isn't in it any more – he's lost his motivation and so feels he's not delivering his best. A pretty classy attitude. But noble gestures of renunciation don't look quite so noble when they come from a man who's already a dollar millionaire and can count on earning two more over the next four years doing PR stuff.

I wonder if anyone pitches or hits his best when he's aware that sort of money is riding on his shoulders all the way to the bank? Which still doesn't explain why great players like Baresi or Baggio, who clearly don't need to do another day's work in their lives from a money point of view, still keep turning in world-class

11

performances. Pride? The dream of playing one totally perfect game? Maybe that's the secret of a superstar.

Cheered myself by taking it out on Mary-Beth again.

'Got the time, love?'

'Five of one.'

'Check.'

'You're welcome.'

Strike two!

Wednesday 15 June

The World Cup kicks off in two days' time and today the flags of all the competing nations are fluttering on the lamp-posts lining Orlando's main tourist drag, International Drive. It's a gesture – but a pretty token one, I'd have to say. Although Orlando is one of the tournament venues, so far I've clocked fewer obvious fans – about twenty, maybe – than qualifying teams. You can buy all the predictable spin-off/rip-off souvenir stuff in the shops but it's not being pushed any more than the baseball, basketball, American football and this is what Agassi's using today goodies. The Americans have a very useful side in the finals, but I wonder how many of their fellow-countrymen know as much.

I think it's significant that the American who thought I must be 'seriously rich' never put two and two together to deduce (wrongly but logically) that I was in Orlando for the World Cup. He just didn't seem to be aware of it. It's in America, of course, because of the *worldwide* TV coverage it's going to get (perfect prime-time scheduling for Europe) with all those commercial break opportunities for the multi-nationals.

I'm willing to bet all the bonuses I'll be copping this coming season – even some serious money – that there's no way that, as a result of this World Cup, soccer gets off the ground as a major spectator and participant sport in the USA. The land that invented instant coffee wants instant results, instant world champion status. Baseball's 'World Series' isn't anything of the kind, of course – just ask the Cubans! – but so long as the event can carry that artificial label, every good old boy can go on believing the home of the Braves is the land of world beaters. Because the World

Cup is exactly what it claims to be, and whoever does win it in '94 it certainly won't be the American side, soccer/football is going to resist all the commercial efforts to catapult it into the big bucks stateside. It will remain the passion of the ethnic minorities and the 'safe' game that middle-class Wasp kids are allowed to play before they're considered mature and tough enough to play American football. For this tournament they're covering over the artificial surfaces of some of the stadiums with real grass. That's pretty symbolic. Staging the World Cup over here is an artificial, and therefore cynical, exercise and you've got to feel that the first and last object of the exercise is to make FIFA as much money as possible. If the temperatures stay up in the nineties where they are now, the matches down here are going to be as much about sweat glands as they are about skill on the ball.

Triumph for me, though. Struck out Mary-Beth.

'Watch this,' I said to Chris as she came swaying towards us with her loaded tray. 'Got the time, love?'

'Sure do.'

Down tray, slow look at watch.

'I have a quarter after one . . .'

Changing-room level, I know, but the fifteen per cent tips for all of the people all of the time rankles.

Friday 17 June

What a day! But not on account of the opening World Cup game. Germany–Bolivia was shown live on American TV, but I think you can get an idea of how your average American was supposed to respond from the fact that CNN only gave thirty seconds of screen time to it and that to cover President Clinton performing the opening ceremony. He must have got a surprise at the size of the ball he was supposed to throw out. I don't suppose he played much soccer at Oxford. It's a contact sport and he might have got hurt.

The World Cup placed nowhere today. It was upstaged by American football colliding with Hollywood. The TV lenses have been unblinkingly glued to the O.J. Simpson affair. How nice of America to keep this bit of real-life drama-doc as our end-of-holiday cabaret. Unbelievable. Freeway chase, gun to own head in back of car, thousands lining path rooting for him. Only things missing were cheerleaders and Leslie Nielsen making the collar. In fact, it's so unbelievable the mind rejects it. It's comic-strip cliché. American dream turned into American tragedy. And then TV-trial soap. It's six corny movies rolled into one so that all the millions of words that will now follow are already too predictable. Moral here for me. No way I was ever going to be nominated to the All-American Soccer Hall of Fame. No Hollywood contracts for me. I haven't been man of the match since Bryant and May went out of business. And just as well out of it, it seems.

Sunday 19 June

When the glossy ads sell you Florida in a big way they don't mention the tropical storms that can tear their 'Paradise' to ear-splitting shreds in seconds. They don't mention the mosquitoes either. Carole and the kids were having an early night before departure day, so I sat outside by the pool. Had to make myself suitably repellant first though ('Shouldn't have reckoned that'd be necessary, Nelse, haw haw!'). Bad move. Always a mistake at the end of a great holiday to sit outdoors alone on a warm night. Soon started feeling sorry for myself. There are mental mosquitoes too. I wasn't Ryne Sandberg or O.J. Simpson but Garry Nelson.

I'd as near as dammit 650 first team games to my credit but I'd never played in the top division and I was thirty-three years old. Tomorrow I'd be flying not only home but back to almost certainly my last season in the game. Quite likely not as a first team player. Apart from the little matter of my one-year contract expiring in June '95, there was the common knowledge that Charlton, notoriously a low-scoring side, were in the market for a do-the-business striker to play up alongside Carl Leaburn. Very reassuring and morale-boosting.

Last season I was in and out of the Charlton first team more often than a scalpel at work on a Gascoigne knee. The positional changes made in the effort to stop our slide down the table always involved me. I didn't know for sure whether I'd be running out at Ewood Park and Old Trafford in the Cup until the eleventh and a half hour.

14

Thirty-three. In almost any other job, instead of staring retirement in the face I'd be just hitting my full stride. If I'd taken up the place I'd had at Loughborough, I'd probably be head of a school department now. Or would I have moved sideways into computer programming or import-export or local government? Eight 'O' levels and three 'A's isn't a bad basis for a 'respectable', proper job. Brain surgery, perhaps.

Thing is, if Charlton hadn't blown it this past year I would have had the chance of playing in the top division. My last chance, probably. And it could have been. We were on top of the so-called First Division and thereabouts – well in the play-off zone – for close to three-quarters of the season. Then we got the yips. Miles of territorial domination but our hitherto best-in-league defence leaking silly goals and nothing like enough going in at the other end. The worst losing trot in my whole career – eleven losses out of thirteen starts.

Why? Everyone thought they were doing the same things, displaying the same talents, they'd been coming up with when we were getting results. It couldn't be down to sheer luck – or could it? The feeling that our season's luck had been dished out to us in two lumps, all good at first and then all bad, became an unspoken superstition.

Probably we were trying too hard to make things happen and freezing on the ball. Darren Pitcher's great mid-season form fell away. Trying to have their cake and eat it, the Board hoped for promotion anyway and kept what money they had for ground improvements and not on buying team-strengthening players. Not a totally irrational strategy, be it said, and, had it succeeded, the directors would have been hailed as geniuses. But it didn't. It comprehensively failed. In fairness, approaches were made to a number of players known to be up for grabs. But Charlton didn't have the wherewithal to offer contracts that grabbed hard enough. We emerged from the transfer deadline chase with absolutely zilch.

I think we were tactically sterile, too. Irrespective of how the opposition lined up, we always played 4-4-2. When we were chasing the game with twenty minutes left the substitution was

15

always one forward for another – never a forward for a defender so we could give it a go with three playing up front. When you badly miss out after promising so much, it's a real downer. People look around at others to put the blame on. The old man is an obvious target. If you're losing with twenty minutes to go and they take you off, you usually get a bit of a clap from the fans but you don't have to be too bright to work out that somebody somewhere reckons you're not doing the job you're getting paid for.

Ironically, I emerged from Charlton's nosedive with as much credit as anyone. I got the ball in the net more consistently than in the earlier part of the season and beat the keeper only to hit the woodwork several times more. Against Peterborough (on St George's Day but I don't think they'll be renaming it) I hit the first hat trick of my fifteen-season career. (Don't know whether that's a statistic to be proud or ashamed of.) Hand on heart, I reckon I put at least as much into trying and running and anticipating as anyone in the side. Despite not making as many starts as some, and being pulled off early or brought on late, I ended the season as Charlton's top scorer in the league. Only fifteen – a comment on all of us – but in a kid of twenty it would have been hailed as bloody marvellous and they'd be building the team round him. Or selling him on to pay for a new gents in the East Stand.

But I'm not twenty. In a lot of people's eyes I'm playing on borrowed time. That list of names . . . they're obviously going to bring in new blood. After fifteen seasons I really don't relish doing a Steve Gatting – drifting down to non-league status. All the grief, all the training aggro, and on the Saturday a few hundred's a good crowd . . . No more do I fancy being 'converted' to an occasional utility squad player turning out week-in, week-out for the stiffs on, say, the left side of midfield. They could send me out on loan, of course. Or give me a free. But where? And, at my age, how realistic? All they'd be would be short-term solutions on the part of a club with an immediate problem.

The mortgage is looking large tonight: this holiday a luxury. They're selling World Cup cushions down near the station. I'd better get a thick one for the subs' bench.

16

Monday 20 June

Heading home. Just re-read the last entry. A bit embarrassing in the cold light of day. Strictly 'I could have been a contender' stuff. Ghost of Mary-Beth was around the pool last night looking for revenge. And getting it.

But today I feel better. After all, we all worry sometimes and I'm entitled to as well. But I've also got reason to feel grateful about quite a lot. I'm healthy and fit and had fifteen years earning my living doing something I've always at bottom got a great buzz out of. How many people can truthfully claim even that? And it's not over yet. I'm still in the game. I'm still as fit as ever, probably as fast. I'm a good pro. Good in the dressing room. I'm not that dispensable just yet. Maybe.

Tuesday 21 June

Arrived Gatwick in small hours. Train to Worthing. Not too bad. House in same place. Straight to bed and slept for six hours.

Wednesday 22 June

Renewed my acquaintance with the British motorway system today and drove up to Floyd Road. Not to report for pre-season training, thank God (the weather's scorching: as hot as Orlando only mercifully less humid), but wearing my businessman's hat. Charlton owe me for the framing of a batch of prints and I need to sort out the payment. Looks as if my most realistic chance of getting it squared away is a 'contra' deal – the club 'donating' Garry Nelson Enterprises some advertising in the programme.

There's been further face-lifting at the Valley over the summer and, if you look beyond the foreground rubble and bulldozers you can make out the final configuration. It's emerged as a direct time warp back to the 1930s – a non-matching bicycle shed-type stand at the sides and ends of the pitch, with all of the corners going to waste. (Why does that expression ring a bell?) But I rather like that. I think it's appropriate for Charlton. They've never been a posh club. For years and years they drew their strength from the thousands upon thousands of dockers who'd knock off their week's work (when they could get it) Saturday lunchtime, belt into the pub for a long hour and then go on to the game. That's all gone, of course, but I think the traditional design of the new ground does give a tip of its hat towards those earlier days.

The old Valley, of course, always had scale. The vast open East Terrace always guaranteed that. Thankfully, the imposing East Stand that has taken its place still generates something of the same visual impact. Without it – and the stylish, state-of-the-art floodlight pylons – it wouldn't be too difficult to drive past the ground and remain blissfully ignorant of its existence. The immediate area is, alas, wall-to-wall with the cheap, uncheerful boxes of industrial units, hypermarkets and cash and carry outlets. Until recently, when glimpsed from most angles, Charlton's ground could have been taken as just another temple to the prevailing religion of 'pile it high and sell it cheap'. Now, though, as you glance up from the players' car park the emphatic, confident sweep of the new East Stand proclaims again what the Valley is all about. And once inside the ground, players and spectators alike can appreciate that in an amazingly short time-span, all things considered, the Valley has become a modern, excellently appointed football ground.

When you consider what an out-and-out tip the Valley was as recently as 1990 – weeds everywhere, the terraces crumbling, the ruined stands totally unsafe, garbage dumped all over the pitch – you have to take your hat off to the Board and everyone who's worked on creating the turnaround. What's been achieved over the past eighteen months adds up to a not-so-minor miracle. All this without losing the Valley's essential character.

The new Valley will only hold a fifth of the capacity that used to stand shoulder to shoulder in the great bowl of the old ground. Still, it's all the club's. Gate receipts will soon be maximised and the running financial wounds of, first, ground-sharing and, then, contractors' fees are being replaced by positive cash flow. Supporters will hope that some of this incoming cash is translated into fresh faces on the park. Well, that'll be all right up to a point.

The new stadium is, of course, all-seater. I'm not sure that's an overall improvement whatever the regulations now demand. Word from the supporters is that leg room between seats at the

Valley is now uncomfortably cramped in some places and many fans, maybe most, prefer standing. Standing you get a better view, you can keep warmer on cold days by stamping your feet and you don't have that idiot in front of you leaping to his feet every time the action crosses the halfway line. Hillsborough has a lot to answer for considering most of those responsible for that obscenity of an administrative malpractice haven't answered for it at all.

But football's ironies, large and small, are non-stop. I'd done the business over the advertising space when who should I bump into in the car park but Kim Grant. Kim's twelve years younger than I am and, even more than I, was Charlton's number one twelfth/thirteenth man on the subs' bench last season. When we weren't playing alongside each other we were competing for a place. Kim scored two or three blinding goals in the course of that campaign but missed a couple of sitters too. His speed and talent are obvious, but without a sustained run in the side he ended up just as visibly lacking in confidence. Know the feeling. And what Kim had to tell me didn't do too much to boost our joint morale now either.

He had just picked up the news – straight up, no longer rumour time – that Charlton are taking on Paul Mortimer (former player) and David Whyte (former loan period with the club) from Palace and Scott McGleish who's been banging in goal after goal for non-league Edgware Town. That long list of 'maybe' names that Chris Carter unrolled in Florida has thus come down to three definites. It could be worse. Marginally. One of them isn't an out-and-out striker.

I've seen Kim looking happier, too.

'What's brought you in so early?' I asked him, although I had a pretty good idea.

As I'd suspected he'd come in to discuss his contract – whether to sign for two years, one year or not at all. He's about the last squad member who's not committed himself. His hesitation stems from his feeling he could get guaranteed first team football with another club.

'Like who?' I asked.

He named a couple of lower division sides.

'So what's Charlton's offer?'

He told me.

'That's reasonable going on generous,' I said, calling to mind that my own terms hadn't altered since I first signed three years ago.

'What would you do if you were me?' Kim asked. How many times have I been asked that? It's always the cue to go into PFA rep mode. Now I told Kim what I thought would be best for his long-term career – to sign on again at the Valley.

'The clubs you're talking about won't be able to match your wages here,' I said. 'No way. The facilities won't be anything like. And there's going to be no absolute guarantee of a first team place wherever you go.'

Kim nodded.

'That's what all the other lads've been saying,' he said. 'They all say I should sign on again here. Reckon I'll think about it a bit more but I probably will.'

Good old Uncle Nelse. There he goes giving his best advice and maybe cutting his own throat with the same gesture.

Monday 27 June

Scorching. All the same went for a four- or five-mile run in the late afternoon. Afterwards sit-ups and press-ups. This time last year I worked on the principle of relaxing completely so as to recharge the batteries and totally eliminate any lingering niggles. The result was that at the start of pre-season training I really felt it. Different this time. I'm going to run myself into a state of fitness better than most of the lads. I'm targeting two hundred press-ups and four hundred sit-ups a day. Kim has signed on again so that's one chore the less.

Wednesday 29 June

Scorching weather continues. So does running. Slight stiffness in muscles, soreness in joints afterwards. But very minor.

Bulgaria eased past Maradona-less Argentina (many a true word spoken in Nelson jest) today. Wish I had Lechkov and Balakov behind me. Millions of miles of worldwide newsprint devoted to Diego being found positive but personally I've only one reaction: they must have convinced him it would be masked. Ah, well – poetic justice. The centrifuge of God.

July

Monday 4 July

Not so many celebrations for the Boston Irish, I imagine. After boring their way past Norway last week Ireland found their true level in the World Cup's second phase today, losing 0–2 to Holland. The pundits tried to let them down lightly (and Big Jack *has* made a little go a long way) by saying that they didn't have an outstanding player who could 'turn the game in a single moment'.

Not true – not when you look at it negatively.

The match contained one of the game's all-time clunkers and you have to feel sorry for the player concerned. Robert de Niro, Brian Lara, Pavarotti – I don't care who you are and how kissed by genius, you're human and sooner or later, you'll drop a mighty ricket. I've even missed the odd tap-in myself. Maybe you'll be lucky and it won't be in public. But when a goalkeeper gets it wrong on a world stage there's no hiding place. It makes you feel grateful you're a striker.

And not a centre back either. A couple of days ago Andrés Escobar, the defender for the very disappointing and eliminated Colombian team who put through his own goal, was shot dead outside a Medellín café. There are own goals and there are own goals. I don't suppose we'll ever know what really happened. And tomorrow, as far as the world's media are concerned, it will be ancient history. I shan't quite be forgetting it, though. First off he was a human being. Secondly it's a reminder – grim but, amid all the World Cup hype, timely – that football isn't finally that important. There's more to life than kicking a ball around a field and Bill Shankly's famous remark to the contrary is funny – as he well knew – precisely because it *isn't* true.

Thursday 7 July

Another run. Encouraging. For the first time since the holiday I floated off on to that level of equilibrium you reach when you're getting fitter. As I slogged uphill away from the coast towards the Downs there was the familiar moment of wondering why the hell I should be bothering with all this at my age and the usual sense of having done it all too many times before – not surprising since I'm literally following in the footsteps of all the training runs I've put in over this terrain wearing a Brighton shirt. But that passed and as I neared the top and it flattened out I came back to the present realising I'd covered a goodish stretch pretty much oblivious of my whereabouts as a result of being tuned in to my mind rather than my body. When you're consciously monitoring the effort going into every stride, it's a sure sign you're short of maximum fitness. When you drift off, though, fantasising about getting the winner at Wembley or remembering the MOT needs renewing, it's evidence you're no longer running on empty. I won't pretend I enjoy the running for its own sake, but I do enjoy the sense of heightened fitness it leaves me with. Another plus this time of year are the stunning views you get on all sides once you top the Downs. Not a glimpse of Canary Wharf in any direction. They're a real boost to the energy bank in themselves – and completely undetectable in any random testing. There are some tonics you just can't buy in a chemist's shop.

Monday 11 July

Back with a vengeance. Pre-season training started today at the New Eltham ground and – surprise, surprise – today was officially clocked as the hottest of the year. Anyone planning a UK holiday has to do only one simple thing to ensure cloudless skies and blazing temperatures: book it for the same date the Football League clubs are scheduled to reassemble.

Came up as usual on the Gatwick Express. Not a BR special but one car, four players. Three other Charlton South Coast residents,

Steve Brown, John Robinson (like me once with Brighton) and Kim Grant, join with me in rotating the driving. They motor up from Brighton to meet me at Pease Pottage; we park up and then come on together in one car. Three trips out of four it gives us the illusion we're chauffeured superstars. It also saves on petrol.

Today we were rather subdued. We wouldn't have impressed anyone with our livewire camaraderie as we seemed just a bunch of everyday commuters. Which, of course, is what we are. First day back blues? More likely the fact no one had brought a paper along. The only relief to the general lack of communication was our collective pleasure we took from Bulgaria beating Germany the night before on clear merit.

At the training ground my first impression was of the usual swirl of smiles and back-slapping with lots of familiar faces swapping places around me as a few unfamiliar ones hung around the edge of things. Everyone in the lightest of casual gear but all perspiring buckets before moving a single muscle in anger.

The verbals and put-downs started flying about at once as everyone put on their public face to play up to the first day back at school atmosphere. Mark Robson was out of his cheeky chappy blocks in nothing flat, kidding around left, right and centre exactly as on a good day he'll wisecrack his way all over the park. Mr Blobby (Peter Garland in our case but every club currently has one) drew a lot of flak for rolling up (ho! ho!) at least a stone lighter than he ended the last campaign. With Darren Pitcher off to Palace, Peter has every chance of establishing exclusive rights to a midfield place and it doesn't take much to see the boy means business.

One thing I speedily clock is that, set aside managers Alan Curbishley and Steve Gritt who are still registered as players, I've now succeeded retiring goalkeeper Bob Bolder as the squad's oldest player. It's a fact that doesn't escape Alan Pardew's sardonic observation. Alan's humour has real bite and he shoots really straight. And not only in my direction. There aren't too many who escape being its target once they've laid themselves open to a corrective put-down. I can naturally be very relaxed about his calling me 'Grandad' and such, because I recognise that this is all a pre-emptive strike. Alan's adopting an 'attack is the best form of defence' policy because he knows that he's next in line for the 'senior pro' label. And while his birth certificate may make him my junior by a month or two, this is really only a technicality. Compare his greying hair with my own golden locks, emerald green eyes and Adonis features and there's no question which of us is the younger at heart.

As the giddying confusion takes on a bit of stability, one newcomer I'm pleased to meet is Andy Petterson who's reached us via Oz and Luton and so should raise the club's cultural profile. His arrival could be timely because Mike Salmon, our first-choice goalkeeper last season, is carrying a torn stomach muscle – an injury picked up bowling in a charity cricket match. Mike also seems to be carrying Peter Garland's lost stone. Already, a ball not kicked, we've got a significant injury list. Stuart Balmer, player of the year two seasons ago, has some mysterious trapped-nerve knee problem.

Suddenly it's shock-horror time. Like so much beef we all troop forward on to the scales to have our weight recorded. I'm clocked at 12 stone 6! That's six pounds heavier than I've ever been! Now everyone can be sure I've been skiving during the break and eating America out of junk food. Who *has* ate all the pies, then? So much for the running and the sit-ups. Come on, Nelse, I tell myself, it's got to be enhanced muscle and sinew . . .

We all get down to some work. It includes some interval training. Ten two-minute runs. I feel fine despite the heat. More than hold my own. But now as things begin to fall into a pattern and I'm taking the odd semi-surreptitious look at how the others are managing, one player is very conspicuous by his absence. Paul Mortimer is languidly present, but where's his ex-Palace team-mate, David Whyte? Rumours and jokes start to multiply. Hung over? In Milan signing for Inter? Protecting his complexion from the blazing sun? Lost for ever in the Bexley triangle? A chance, a less than generous part of me can't help thinking, would be a fine thing.

Other faces are missing today, I now notice. Today and every day henceforth. They belonged to the lads from the junior

26

teams who haven't made it and have been let go. There you are, eighteen, let's say, and your career, your hopes, are all gone. You're holding zilch. For a while it's the end of the world. And for some it stays that way. The trouble with discovering at eighteen you've made a false start is that eighteen can be an age when you don't have vision to see there's still plenty of time to build a new career and don't have the patience to set about it. No one's older than an eighteen-year-old in a hurry. The PFA under Gordon Taylor have put in a hell of a lot of work encouraging apprentices to get second strings to their career bows via day-release schemes – not to mention encouraging clubs to release them. In my twenties I got my own HNC in Business Studies in precisely that fashion, training by myself to make up for the lost sessions.

For those permanently dropped, though, insult gets added to injury. The clubs tend to rub salt in the wound. They go from Mr Nice to Mr Nasty overnight and suddenly don't want to know the kids that just a short while earlier they were doing everything in their power to attract. I suppose they can argue a clean, total break is best all round. But it's not always so clean.

When I was at Brighton a young Irish lad got axed. He was distraught. Another set of the same dreams had been blasted. But he had one small crumb of comfort to ease the pain. His contract stipulated that he was allowed four free return flights to the Republic a year. He still had two to his credit. Using these he could at least get his bits and pieces back home without bankrupting himself. Brighton FC, however, deemed otherwise. He'd been released: end of story. No way, lad.

He came to me as the PFA representative and I got on to them. The two upshots were, first, that he got what he was entitled to and his little clutch of possessions back to Ireland free of charge to himself and, second, that I had endeared myself even more fondly to Barry Lloyd, the Brighton manager, and his Board.

Lose some, win some. A clutch of apprentices out. A batch of trialists in. Temporarily. Here because of a motley collection of reasons, virtually none of them has any more chance of sticking than would the first half-dozen you picked at random, men, women and children, from a bus queue.

Mid afternoon we were finished. In more ways than one. By then, I weighed 12 stone 2.

Tuesday 12 July

Still baking hot. Still no David Whyte. A reassuring sense of the familiar provided by Andy Petterson being fined a tenner for turning up late. His excuse that he finds it difficult getting about the right way up was not accepted.

For those who were present and more or less correct, an escalation in calorie-burning in the form of hill runs up Shooters Hill where the stage-coaches used to stick. Gruelling – but I was feeling fine after the first day and my work on the Downs stood me in good stead now.

Alan Curbs gave us all a little pep talk later in the day. It was the one about how he and Gritty had no preconceptions regarding team selection and it was what we all did in training and the pre-season friendlies that was going to count. As we listened, most of the more experienced, and hence cynical, pros crystallised the contents of some of the buckets of sweat we'd filled up, thus supplying ourselves with a handy grain or two of salt to swallow along with the fairy tale.

Wednesday 13 July

Drove up alone today. My car, for the record, is a Fiat Tempra, on the H, John. It's the survivor of a PR thing I was once involved in with a dealership during my Brighton days and its chief automotive attraction was the pretty good price I got on it. Plus, being Italian, it's got a bit of soul. And no air conditioning. Sticky now as well as hot. Florida all over again.

Still no sighting of Lord Lucan, aka David Whyte. We did our first ball work today and, as requested (Quasar, the manufacturers of our training gear, not having divvied up yet), brought our own kit to kick about in. You haven't seen such a ragged-arsed army since Napoleon's lot got back from the away leg in Moscow. Universal truth: no pro footballer has any decent gear of his own. He expects it to be all there waiting for him in the changing room courtesy of sponsors and boot boys.

The day ended with a surprise. The Board, via the management, sent down the bonus sheet – details of what bunce we're on for a win, a draw, gaining promotion, putting together a cup run. By hoary tradition the sheet doesn't materialise until the last minute, the Thursday maybe, before the season's first kick-off. That way, of course, there's a minimum of time left in which the preoccupied players can muster objections.

It's certainly not on account of its munificence that this one should have appeared so amazingly early. There have been a couple of cosmetic tweaks, but essentially it's the same deal we've been on for the past two years. We all said we'd go away and have a little think.

I drove off and what should I see on the side of the road but a thoroughly bad smash. Blood and glass all over. Am I getting hyper-sensitive about these things or is someone trying to tell me something? I suppose, the miles I do, the law of averages means I'm going to pass a fair old number. But, please, O Lord, grant that I may continue to pass by on the other side.

Arrived safely, nonetheless (or because), and later on watched Italy squeak by Bulgaria in the first World Cup semi-final. I was intrigued to note that I wasn't football fan enough to stay up all hours to watch slightly misfiring Brazilian flair run into Swedish dourness.

Thursday 14 July

David Whyte showed up today to put an end to the jokes and mystery with a big anti-climax. He's merely been ill with some sort of a common-or-garden virus. He picked a bad day to feel better. The sun was still hammering down and we were all despatched into Greenwich Park to do thrust runs up the precipices there.

Historic setting and all that. The Queen's House and over the river the Isle of Dogs where the Tudors kennelled their hunting dogs. But no time to enjoy the views. We had our managers snapping at our heels. I gave the murderous hill runs my best shot and was pleased to see that I was up with the leaders every time. Not a case of the old man gradually slipping back down the queue this time. Afterwards I got my reward.

'Didn't really notice you today, Nelse,' Curbs said. 'Where were you? You've put on weight, haven't you?'

When you're more dead than alive it's nice to feel your efforts have been appreciated. Especially by the eagle-eyed. Or short-sighted. In the afternoon we were back at the training ground being asked to do more ball work. Because we were knackered, what we responded with was crap. After the morning's duel in the sun with the assault course everyone's legs were twitching as if they had completely independent nervous systems. It's impossible to display silky skills on the ball when your knees have turned to water. Two heads being better than one – allegedly – you'd have thought our managers would have had the common sense to acknowledge the conditions and show sufficient flexibility in their thinking to alter the original training programme to something that would stop short of giving us all perpetual cramp.

Friday 15 July

David Whyte's no fool. One look at us and our methods, and he's off sick again today, the virus still bugging him. I don't blame him. If he was less than a hundred per cent, he couldn't have found yesterday much fun.

His absence was compensated for, to a degree, by the arrival of a further newcomer, Mike Ammann. Mike was in the American B squad during their World Cup build-up which is a pretty high recommendation considering the choice of goalkeepers the US enjoys. His arrival among us (after his marriage to an Italian girl had cut through all rain forests of work permit red tape at a single EC stroke – where's the logic, I ask) means that Charlton now have two keepers from the colonies. Hand on heart I'd find it very hard to pick Mike over Andy Petterson or vice versa. They're both more than useful, and a fit and on-form Mike Salmon is going to give us a real embarrassment of riches in that position.

In the afternoon, sprawled out on the training pitch we held a players' meeting to discuss the bonus sheet. As skipper, Alan McLeary was the unofficial chairman and the meeting was infinitely more grown-up and well mannered than you'd ever experience among all those verbal hooligans at Westminster.

30

Consensus was that the terms were far from being the greatest but that the club wasn't being deliberately tight-fisted. Charlton aren't a rich club and that just about said it all. The news had just been confirmed today of Chris Sutton's move to our rabbits, Blackburn, for £5.5 million, plus all the trimmings. It moved us, I think, much more to resigned shrugs than open rebellion. There was all-round tacit agreement that the man never said that football was a just game. We might argue about whether Sutton is worth all that money (for mine he's not, but he's already got more than I'll ever have so he should care), but none of us could deny that our own combined worth in the transfer market *as a squad* wouldn't top Kenny's latest little flutter.

It all made discussion of what we ought to rate week-to-week in the way of a bonus seem rather irrelevant. All the same I did come up with one suggestion: that there should be a two-tier system and that so long as we held a place in the top half of the table we should get a touch more for good results. The logic of this, of course, is that in the top half we'd be attracting bigger crowds and generating more revenue. This proposal was, in fact, carried and we'll be putting it to the Board. More, it might be said, in a spirit of hope than anticipation.

Wednesday 20 July

Kicked first ball in anger today. Sort of. We played a 'behind closed doors' friendly on the training ground against Leyton Orient. Essentially a 'remember how it all goes pre-pre-season game' with an agreed format of three thirty-minute thirds and substitutions ad lib. A hitch in these civilised arrangements for Garry Nelson, however. Carl Leaburn, Kim Grant and David Whyte all picked up knocks. My lucky day. As hot as ever and I get to play ninety minutes first time out.

Orient scored twice in the first fifteen minutes and that's how it stayed. Meaningless as a result. They'd started training a week before us and were that much fitter and sharper. At our level, a week's head start really is a difference. For that reason, though, a useful exercise. You can do all the running in the world but the only thing that makes you match fit is playing matches.

Saturday 23 July

No let-up in the heat for our first friendly proper – a traditional annual fixture against Vauxhall Conference neighbours Welling United. Park View Road is literally closer to home for many Charlton fans than the Valley, so the 3,000 or so gate always reveals a heavy preponderance of red shirts on the terraces. Our supporters turn up full of great expectations convinced we'll roll over the non-League minnows in a comprehensive victory. It's never quite that easy. Welling are a useful side; we're still working our way to fitness; the pitch is tight; the heat a great leveller. While we were warming up (as if that were necessary) I heard the Tannoy announcing the day's raffle prizes. One was 'a pork pie and three video tapes'. Apt. It was a job lot of a match too.

The first half was fairly even but we made a difficult task near to impossible by conceding a goal right on half time. This is a cardinal sin in any game, but against a non-League side with a point to prove it's arguably worse – a recipe for humiliation. In the event we won 3–1. The differences, finally, were a superb Colin Walsh long-range shot and our full-time pro fitness as against their part-time. I started the match but came off through the non-stop revolving substitution door ten minutes into the second half. Limping. It was the reward for having made my debut in the medium of black comedy.

Ten minutes into the game Shaun Newton was sprawled on the pitch out on the right wing signalling for treatment. In vain. His injury was pretty obviously more than trivial but the referee was allowing play to continue. Our defence had control of the ball and I made an anticipating run into the channel concentrating solely on the ball – now coming my way through the air. Thunk! In a moment of broadest farce, not without its Schmeichelian nuances, I had crashed into the still prostrate Shaun kicking him hard enough in the head to hurt my left ankle quite enough to make my own eyes water, thank you. The crowd's laughter – such a comfort to those in distress – was shot through with 'oooohs!' of disbelief.

Well, it's always funny if it's not your own foot that went down on the banana skin. But while *I* was getting attention, I could only think that one serious injury at this stage of a career could be it.

Curtains. Taped up, I got to my feet to run the knock off now thinking that it would have taken a hell of a lot of accepting if, after years of being on the receiving end of take-no-prisoner tackles from some of the hardest men in the game, I'd been permanently sidelined in a Keystone Kops collision by a self-inflicted wound.

There were no hard feelings from Shaun – head apart – but I took some stick from the other lads as immediately after the game we packed for our five-day pre-season trip to the South Coast.

Sunday 24 July

Dormy Hotel, Ferndown. This is our base for the short week we're 'on tour' and very nice it is too. It's good management to bring the squad here for a concentrated 'shake-down' period. It's a small squad, mind you, at eighteen, and there's disappointment for the injured and the young pros who've missed out on the low-level 'dolce vita'. For the latter, of course, there's the added downer of gaining fairly certain confirmation that, whatever degree of preconception Curbs and Gritty may have laid claim to a fortnight ago, the first team-sheet is unlikely to be decorated with new blood as opposed to old sweat.

Purely to boost team morale and accelerate the knitting together process, you understand, those of us who did make the coach (happily for me the Welling knock only lastingly bruised my ego) had a very satisfying night on the town in Bournemouth – it can be done – secure in the knowledge that today would be a rest day. Not for all. Putting the Dormy's superb facilities to good use, the more energetic squad members are engaged in a highly competitive tennis tournament played, be it said, at a well up to snuff level. The more wily campaigners are saving their energies by relaxing over a few drinks at the pool-side bar. No prizes will be awarded for correctly guessing where this diary is being updated. Or who has experienced a sudden nostalgic pang of near affection for Mary-Beth and her great big trays.

Monday 25 July

After a morning's training and afternoon's sleep, we took on Bashley in an evening game. Relegated from the Beazer League

Premier Division last season, Bashley are something of a one foot in the career-grave side for ageing Southampton and Bournemouth players and have had their moments in the recent past. The ground's location must be one of the most picturesque I've ever come across. But it proved to be a case of the beauty being overshadowed by the beast. Judging by the conditions tonight, Bashley programmes should carry an FA health warning of the 'playing on our pitch can seriously damage your health' variety. Giving your ankle or knee a long-term injury on such a thick, clinging surface can be the result of no more than a quick turn, a sharp start. In football you have to take the rough with the smooth, but the Bashley pitch demands a nine iron. I started the evening on the subs' bench and could see Alan and Steve getting increasingly concerned about the wisdom of committing us to this fixture.

As I warmed up for the second half (the first was lacklustre and scoreless) a middle-aged Charlton fan came up asked if I'd pose with her for a photograph her mid-teens son would take.

'Of course, love,' I said.

I watched the birdie and said 'Cheese!' and she thanked me as did the boy. He then advanced upon a further topic of conversation. 'You know, Nelson,' he said. 'You're useless these days. Rubbish. You ought to be packing it in.'

Ah, the beautiful game! Don't you just love moments like that! Every player runs into them, of course. You continually meet the fan who knows best – what jockeys call the rider in the stands. Their opinionated comments ought to be water off a duck's back. But the game's not that kind. However misinformed or based on ignorance it may be, what is said still touches a raw nerve in virtually every player. And never improves his game. Think about that the next time you feel like slagging off somebody having a 'mare of a game. Put it this way: do you really think he doesn't know already?

My game wasn't improved, anyway. Coming on for the last twenty-five minutes I was presented with a gilt-edged chance. I hit the bar. Thanks, pal.

The 1–0 win was an irrelevance. I think I can write without too much fear of contradiction that, against the odds though it was, we all left Bashley without too much of a wrench.

Wednesday 27 July

League opposition for our friendly tonight. Bournemouth. And for me an added reunion element. My Brighton room-mate of three years' standing and close friend, Mike Trusson, is their first team coach. And another former team-mate, Gary Chivers, who a year ago was in the Charlton Dormy squad is in their team. Further, instead of moving up the motorway to Charlton, I came very close to signing for Bournemouth myself three and a bit years ago.

Looks like I got it right for once. The 'AFC' with which Bournemouth pretentiously preface their name seems to stand right now for 'Absolute Footballing Chaos'. A sense of terminal decline hangs in the air over Dean Court. There's a running debt of £2 million and rising, a complex but stumbling game of musical chairs being played in the boardroom and the open secret that, living on borrowed time, the manager is counting not the days but the hours. The name of Harry Redknapp, the high-profile and longish-serving manager of Bournemouth's more successful past is on everyone's lips. You can only sympathise with players being asked to motivate themselves for the coming season in the context of so much club and individual uncertainty. No one likes it when the goal posts are moved but footballers find it particularly awkward.

Nor is Bournemouth's plight so untypical. It's a more extreme example of what a great many sides in the lower divisions have to contend with week after week after week. There's many a once-thriving and illustrious club that could be kick-started back upwards if a cheque for the odd million or two with John Paul Getty's monicker in the bottom right-hand corner were to drop through the letterbox. There's many a management that would be happy to have the amounts United pay Cantona and Giggs, Blackburn pay Shearer and Sutton, each week with which to meet the wages bill for their entire squad. Yes, I know some players are kissed by genius and magic on the ball and are telegenic and boost

35

ratings, gates and product-awareness percentages. But do they do the game as a whole a service? Their demands – or those their agents put into their mouths – carry us towards the telephone numbers, Ryne Sandberg scenario.

If Shearer is paid so much that the press/publicity machine has to be geared up to get the last pound of spin-off financial return on his career, then the people who live in Burnley and Preston will be drawn in. Their impoverished local teams will lack glamour in the eyes of youngsters. (Ten year olds, by and large, are only interested in climbing on winning bandwagons. It must be better to support Blackburn because they're on telly more. Who wants to go around wearing a rotten old Burnley shirt – or a United shirt that's a whole month out of date?) But small, impoverished local teams will also tend less and less to attract the uncommitted, occasional spectator. The man who once would have gone to watch a dozen live games a season will now buy a satellite dish and, staying in Monday nights, become a couch potato. He will, by and large, see better games. But he'll see them at skin-deep level and they'll soon begin to blur in his memory. He won't be nearly as involved. He won't see the whole picture – television never shows it – the running off the ball, for instance. He won't get as much out of the experience. Every time a dad in Devon buys a United shirt for his kid, it's bad news for Plymouth, Torquay and Exeter.

Ominously – a pattern is emerging – I began the Bournemouth game on the bench once again as Charlton started with Carl and David Whyte up front. It was no classic but, clearly fitter, we had some goodish spells and should have won by two or three rather than the game's only goal. Symptoms, alas, of our chronic disease – indifferent finishing, a lack of goals in numbers – are beginning to re-appear already. And, alack, with an indifferent contribution towards the end of the game I did little to instigate a cure.

In the players' bar afterwards I couldn't help but feel time is running out for my mate Truss. He's always been one of life's enthusiasts, someone who has always thought positively. But a couple of years in the debt-ridden lower depths of the Football League seem to have taken their toll. When I quietly wondered aloud about his ongoing prospects he rolled his eyes to heaven and changed the subject.

Saturday 30 July

One door shuts, another one closes. No more Dormy Hotel pool but a return to motorway rat-running and a week at the training ground trying to move up a gear for today's visit by Chelsea. In an equivalent game last year we outplayed and beat Arsenal and came out of the league starting blocks like Linford Christie.

During the close season we (under)sold our far-and-away best player, Scott Minto, to Chelsea. When the teams ran out it was great to hear the lovely 'thanks for everything, Scott' reception he got from the Charlton fans. This was soccer supporters at their best and I know Scott was genuinely touched by the warmth of the response.

Not without wit, the same supporters serenaded their Chelsea counterparts with 'Blue Moon' choruses of 'Three-one ... we only lost three-one...' a reference to our respective defeats (1–3 as opposed to 0–4) at the hands of Manchester United in last year's FA Cup. Unfortunately, our lot got the tense wrong. It should have been the future tense. The lyric was prophetically accurate for today's game. Instead of 'Blue Moon' it was largely a case of chasing blue shadows.

Chelsea passed the ball beautifully. Glenn Hoddle has transformed them and his genius has rubbed off on all his team. They're a very well-balanced outfit now who must do well this coming season. Scott looked totally comfortable – his game is dead right for them – and, more to the point still, they looked comfortable with him. I'm confirmed in my opinion he's got full England caps to come. And sooner rather than later.

Once again I spent the first half as a spectator. I then had the dubious experience of witnessing the half-time firework display. In the Charlton dressing room.

We'd gone in lucky to be only one goal down and knowing it. When the other team are making you do all the running on what is another inferno of a day, frustration tends to run high. Big Carl is never one to keep his irritation to himself and he now made his feelings loud and clear. The upshot was that, by way of counter-blast, he drew down on himself the biggest bollocking that I have ever heard in a Charlton dressing-room – certainly in the context of a July pre-season friendly. Snail's pace, the bottom line was, would be a compliment for his work-rate. The second outcome was now predictable. Leaburn off. Nelson on.

I didn't quite turn the match. We did step up a bit and put together some neat approach work, but their cool reply was yet again to pass the ball right through us from the back and score a textbook second goal. A moment of vision from Mr Peacock's little boy Gavin and a dummy that gave him an acre of space had made a nonsense of doing-it-by-numbers man-to-man marking.

Then another twist. David Whyte went off nursing an injury. Carl, it being a friendly, was given a reprieve. Geed up for some reason or another, he earned a penalty and, for his pains, picked up a knock of his own – a heavy-duty one. Being selfish, that could have been the most significant aspect of the game for me.

More significant, being unselfish, had to be the appearance on the field for the last fifteen minutes of the Chelsea player-manager. Five or six of his passes later and both sets of players and supporters had exhausted their drool. It must be a joy to play in front of him: time your run right and there will be the ball in front of you, the back spin bringing it nicely on to your boot. Glenn is another example of a superstar who has made a fortune from the game. You can't begrudge him a penny. Why not? Because of what he does on the pitch. Because of what he's putting back into the game.

'Three-one . . . we only lost three-one . . .' The final score must have given the managers a lot to think about. This season we look like coming out of the starting blocks like Julie Christie. However, I remain at heart a fan of the beautiful game with a deep admiration and respect for those who through correct technique can make it seem so simple.

AUGUST

Tuesday 2 August

More Premiership opposition tonight, although against more of a known quantity, Crystal Palace having just gained promotion from our own division. The fixture's potential focal point, however, was the promise of Darren Pitcher's speedy return to the Valley. During the close season we sold Darren to Palace and the word was that he'd be in for a far less welcoming reception than Scott.

Up to and including our fourth round FA Cup ties with Blackburn, Darren had an excellent ball-winning, ball-distributing season in our midfield. In both Blackburn games he was outstanding, making his obvious opposite number David Batty look like a very ordinary work horse. But then we all had good games in those ties. Our win at Ewood Park was a magnificent team effort – great keeping from Mike Salmon, superb defending from Stuart Balmer, Scott Minto making telling runs from defence on top of blanking out Stuart Ripley. In both games we were the better team overall. It was from this launch pad that Darren scored the one (and, in itself, lucky – the ball took a huge deflection) goal.

As the scorer, though, Darren grabbed all the headlines the next morning and, lo and behold, there suddenly at his side was agent Eric Hall. It was like Mary and her little lamb. And now, would you believe, Darren was making it very clear that he wanted a lot more money out of the game either from Charlton, the club who had developed him from a junior (some chance – the other headlines had been that every player in the Blackburn team had cost more to acquire than the entire Charlton side), or from the obvious main chance of a transfer.

Eric Hall was by now employing the basic tactic of promoting Darren, rather as Max Clifford handled Antonia de Sancha, grabbing him, briefly, a sky-high profile in the papers complete with matching price tag.

Mary was trying to pull some of the little lamb's wool over quite a few eyes and the OTT nature of this tag – £1.5 million – was regarded in the Charlton changing room as a joke. Less easy to handle was Darren's lack of inhibition over keeping the rest of us updated on the endless stream of Premiership clubs lining up to secure his autograph on a contract. It didn't do too much for our collective morale.

High profiles are two-edged. They are dangerous things to carry around. As if believing overmuch in the inviolability of his own publicity – that it would do the job for him out on the field – Darren allowed his own form to nosedive dramatically. It was at this point that the whole team went disastrously off the boil. Probably because of the publicity he was receiving, a lot of the Charlton supporters chose to vent their frustration at Darren's expense. Thanks a lot, Eric.

Such vocal disappointment went up a few illogical decibels when Darren finally did choose to move – at a fraction of the initial asking price – to Crystal Palace. Given the hostility, rather artificial though it may be (does every club *have* to have a deadly rival?), that has existed between Charlton and Palace fans since the ground-sharing days, this was a move calculated to rub salt in the wound more than absolutely any other.

So – stand by in the stands to hiss and boo. Only, big anti-climax. Neither potential nor promise was realised as Darren didn't show. Not his fault, I'm sure, but Palace discretion being the better part of Valley hostility, they had coolly agreed to play *two* games that evening and field Darren in a testimonial match at Crawley. We were pitted against an alleged second team.

Or not. With two million-pound centre backs (Young and Thorn), a million-pound striker (Bruce Dyer), another valued at

£350,000 (Andy Preece) and in right back John Humphrey a better player than any of them, they didn't strike me as too much like a Combination team. In fact, though losing 0–1, we were by some way the better side on the night, largely dominating the game. Carl's injury keeping him out of the running, I started the game and had by some way my best pre-season match. Almost everything I tried came off. My reward was to be substituted ten minutes into the second half. Just pre-season egalitarianism, I'm sure.

Wednesday 3 August

A day off. No M23, no M25, no cones – and no scribbling myself into writer's cramp. Luxury.

Friday 5 August

The kick-off to the season proper eight days away, the bonus sheet has re-appeared. The Board's overriding immediate concern seems to be to correct an area where, first time around, they got their sums wrong. They obviously feel – and they're right – that the original bonus proposed in the event of our making the play-offs but missing out on promotion is too generous. They're desperate to cut it back. With so many experienced pros around, however, who know a good thing when they see one, I reckon there's scant chance of their getting their rethink implemented. I've a hunch that as the season progresses they'll not find themselves losing too much sleep over this clause anyway.

As regards the bonus sheet as a whole, the Board are playing the same swings and roundabouts game as a Tory Chancellor – giving with one hand and taking with the other. My two-tier suggestion has died a quiet death and, with time running out and the players working through the ACAS-like third party of the management, I'll be very surprised if anything is materially altered from last year.

As the PFA rep, I should maybe be a bit more proactive – perhaps setting up a face-to-face meeting with the directors. But the reality is that the money isn't really there to begin with. And do I need all that extra hassle at my age? All the extra risks? Sour memories of a previous bonus go-around at Brighton come flooding back to persuade me the answer is almost certainly a resounding 'No!'

The problems at Brighton started with the ink almost still wet on the contract I'd signed to move there from Plymouth. Brighton had just been relegated to the Third Division but still had seven or eight players on their books going back to the heady days of the early '80s. These were on a very large bonus. More recently it had been deliberate policy to bring in non-League players at a fraction of the terms enjoyed by the older, established hands. Being as green as grass and desperate for a chance with a pro club, the newcomers had signed a bonus sheet without giving it more than the most superficial of glances. It was only later that it dawned on them that several of their team-mates were earning six times as much for a win as they were.

In the summer of '87, which is when I signed, Barry Lloyd was given some extra cash to bring in some more experienced players. In no time, the bonus imbalance had become an issue. Frantic discussions and negotiations ensued and an improved bonus sheet did materialise. It was a distinct improvement for the former non-League lads – but still fell a long way short of the rate granted the club's old-timers. Talks were still taking place and after initiating discussions between the PFA and the Football League, I obtained a two-week extension to the general bonus sheet deadline in the hope that differences could be resolved once and for all. Then the Brighton Board played their trump card.

The Thursday before the season's start, the first team squad found themselves training separately from the rest of the professionals. Rather strangely, the youngsters were allowed to finish a good deal earlier than the rest of us. It was only after we had at last returned to the changing rooms that we learnt that the club secretary had materialised to secure the signatures of all the young pros for the new – i.e. Board-approved – bonus sheet. The big earners were – quite rightly – staying at their existing level. But this left about half a dozen of us in limbo and with nowhere to go. It is fair to say that the six of us – Kevin Bremner, Alan

Curbishley, Mike Trusson, Dean Wilkins, Doug Rougvie and myself – played a key role in winning Brighton promotion that year. Our reward was half that of five other first team players.

It all left a nasty taste and the problem was never far below the surface. In my last season at Brighton it flared back up again. The terms hadn't been improved for the past two years and now, much to the senior professionals' disgust, it looked like it would be another case of 'No change, lads'. As PFA rep, I always acted as per the wishes of the other players after they had been established through a series of meetings and discussions involving every player. Now it was felt we had a lever with which we could exert pressure in negotiating with the Board. Looming up was a potentially truly bummer of a trip to a Romania where the bullets had only just stopped flying following the overthrow of Ceausescu and everything was manifestly close to total chaos. Since we'd all been through the mill of an utterly demoralising trip to the Soviet Union only three months earlier, nobody, truth be told, relished the idea of trekking across Europe once again to spend a week alternating being kicked up in the air with drinking cabbage soup. The players thus came up with a collective solution. Refusal to go. Strike.

I, however, knew that the PFA would never sanction such a course of action. The strike would be unofficial. I counter-suggested that it might be cannier to make the trip but, having reached Romania, then inform the chairman and manager that, unless they sat down with us and addressed the bonus question properly, we would refuse to play. The players, though, were unanimous and adamant. If we didn't get the (far from extravagant) bonuses we were asking for, we should refuse to go at all.

I was uneasy. But I was the players' representative. It was my job to put their case. The players right behind me, we all trooped in to a meeting with Barry Lloyd.

I put the players' arguments as simply and unheatedly as I was able. 'Isn't that right, lads?' I ended by asking.

A dozen or so eyes looked out of the window, inspected the shine on their owner's shoes, stared into infinity. Suddenly they weren't behind me at all.

Barry Lloyd's response was statesmanlike – if you consider Hitler was a statesman. He threatened to sack us all on the spot. I tried to calm things down but the damage had been done – damage I sensed might be irreparable. I felt a deep gush of warmth run through me. It wasn't gratitude for the solidarity displayed by those I was representing. I'd been elected PFA rep. Now I'd been cast as chief trouble-maker.

The upshot was that we did go on tour – the soup was all we'd expected – and two days after we got back Lloydie phoned me up to say that I could go.

The bonuses remained unchanged.

Saturday 6 August

Away to Gillingham. The last game in our pre-season programme. Full steam ahead, then. But not on the Gatwick Express. Dispensation granted, three of the four South Coast commuters had elected to drive straight to the ground thereby gaining the extra odd half-hour in bed. The chauffeur? Well who better to drive into darkest Kent than the proud Essex born-and-bred owner of a four-year-old Tempra? With me at the wheel we could make a bee-line for Priestfield.

Forget it. Huge tailbacks were turning the M23 and M25 into ribbon configuration parking lots. No problem! We opted to go cross-country via Lewes, Tunbridge Wells, Maidstone and the Upper Volta bypass. The next time you go to slag off a player who hasn't got high enough off the ground, stop to wonder whether his vertebrae have had time to recover from three cramped hours in a coupé.

For us, bad went rapidly to worse. Or, rather, not rapidly. After stopping for petrol I was charmed to discover my starter motor had died. With fifteen miles still to cover we not only had no forward movement (what else is new?) we had just twenty-five minutes between us and a fine for turning up – if at all – late.

Necessity is the mother of push coming to shove. Brownie and John Robinson made with the feet and we engineered a perfect bump-start. We made it on time. The team coach was late.

After the game – it was a totally forgettable goalless draw, if memory serves – we again had to bump-start Signor Agnelli's heap of tin. I trust he gets better performances out of his Serie A boys. Our antics occasioned the predictable mirth from several press men and match officials.

'Get a decent car. You can afford it on your wages,' one hack surpassed his usual level of informed commentary with. I thought at once of the American I'd met in Orlando who equated professional sportsman with mega-bucks. It's happening over here. Thanks again, Eric. Football agents' PR announcements are helping stamp into everyone's mind the certainty that all footballers are rolling in it. People who believe that should spend a few minutes studying a Gillingham or Bournemouth player's tax returns. That we're all rich beyond the dreams of avarice is, believe me, a load of Hall's.

Tuesday 9 August

Early start today for what I grudgingly concede is a useful purpose. All players have been instructed to attend a meeting addressed by ex-FIFA referee John Martin. The object thereof is to outline and explain the new rules the English game will play to until further notice. These variations are plainly fallout from the just gone – and largely already forgotten – World Cup. We listen with a mixture of genuine interest and scepticism, clocking what seem – on paper – the pluses and minuses.

The most obvious plus is the crack down on tackles from behind. I feel my Achilles' tendons twang with approval. As a striker, I can't get too upset about the decree that linesmen are now to incline towards favouring forwards when ruling on marginal offsides. Similarly the 'not interfering with play' status of a player otherwise offside is to be more liberally interpreted – even to the extent of his being allowed to join in the same move downstream from its beginning. This will make it a more attractive proposition to close down a keeper dealing with a pass back.

And now the bad news. The big minus is the (surely) Draconian edict that swearing at your team-mate, the opposition, their bench, your own bench, the ref, the linesmen or the reserve official's cat are all alike to be adjudged a red card offence. Yes, OK in principle, but interpreted to the letter, this new rule is going to curtail the length of time spent out on the park by scores of players. We broke up from the meeting with our eyebrows raised pretty high and a feeling that there's a real danger of confusion reigning as a rash of red and yellow cards transform the pitch into something resembling the pavilion at Lords.

I was amused when John Martin got to the 'Any questions' stage. All the hands that shot up were attached to the arms of defenders. Defenders are such sticklers for doing everything by the book! But, again, on balance over the past few years they've been the ones drawing the short straw with regard to most 'improvements' to the rules.

Friday 12 August

Eve of the season proper's kick-off and an early start – 7.00 – in the Nelson household: bags to pack for overnight stay in Manchester. Gallant to a fault, I opt to take off in Carole's old wreck of an Uno. It's going to have to sit out on the streets of crime-ridden Pease Pottage for two days and I don't want to risk my H-reg dream machine being stolen. Not now I've lashed out on a new starter motor.

I meet up as usual with the other three South Coast commuters. Only this time it's a touch different. Already there's tension flitting about. Will Brownie be fit? Will Robbo be playing? Will Kim be travelling? The first game of the season is always special. It seems almost like a Cup final. It's a one-off that everyone wants to play in: that everyone reckons they should be playing in. It's illogical, if you take the long view of our maybe sixty-match season. But it's not often players do take the long view. And certainly not at the season's start. Before today is out, before the league programme is under way, there's going to be multo disappointment for quite a few.

First off, though, it's hilarity for us all. On our arrival at the training ground, we're issued with our new tracksuits, T-shirts and club blazers. Put-downs ricochet around. Footballers are

46

renowned poseurs. The young, single players – well, those without large mortgages and kids and, it has been rumoured, with birds to impress – see themselves at the cutting edge of high fashion. Some, indeed, are known to sartorially go where no man has gone before. And never should have. Certainly a great deal of time, effort and money goes into getting the appearance right. Or otherwise. Whatever – being forced into a latterday school uniform, as it can seem, has been known to bring forth the occasional not altogether unpredictable tantrum from the Beau Brummels of the younger set. I'm not without some sympathy for this viewpoint. We're not expected to be clones on the field. We should arguably reserve the right to 'express ourselves' – however extremely – off it.

But the argument can be turned around. Yes, we are individuals. But we earn our money working and thinking as a team – a cohesive unit. The other school of thought, therefore, – one that Alf Ramsey certainly subscribed to – is that anything which promotes the sense of unity has to be insisted on. If push came to shove, I would probably put myself down in the dedicated followers of fashion camp. Though not vice versa. But it's not an issue I feel that strongly about. In working reality, it probably largely comes down to the quality and style of the gear that the clubs dish out. I still shudder at the memory of the blazers Brighton stuffed us up with one season. They had been tailored (with pitchforks, I believe) in pre-*glasnost* Czechoslovakia. They must have cost pounds. Which says it all, really. As so often in British soccer, we come back to the penny-wise bottom line. You can't see clubs like Brighton and Charlton earmarking scads of money for the top priority of kitting out the lads with decent travelwear.

One item of clothing is in no way subject to the faintest possibility of rejection. Like the Tour de France, CAFC is characterised by the hallowed tradition of the yellow jersey. Ours is possibly less coveted. It goes not to the leader of the pack but the player adjudged to have turned in the week's worst training performance. Today there were no real contenders so, with rough but apt justice, the *maillot jaune* is awarded to coach driver

47

Pete, now held singly responsible for the team's late arrival at Priestfield.

After the fun and games, business as usual. The light-hearted atmosphere vanishes in micro-seconds as the eighteen-man squad for Oldham is called to a private meeting. The eleven who'll start are announced right away. I'm in. I owe it to Carl Leaburn's graunched knee ligaments, I know, but to be going on with it'll do very nicely, thank you. The anxiety flows out of me. I relax and listen hard to a detailed and genuinely informative guide from Curbs and Gritty on Oldham's style and tactics, and the individual ins and outs of players we're likely to come up against. I take a quick glance round. Anyone arriving late could tell from the facial expressions on view who is fuming at being left out, who is gutted, who knows for a fact God's in his heaven. I reflect again on Carl's injury and that it's no time to feel complacent. It's only that knee injury which has kept me from sitting with brows even more knitted than usual and from joining the queue looking for a quiet chat with the management the moment training is finished.

The time comes to follow the yellow-clad driver aboard the coach (hired – like most clubs, Charlton can't afford their own) and to rediscover all the joys of tedium on wheels. Long motorway journeys, spending countless hours crawling towards all parts of the country is an occupational hazard that comes with every footballer's territory.

We have it a lot easier now than they used to. The motorways, for all their evils, are a better way to fly than surface roads. We have TV, a coffee-making machine, toilet facilities, tables for cards. For the 'game boys' in our midst, if you catch my drift, there are the mentally retarding delights of Sega and Nintendo. Yes, inside as well as outside the coach, it's diversions as far as the eye can see. And it's all still such a bore.

Compared to the coaches of other clubs I've been with, the Charlton bus has always seemed to me to be relatively sedate. Perhaps this tone is set by Carl whose first action on boarding is to make straight for the rear bench seat. His second action is to stretch out right across it – the coach builders having made it just wide enough to accommodate that endless length of leg. This sleepy hollow attained, his third and last action is to lapse into a coma and, indeed, Lewisham probably has in Carl a viable contender for Rip van Winkle's title. Another to go into sleep mode at an early stage is David Whyte; but he needs a lullaby or two before escaping to the land of Nod. Accordingly, he comes equipped with a Walkman.

The rest of us aren't blessed with a built-in 'snooze' button and are obliged to generate more active forms of diversion therapy. The younger members tend to gravitate to the crèche, as it's called, the novice card school. This, by time-hallowed tradition, forms at the back of the coach whence cometh, quite coincidentally, of course, most of our journeys' undue hullabaloo and dispute. Frequent are the bitter squabbles that erupt from these apple (and damson) cheeked cherubs over such weighty issues as who first yelled out 'Snap!'. In time, being ripe for fleecing, the little lambs may graduate to the mid-section of the coach. It is here that several senior members foregather and, before the cards are reached for, read the papers ('. . . where Charlton may well feel happy to settle for a point.'), swap old stories and chart the onset of rigor mortis.

I always contrive to enroll in the serious card school nearer to the front. Serious up to a point. 'Nominations' (forecast whist) is the name of our game, but to my mind it's a poor substitute for the poker schools of Plymouth and the Chase the Lady sessions at Brighton. Also enrolled in my school are Alan Pardew and Peter Garland who in a previous life must have been a river-boat gambler. Our fourth is the club physio, Jimmy Hendry, who in *his* earlier life must certainly have been cashiered from the regiment (or taken out behind the saloon and shot) for non-payment of his gambling debts.

The very front seats are reserved for the managers and the directors. What game they are all up to is, of course, something no one has yet quite succeeded in working out.

Foremost of all, naturally, is Peter our driver manfully wearing his bright yellow jersey without a trace of jaundice. Our safety is very much in his capable hands and it speaks volumes for his expertise that boredom, not terror, is the bane of these trips.

Although hired in with the coach, Pete is really very much one of our team and a man of no little 'previous', with three marriages and a London marathon on his CV. This tendency towards masochism is further underlined by his earlier choice of career – nightclub singer and entertainer.

This last revelation acted on us like a red card to Steve Bull, but all our attempts to get Pete to warble a few bars proved fruitless until a memorable evening at the heretofore cited Dormy. His tonsils lubricated more than somewhat, Pete was finally persuaded to join our own, our very own, karaoke kid, Mark Robson, in a series of Elvis and P. J. Proby numbers. Thus the Dormy did, indeed, become a heartbreak hotel. But there was a still greater challenge for us to rise to. A little detective work and a great deal of Bacardi-and-coke bribery finally elicited the startling discovery of our coach driver's erstwhile stage-name. All was now revealed. We enjoyed the privilege of being driven across England's green and pleasant land not by a mere Peter Tuffin but by none other than – as he is henceforth condemned to be forever known – Ricky Towers. We wait with scarcely contained anticipation for the day when he will introduce us to his aristocratic brother, Alton.

The for'ard card school was soon reduced to three. Realising he was about to lose another £4, Jimmy Hendry had abruptly remembered (i.e. invented) an obscure Scottish variant on the rules of the game which being interpreted into Sassenach conveyed the basic message that he was a tight-fisted git and wasn't going to shell out. He was instantly red-carded from the game.

Four hours of snails-pacing had brought us as far on our way as Stoke and closer still to going stir crazy when a momentous event occurred which all but precipitated a ghastly accident. Whether turned on by the prospect of self-exposure to a coachload of assorted males in the prime of life or, more likely, merely desperate to relieve her own tedium, a young lady caught up in the jam alongside us was so forthcoming as to enliven her journey – and certainly ours – by favouring us with a feminine version of a 'moon'. In a manner making nonsense of the adjective 'topless', this well-blessed damsel revealed the full splendour of her breasts to the off-side windows of our coach. The instant lateral movement left to right all but caused the vehicle to turn turtle. It was undoubtedly some of the best movement on or off the ball certain players had managed in the last four weeks. This was definitely the Valley party's Popular Front candidate.

Naturally, as the side's chronologically senior pro, I felt the need to set a standards-maintaining example. I remained steadfast at the table making notes for my diary. I was thus not able to see that the left one was slightly plumper and featured a distinctly superior nipple development.

By 7.15 p.m. we were in Manchester but not, alas, at our hotel. Oblivious of our cramped muscles and tightening joints, Ricky was set on giving us a little treat – a quick guided tour of the regenerated Salford Quays area.

Urban development was not his motivation. Memories of his former showbiz glory still hung about him. He was searching for the *Coronation Street* set and – who knows? – that magic moment when, plucking him from behind the wheel, a discerning producer would make him an overnight star.

We got to the Copthorne Hotel stiff and brainwashed. Ricky got to go on wearing the yellow jersey.

Saturday 13 August

Kick-off day to another new season. Probably/possibly my last. The sun is streaming down everywhere. The Pennines way off on the horizon shine like the frontier of an unattainable kingdom. No time for that. Second out of the tunnel, holding a ball (my superstitions), I'm very much down to everyday earth. Or, more precisely, turf. As a nostalgic overlay of quick-fire memories of past seasons blurs my reactions to this new one I am, nonetheless, struck by the beautiful grass pitch that now graces Boundary Park in place of its former, unspeakable surface. A few years ago Oldham's artificial surface was arguably the most potent factor in their gaining promotion from Division Two. It wasn't the only factor, I concede, but their enjoying a thirty-something games unbeaten home record cannot be entirely unconnected with their one-off pitch – as QPR and Preston might agree.

The whistle blows and there's no time for further trips down memory lane as – for a neutral – the game develops into a thriller. Seven goals and some great end-to-end play. Unfortunately for Charlton only two of the goals were ours and in the second half all the great play came from Oldham.

I started the season on a high, getting the ball on the left with not much room to work in but still taking it past two defenders before drawing Jobson, Oldham's classy centre back, and then going past him. I feinted to shoot and then knocked the ball sideways to David Whyte. He thumped it home from about five yards. The first goal of the game, the crowd going wild and me feeling the self-inflicted razor wound extending further across my throat. Still, come on, Nelse, it's a team game.

We weren't too downcast on the way back. Not too many will come away from Boundary Park with a result, we rationalised, and there's forty-five games to go. The modest allowance (apt word) of alcohol ('Win or lose/We're on the booze' as Keats so poignantly expressed it) helped keep our morale in some sort of shape too. So did the lively school of shoot-pontoon which developed with the sharks exploiting the naïvety of those crèche members who'd ventured forward into the deep end.

The one downer, as always, was the fish and chips. All the club stands us. Eighteen to twenty souls on board and the allowance for our group Saturday night dinner is a munificent £100. Further, your innards scaled out to hollowness by the afternoon's exertions, the last thing you want is a dollop of hot greasy food minutes after starting for home. But that's always when it comes. Take it or leave it time again.

On the night roads, the trip back to New Eltham was much quicker – three and a half hours. All the same I wasn't turning the key in my own front door until the Sunday small hours. Thirty-nine hours, door-to-door, with only ninety minutes of that – well, ninety-five – taken up by the game. It's not all about kicking a ball.

Wednesday 17 August

My first trip to the medical room this season. The slight niggle in my knee I've been feeling since the Dormy trip is making its presence felt a bit more insistently: ice, deep friction rubbing on the tender area and acupuncture. The needles are a relatively new weapon in Jimmy Hendry's armoury. They were greeted with a great deal of scepticism when he first introduced them and there are still some devout doubters. Aka cowards. But then we've all seen him try to play darts. I have to say that they work well for me on minor problems.

Thursday 18 August

A day off – in theory. I could have taken the easy option and keeping quiet about the knee, enjoyed the day as a temporary gentleman of leisure. In hard, tiresome fact it was troubling me, so, making the sacrifice, I exercised it on the car's accelerator all the way up to the training ground. A 150-mile round trip for about half an hour's treatment.

Friday 19 August

Virtue rewarded. Nelson, anyway. The needles have worked wonders once again. The knee feels a lot better. Declared myself fit for tomorrow.

Saturday 20 August

First home match of the campaign. Barnsley are our opponents. A 2–2 draw is the result, with the game ending in a roller-coaster ride. Into added time, Phil Chapple headed us into a 2–1 lead. Thirty seconds later we gifted them the softest of equalisers. Psittaceous nausea time. But overall we probably would have to say we nicked a point. Barnsley's precision passing cut us apart for long periods and it took a lot of last-ditch clearances to keep us in it. Our midfield was conspicuous by its absence and I spent the afternoon trying to live off 'anywhere will do' scraps.

Afterwards I had a word with the club doctor about the knee. He advised me to take things easy in training. If it's still a problem two weeks from now, he'll give it an injection. That will deal with the symptoms; what it does for the problem is rather less definite.

Monday 22 August

One of the down-sides of being an army general used to be that, after a battle, you were supposed to visit field hospitals to see the results of your work the day before. With footballers it's the video of the game just played. Charlton, praise be, don't set great store by collective post-mortems and, as a rule, it's usually the two managers who laboriously pore over the latest video nasty we've enacted. The premise, of course, is that it's absolute reality. There's no distortion of truth because the camera never lies. Hmmmn . . .

Today we were all asked to sit through the video of the Barnsley game. This less-than-inspiring or epic preservation of Saturday's thud and blunders for posterity only strengthened my personal view that the camera does lie. It diminishes things you thought were excellent and makes poor games seem even worse. As we trooped out of the meeting someone had the sense to flip the lights on immediately. It's in the dark that nightmares recur.

I was granted the respite of some sick leave anyway. Curbs told me to rest and not to train. Had a few needles in my knee and – to deal with an old problem – my lower back. Enjoyed a good wallow in the bath. This is the life after all.

Wednesday 24 August

A day off. And the glutton for punishment in me knows just how to spend it – journeying up to London. Since, though, a change is as good as a rest, it's North London this time and White Hart Lane. Moreover, I'm in the company of two different motorway companions, Derek Steel and Adie Cooper. Between us we make up arguably the entire West Sussex chapter of the Everton fan club. Yes, the object of the away-day excursion is to be present at the eagerly awaited debut of Herr Sturtzbomber against my team, Everton.

'*Your* team?' Derek asks me as we plough on towards London. 'What's a nice Essex boy like you doing supporting a Scouse side? It's not as if you've ever played for them.'

It's a fair question. When Derek, Adie and I met up during a party for the adults who'd supported a local youth tournament a

54

couple of months ago, we were so chuffed to discover that we had being exiled Evertonians in common I never got around to explaining the reason for my own lifelong allegiance to the Blues.

'A chance would have been a fine thing,' I say – and take him through it.

Both my parents come from families long settled on Merseyside. Soon after their marriage, however, my father broke away from his boyhood haunts. A worker in the printing industry, he moved down to Essex to take up a better job with, as it then seemed, better long-range prospects. As a consequence when, not long afterwards, I was born, it was not in the romantically hard-nosed city of Liverpool, even then being discovered by the world's media, but in Braintree which still awaits the global recognition as yet so cruelly denied it.

Family visits, though, were regular events and as a toddler I soon made the acquaintance of all my northern aunts and uncles and grandparents. It was my grandad who took me, at the age of five, to the focal point of all the family's football fervour – Goodison Park. It would have been unthinkable that any new-comer to the clan should begin his soccer education anywhere other than at the pure fount of soccer science.

I seem to remember that day vividly. The blue and white, the huge press of all the world's grown-ups in the same ground, the giants and gods who were down there playing on the brilliant green pitch. As we walked to the ground a coil of excitement seemed to be unwinding itself deep inside me. I felt glee bubbling through every nerve and vein. I was holding my grandad's hand, but I was walking inside an invisible envelope of happy expectation.

An experience like that stays with you. Semi-literally, Everton were in my genes and blood. From then on, the shining jewels in any family trips to Liverpool were the Everton home fixtures falling within our stay. Later, as a young teenager, I fantasised constantly about running out with the Blues into the Goodison roar. Roy of the Rovers never got near to my exploits. I did all this in the face of all geographical logic. The nearest coastal town, the nearest Football League team, both went by the same name.

Southend. When eventually I did run out in a league match I was wearing a blue shirt but it was theirs. Not quite the same. No disrespect. It's just that, as all the world knows, we never completely get over our first love.

I see from the increasingly glazed looks on Derek's and Adie's faces that I'm committing the cardinal English sin of declaring a passion. I hastily change the subject and apologise for the fact that we've all had to fork out a score for the tickets. But that's sports-page hype for you.

Naïvely I had counted on benefiting from the old pro's discount of one hundred per cent and copping the tickets for nothing. But I'd been thinking in pre-Klinsmann, pre-Dumitrescu terms. Hard on the heels after their arrival at White Hart Lane were not only countless journalists but the 'House Full' signs. It took a last-ditch effort by the Charlton club secretary to salvage our evening.

Spurs have spent millions on a beautiful stadium and, on the evidence of what we saw in the first half, a beautiful team. But it very much surprised me that their financial outlay hasn't made provision for state-of-the-art turnstiles capable of doing away with the century-old crush ten minutes before the kick-off. This could be an example of spoiling the ground for a ha'porth of sugar, because for the first quarter of an hour our view was consistently blocked by late arrivals shuffling past. At £20–25 a ticket you would have thought they'd be desperate to see the entire proceedings. I know I was.

Nor was it any consolation whatsoever that everyone was properly installed in his own seat in time to leap up from it again both times Klinsmann put the ball in the back of the Everton net. He might have had a dream home debut hat trick when, on the stroke of half time, the Aryan-looking linesman awarded Spurs a very dubious penalty. It was Sheringham, however, who put the ball on the spot. Magnanimous to a fault, Klinsmann took it in his stride. Sheringham, unfortunately, didn't. Leaning back he delivered a strike that would have cleared the cross bar of the Brandenburg Gate. Jürgen was diplomacy itself as he forbore pointing this out.

A minute into the second half the script was rewritten as the

Blues pulled one back. Secure in the knowledge that by putting seat prices up to a level only nice people can afford, soccer has eliminated the hooligan element, my fellow toffeemen sprang to their feet exultant. Not entirely wise. To judge from the abuse that was heaped on us from all sides somebody somewhere has got their social classifications in a twist. You don't have to be skint to be a hooligan.

Losing their respect for the opposition, Everton pleased me by playing very well in the second half on the back of a lot of intelligent commitment. On tonight's form Everton are where they deserve to be. In the top flight.

Friday 26 August

Worked long and hard on how we are going to play against Portsmouth and what we can expect from them. Curbs and Gritty full of confidence. They expect a result.

Saturday 27 August

Away at Fratton Park. Virtually a home game for the Gatwick Express commuters. Thirty-five minutes to the hotel and the prospect of getting back home in time for the six o'clock news. It felt odd playing in front of a largely standing crowd once again. Portsmouth seem to have done nothing to their ground. I don't begin to understand the logic behind the Football League's thinking but, apparently, because they have ground improvement plans in the pipeline, Pompey don't have to conform to the recommendations of the Taylor Report.

Stuck my first goal of the season in today, a left-footed thunderbolt that Mark Hughes would have ... well, maybe not quite, actually ...

It was, in fact, a slightly mis-hit half-volley that beat the keeper on its second, awkward bounce. To my credit, I did react quicker than anyone else when Peter Garland sent a botched corner kick pinging in towards the penalty spot. My overwhelming personal emotion was relief. Always nice to break your season's duck, of course, but these days whenever I get the ball in the net it's always more a matter of feeling relief than joy or excitement. A pretty revealing comment, I suspect, as to where I've got in the game and the confidence I've got about being a regular on the first-team sheet.

When I was sixteen or so banging in goals week after week in junior league matches, they came with a sense of inevitability. I expected to score. It was in the natural order of things.

Today Charlton weren't allowed to experience relief or any more positive an emotion for more than a moment. Portsmouth equalised straightaway. These two efforts, though, marked the end of the scoring so that we came away with a distinctly creditable draw. I came away personally in sharpish fashion so as to reach home on the stroke of six o'clock and enjoy the bonus treat – it's by no means always possible – of playing with the kids.

Monday 29 August

Bank Holiday Monday – traditionally the last day-trip of summer and the boot is pleasantly on the other foot for once. We working lads head unimpededly north while the southbound lemmings sit happily for hours in the mandatory South Coast tailbacks.

Today is all about preparation for tomorrow's evening game against Sheffield United. They're a side with more corner and free-kick variations up their striped sleeves than our three previous opponents rolled in to one. Gritty is having to work overtime on his Bank Holiday.

Boredom, though, sets in early. The session, I sense, is deteriorating. The management keep stressing the need for vigilance and concentration. I start to feel I could be at a Neighbourhood Watch committee meeting. We'll see tomorrow if it was all taken in – or whether Steve and Alan were.

Tuesday 30 August

As usual I left home at 4.30 p.m. for tonight's 7.45 kick-off. A moderately affluent club wouldn't give this routine house room. Instead, they'd give me house room, so to speak, by paying me a salary sufficient to justify buying an (overpriced and over-rated) house somewhere close to the training ground. It's not a question of my wanting to have barristers and commodity brokers for my

58

neighbours. I like to avoid the hooligan element in my leisure hours. It's all about my not having to turn up for a game half-brainwashed from the motorway slog and the base of my spine nudging me in the brain. At the least, Charlton could make an arrangement with a hotel for its commuters to have an afternoon's rest and recuperation facilities. Given the quarter of a million that Blackburn bunged Chris Sutton as a little something extra to help him set up home, it doesn't seem an exorbitant request. Only Charlton aren't Blackburn. The reality is that my being condemned to 25,000 miles behind a steering wheel a year is the club's financial necessity.

Still, I got there. Not for much. The game was a bore with Sheffield largely bullying us into playing at the tempo and in the long-ball style that suited them. It all ended in another 1–1 draw. The most satisfaction we derived from the evening was the hard graft we mustered and sustained. Nor did they score from a set piece despite having twenty-odd corners. Score one to Gritty instead.

And maybe one against Curbs. Something that will remain in my mind for longer than the memory of this indifferent game – because it rankles – is a quotation attributed to Alan in the 'On Line With Clubcall' feature in this evening's programme:

> With Darren Pitcher and Scott Minto having left the club and with Carl Leaburn injured we are going through a transitional period. I think when we get Leaburn it will be a different picture and his partnership with David Whyte should be fruitful, but for the moment things are a bit of a battle for us.

I appreciate there's quite a bit of hidden agenda here. After the team's indifferent start, Curbs has a natural tendency to want to protect his back. We all say things – especially in front of microphones – that we wouldn't have let slip if we'd heard them first. I know there's tremendous pressure to come up with fresh copy for two programmes in the same week. All the same I could have wished someone had thought a bit before committing this gem to hard print and the cold light of day. A moment's consideration would have pointed out that it's less than flattering and potentially thoroughly demoralising to the player who currently happens to be partnering David Whyte. Tact is supposed to be one of the good manager's characteristics. If tact is, as they say, knowing how to go too far without going too far, this goes too far. I think I may well have to have a quiet word on this one. But I'll take my own advice first and give it a moment's thought by sleeping on it.

Wednesday 31 August

Brighton versus York. No problems with complimentary tickets here, although – twinge of guilt – Brighton could certainly do with the money.

In the three years I've been gone, the old stomping ground hasn't changed a bit. Which is to say most of the old problems remain. A severe cash-flow crisis – i.e. poverty – has left Liam Brady without the option of buying in and, judging by what I saw tonight, a place in the play-offs would seem Brighton's best hope.

In many respects, I would think, promotion would come as a severe embarrassment. The Goldstone is typical of so many grounds – no room for expansion, difficulties regarding planning permission to put roofs on stands and a total reliance on the Football Trust to finance such work as might succeed in getting an approving nod. Relocation would seem a sensible alternative. But Sussex's coastal strip is fully occupied and inland from the Goldstone is one of the nation's most idyllic stretches of countryside, heavily – and most properly – protected by the National Trust.

With that sort of backdrop to their games Brighton must look upon a win as something of a mixed blessing.

60

SEPTEMBER

Friday 2 September

After training met up with Carole, Carly and Christopher at a Bloomsbury hotel. It's the end of the kids' summer holidays and the idea is to show them there's more to life than Orlando by giving them a quick whizz around some of the sights of Old London Town.

Saturday 3 September

A different journey to work today: tube to London Bridge and then – luck having it that it's a non-strike day – BR to Charlton station. A very welcome change for the better. I had time to watch 'Football Focus' and arrived at the ground far more relaxed than is normally the case.

The team-talk was different today as well. It was 'No more Mister Nice Guys' time. Forsaking their normal approach, Steve and Alan opted to give their red-and-white army a right verbal pasting – running us down in the pious hope it would provoke us into bouncing back out there on the field. We all came in for some of this subtle deployment of psychological encouragement and the fact that today represents a small milestone in my career – my 650th first team appearance – didn't save me from copping my share of the flak.

In that we notched our first win of the season – 3–2 over Bristol City – you could argue that the change of managerial tack worked. But only just. Less arguable was that we were pretty lucky to end up with any points at all. As Bristol City came at us in the last twenty minutes our defence went limp at the knees and it was as much luck as any other factor that kept our noses in front.

On one front we had been more than half expecting the worst. Our fifth round FA Cup tie at Ashton Gate last year had left a particularly nasty taste in the mouth. It had been characterised by a sustained and clearly calculated stream of racial abuse. Just two players were involved. On the receiving end had been Carl Leaburn. Spewing out a torrent of racist filth had been a Bristol City player. The rest of us were convinced it was far less a working demonstration of National Front mentality than a cynical attempt to wind up Carl and get him red-carded off. We tried to get this across to him but it was clear that, although he avoided crude retaliation, it was getting to him. Then at half time in the tunnel fists flew.

Unofficially, luckily. The second half was acrimonious going on dirty and not helped by some distinctly indifferent refereeing. The new regulations would, in theory, have seen Carl's tormentor himself dismissed. But not, I think, in practice by this particular referee. Bristol City had gone ahead quite early on and if they'd concentrated on playing tight football might have maintained that lead. As the game got heated and ragged, though, we came back into it and scored a deserved equaliser.

Possibly because neither of the protagonists from that go-around were on the field this time, today's game was totally free from any such unpleasantness and produced very few free-kicks. I didn't mark my milestone with a goal, but I had a minor hand – foot, actually – in the build-up to two. In both instances it was David Whyte who got the final tap/nod-in. Well, it's the result that counts, give him credit for being in the right place at the right time. But let's give his apparently temporary partner a bit of credit for knowing how to find him. I think *pro tem* I'll not take Curbs to task but try to let my form do the talking on the park. Perhaps that was his idea anyway.

Not having to play Stirling Moss on the way home tonight, I enjoyed the luxury of a few beers after the game before setting off to catch the 6.24 p.m. train back to London.

I hadn't indulged in too much forward thinking. As I stepped onto the Charlton station platform the air was thick with West Country burr and a considerable amount of alcoholic fumes, some of the latter mine. In a suit and holding the footballer's obligatory toiletry bag, I stood out like Paul Ince at a West Ham Supporters Club AGM. Two or three Bristolians wandered over, followed in a slower stagger by four or five of their mates.

The fact that, on top of knocking their club out of the Cup last season, we'd just won again today flashed across my mind and deep inside me a small still voice screamed 'RUN!' But I told it to shut up. If I believed most fans are nice fans why shouldn't these be? Time to step forward and be counted.

'All right, lads,' I said, 'I'll say it first. You were a bit unlucky not to get a point today.'

They *were* nice. Ignore the large number of expletives (they weren't exactly drawn from the *silent* majority) and they were politeness itself. We shared the fifteen-minute journey to London Bridge like the oldest of mates while they told me quite a lot about football. Then it was handshakes all round and, as I walked off, the essential pride-saving, follow-up cry: 'Wait 'til you come down to Ashton Gate.'

They may be right.

Monday 5 September

What a difference a win makes. A much happier atmosphere at the training ground this morning. With the first win of the season (just!) our league position is already looking a bit healthier. The added bonus – I speak figuratively, of course – is that we're not confronting a midweek game.

I soon put a stop to all this sweetness and light. I inform everyone that their October pay packet will be lighter to the tune of £40 – the cost of a year's subscription to the PFA.

Soccer is often a game of instant retribution. I immediately find myself made responsible for picking a side for a small-sided game, eight v eight. I make a point of selecting from those who despite – or because of – our victory haven't had too good a weekend and a few who I know feel generally narked about the way they are being treated by the management – one of whom, I

63

clock, is stripping off so as to show us lads the maestro's touch.

In fact, the morning developed into a rout as Nelson's Nomads toyed with Curbishley's Corinthians, so utterly beating them in the end that it became necessary to call in the emergency services to prevent outright massacre. The boy, as it turns out, done good.

The aftermath was predictable. While my lot enjoyed a nice cuppa on the sun-deck, Mr Curbishley assembled his clod-hoppers to run the legs off them in what could only be described as a punitive extra session.

My glee proved short-lived. Finished with training by 12.20, I belatedly realised that two season-ticket holders on the Gatwick Express were faced with an extended work session with Reserve Team manager Keith Peacock in preparation for their midweek game at Oxford. No quick return to the grown-up world for me then. Instead the prospect of two hours spent developing my thumb-twiddling muscles.

But always improve the shining hour. Gathering together the new intake of YTS lads, eleven in all, I set about explaining my role as the club PFA delegate and what benefits membership of the PFA could make available to them. In return for a YTS annual subscription of just £5, these are very considerable. If, I pointed out, they cared to take advantage of a coaching course or vocational training or a return to evening classes all their fees would be met by the PFA.

I would have done better to save my breath for next Saturday. Dumb, blank faces stared back at me, the 'Vacancy' sign nailed up right between the unlistening eyes. None of this has anything to do with me, mate. Don't wanna know. Don't need to. I'm on the road to glory, a guaranteed twenty-two carat super star ... I don't s'pose the PFA can do us cheap insurance on my GTI...

The hard truth is that if just three of the eleven make it even as far as the level of workaday professional it will be a good return. The sad truth is that all eleven are incapable of imagining themselves left out of the frame.

Friday 9 September

No managerial agonising this week. The team picks itself. Curbs and Gritty are probably breathing a combined private sigh of relief that their decision-making has been streamlined by a further injury to Big Carl. His damaged knee having fully recovered, he has now damaged his good knee. It's slight but enough to rule him out of today's trip to Grimsby. It's yet more bad luck for Carl, but rescues our managers from a (mild) embarrassment of riches. Carl is the player with, in every sense, the high profile. But, on current form, dropping either Whytie or (far more likely) me to make room for him would generate a case for unfair dismissal the entire rat pack of the British bar would rush forward to argue. Less selfishly, these past weeks the team has got used to playing the ball in low and short when attacking. Carl's inclusion and the consequent need to feed him in the air could see us developing a stutter in our rhythm.

Saturday 10 September

The scorching August weather has tapered off now allowing us to feel less like Egyptian slaves and concentrate that much more on the game. Today is bright and Humberside breezy. Less so the mood of my room-mate, Colin Walsh, on his waking to discover that overnight he'd picked up my cold. Coughs and sneezes spreading diseases has to be as much an occupational hazard for footballers as for any group working in cheek-by-jowl proximity you can think of.

The name Grimsby doesn't quite conjure the same magical associations as Sampdoria or Celtic or Deportivo La Coruña. I've yet to bowl anyone over by triumphantly announcing that I've played at Blundell Park, Cleethorpes.

But this I can say: if you do play there, you'll know you've been in a game. Alan Buckley has never come anywhere near winning those prestige, showbizzy, Manager of the Year awards but to my way of thinking what he regularly achieves stands comparison with anything Kenny Dalglish, Alex Ferguson or George Graham can point to. Blessed with virtually no investment funds, he consistently fashions teams that, more than holding their own in

65

the First Division, play the game the way it should be played – teams with skill, speed and vision passing to feet.

No less impressive is the playing surface of Grimsby's otherwise homely ground. It suits their style. But unfortunately that style doesn't seem to be to the taste of the club's catchment area. A crisp, sunny day in only mid-September and a gate of less than 4,000. Perhaps the latest fishing regulations are beginning to bite in local pockets.

Those who stayed away missed a very watchable game. I'd have enjoyed it even if we hadn't come away with a thoroughly deserved win – although such talk may be cheap after you've had a hand in Mark Robson's result-deciding goal.

The Great Manager in the Sky, though, (no, *not* Rupert Murdoch) seldom allows you a blemish-free passage. The eighty-nine minutes of good work were all but offset in my mental play-back of the game on the way home by the last-minute Nelson miss. Shaun Newton made a length-of-the-pitch break from our own half and it was down to me to match his speed and time my run for his perfectly struck cross. Here it came! Yes! Yes! NOW!

It was a chance that would have flown in four or five years ago but – DAMN! – today I wasn't quite there and couldn't get my boot to complete what every one of my brain cells was screaming out for me to do: Score! for Christ's sake, score! It's no surprise that, by and large, defenders last that little bit longer in the game than forwards. Still, the miss did offer a tiny speck of binary consolation. A second goal would have broken the symmetry of my six-game sequence of Blundell Park results: 0–1, 1–0, 0–1, 0–1, 1–0, 1–0. We're not sponsored by Viglen for nothing.

Monday 12 September

An excellent piece of man-management by the dynamic duo. For this man, anyway. An extra day off. A heavy cold, a few niggles, a midweek match looming. All makes sense to me. Sometimes being an old git can be good for your health.

* * *

Tuesday 13 September

If sarcasm is the best indicator of heart-felt concern, my team-mates are desperately concerned as to how I am coping with this bloody cold.

My own concern centres on the fact that Big Carl played all ninety minutes in the reserve game last night helping the team to a 2–0 win over our old friends Millwall. That's a league-topping five straight wins in a row for Keith Peacock's side and – God! football turns us all into manic depressives! – the new worry is beginning to be about whether I'll be able to force myself into the Combination team's class act if I get dropped from the first.

From the mundane to the sublime. This evening I watched Newcastle demolish a by-no-means unskilful Royal Antwerp with a mind-blowing display of all-out attacking football. Largely prompted by an inspirational performance from Robert Lee, they homed in on the Belgian club's goal from all angles. Robert's own breathtaking, all-headed hat trick was the core of the 5–0 hammering. The last time he scored a hat trick was for, yes, Charlton. Developed by Charlton, his only other club, all the way up from turnstile operator (a biographical detail that will haunt him throughout his career) 'Lurker' has to be seen as the club's outstanding player of the last ten years. It is a measure of the Board's then financial desperation that when second in the First Division and chasing promotion they sold him to the one team above us. Newcastle went on to clinch Premiership status and we . . . didn't.

But it's proved to be a great career move. Under Kevin Keegan's generous and human guidance, Rob has found that little bit of extra self-belief he probably lacked when playing on the lower slopes. Injury has temporarily delayed Scott Minto forcing himself into the foreground of the Premiership scene but it's surely only a matter of weeks now before Rob's Italianate ability to work with the ball in the thickest of traffic has him running out in an England shirt as the thinking manager's David Platt. One of the pluses of my own career is that I spent a season and a bit playing alongside Lurker. It was an inspiration to see such talent from so close a range. It was to despair to recognise the gap dividing us.

Wednesday 14 September

The day's minor bonus – again, it's only a figure of speech – is the quality of the bacon rolls in the little café in the local parade. The more significant plus is that the ball bounced the South Coast softies' way when, the argumentative dust settling, the route for our away-day in Stoke was decided. The benefit for us of a pick-up just off Junction 9 of the M25 is a later start to the day and, three times more desirable, as much as an hour and a half shaved off the time of our arrival back home in the small hours. Thus the faint irony of three pro players, whose names *might* be in the nation's papers the next day waiting for their lift like any three Sunday League likely lads outside 'The Dog and Duck'. A great leveller, indeed.

Torrential rain as we nose northwards to the Potteries. It's only mid-September but we're looking up from our card games to wonder out loud whether we're travelling to a non-event. No, is the eventual answer. After a couple of fitful hours' sleep in our hotel I wake with a dry mouth to learn that the game is definitely on.

Nothing dry about the pitch, of course, or ambivalent about the Stoke supporters. Their zealous chanting of 'Lou ... Lou ... Super Lou ...' throughout the game affirms that they can't wait for the second coming of the saviour – or do I mean prodigal son? – who managed them a few seasons earlier. As it happens, the same manager, Lou Macari, was the boss for part of my unproductive stay at Swindon in the mid-eighties. On the basis of that experience I'd hazard a guess that the fans' enthusiasm for his return to the Victoria Ground is well in excess of the Stoke players'.

The Inland Revenue might have their own private opinions but, true, Lou's record as a manager is much more good than bad. Fans would argue that's all that counts. But fans don't have to live and work alongside the man, morning, noon and, yes, night.

For a start, Lou Macari has built up a fearsome reputation among players for the huge emphasis he puts on sheer running as the core of training. Not everyone is a natural on the track, but with Lou there's no horses for courses. Everyone grinds out the same mileage. It wasn't, in fact, such a penance for me at Swindon as it was for a lot of the others but I can remember worrying mid-way through lung-bursting, gut-busting running sessions about whether I would be able to recognise a ball again in the unlikely event of ever seeing one. It seemed a strange primary emphasis for a man who as a player was so tricksy and clever on the ball himself.

Losing him the popularity vote even more markedly, however, was Lou's extra-curricular (as it was perceived) habit of regularly turning up at the hostel where many players boarded to spot-check on who was out late, what time they were getting back and what state they were in when they did.

Alcohol is Lou's pet hate or, as some would put it, obsession. He makes it quite clear that the 'win or lose we're on the booze' attitude is tee-totally anathema to him.

Yes, but man doesn't live by running sessions alone. We also require to draw on wit and vision and self-confidence and an inner sense of well-being. We need to feel at one with ourselves if we're going to keep on giving it our best shot week after week after week. OK the game has seen some of the great players – George Best, Charlie Cooke, Jimmy Greaves – cut short their ability to perform at world-beating heights on account of their predilection for the fatal glass of beer or the easily affordable crate of vodka. But every profession has such examples and, apart from having to endure living in the spot-lit, fast lane of the game with its myriad of 'well-wishing' hangers-on, these were players cursed with a specific physiological reaction to booze. It was their biochemistry that couldn't handle the stuff. Discount this specific medical factor and I know of hardly any players who don't enjoy the odd pint or six from time to time and aren't the more complete footballers for it when they run out at five to three the next Saturday.

Because he happened to be 'virtuous' in this respect, Lou felt there should be no cakes and ale for the squad.

To my mind, still less appealing than Lou's untrusting anti-booze snooping was the 'vice' he positively encouraged – to which, indeed, in some strange, almost compensating way, he seemed almost addicted. He wasn't quite in the same league as the legendary Stan Bowles ('A tenner says the next car round the corner is a "T" reg.') but Lou certainly encouraged gambling. A sweep on the arrival time of the last squad member to turn up for training was the standard Swindon start to the day.

At Swindon we were paid weekly and in cash. If you get into the horses or some serious card schools, money ceases to have its basic purpose of paying the rent, buying the groceries. It's just your starter for another bout of adrenalin stimulation. Some lads at Swindon, cash in their hands on a Friday, had blown it before Monday came around. After all, Fourth Division as we were at the time, there wasn't that much to begin with. You have to ask who ran out in a better frame of mind each Saturday – the social drinker or the compulsive gambler with the bookies' heavies breathing down his neck.

Today, alas, Stoke didn't seem to have any problems or any need of a manager. Fifteen minutes into the second half they had strolled to a 3–0 lead as a series of individual errors at the back cost us dear. In the final third of the game, though, we came back at them with two goals, the first of which was one of my rare headed efforts.

Two does not equal three. Travelling south again through the losers' slough of despond, all we could initially clutch on to by way of consolation was a classic misprint in the Stoke programme. Apparently one of the Charlton squad is the gifted striker Carl Lea*bum*. However, as we'd set out believing Stoke were there for the taking, the error was not really adequate distraction from our own bummer of a performance.

Thursday 15 September

A day off. From football. For me, though, the necessary task of re-enrolling in the Chartered Institute of Marketing Diploma course at Northbrook College, Worthing. The elusive element of the diploma, International Marketing (I missed it by a couple of percentage points in the last batch of exams after passing the other three papers), is all that currently lies between Garry

Nelson, Esq, and Garry Nelson, Dip M. (No, it's not an abbreviation of 'dipstick').

I already have, let me remind posterity, that HNC in Business Studies and Finance. This is the qualification that after a couple of false starts at evening class – with midweek games it's next to impossible to attend courses regularly – I secured at the end of the eighties. Since then I've put theory to practice by getting involved on the marketing and sales side of a small picture-framing concern. It's all, as yet, minor league stuff but not, I think, to be despised. It's giving me a good working insight into organising a business and I'm finding that, through repetition, basic skills are becoming second nature to me. As a considerably 'grown-up' qualification, the CIM diploma will lift me, God willing, on to a reasonably rarefied level. Together with my practical experience, it will give my CV some genuine weight.

Just possibly I'm going to need all the qualifications I can get. It's certainly possible Ryne Sandberg knew something last June. Today the week-old players' strike among pro American base-ballers became set in long-term concrete. It couldn't happen here, of course. Anymore than there will ever be a pan-European Super League. Just ask Jürgen or our Ryan or Eric. Ask the other Eric. No, not Idle, Hall. No, no way . . . couldn't possibly happen here, a strike . . . could it?

Friday 16 September

Bad day at New Eltham. No, not the world's catchiest title. Just the truth. Something's going on. Going down. Not Charlton just yet, but . . . something. You can sense it as soon as you enter the training ground pavilion. It's as if somebody's been arrested. Or about to be. What? What is it?

Consider the evidence. A late start to training. No weigh-in. No sign of either manager. This season we've veered from Linford to Julie Christie. Now it's time to call in their Auntie Agatha.

Meantime the rumour-mongers are having a field day. Which is to say we all are. Professional footballers are not only among the world's most self-conscious dandies, they're positively the world's

71

worst keepers of secrets. We spray gossip around more indiscriminately than practice balls.

The signal starts to become fine-tuned. We've signed somebody. No immediate skin off my nose is my gut reaction. This time around there's no way it can be a forward. Who then? By mid-morning rumour has become stale news. It's Keith Jones, a neat, small-going-on-diminutive and very combative midfielder whom we've signed from Southend for – a biggish fee for us – £150,000. The two-way and three-way conversations now, of course, swing to discussing who's going to be put under most pressure by this. Who, in other words, is going to get the chop from the first team. After being so often in that particular firing line myself, I bear up to spotting a few worried faces with commendable equanimity. No, no skin off my nose this time, gents. Suddenly, though, my complacency is shattered. Big Carl has declared himself fully fit. Could be I'm about to be on the receiving end of – as they would put it in Stoke – a bum deal.

Could well be. The day's biggest shock now hits. Skipper Alan McLeary has been axed from the first team. In the past few games he's put in a whole series of last-ditch saving tackles but his demise is clearly linked to the question of why those tackles came to be necessary in the first place. Further, he's not as tall as Phil Chapple.

The rumour mill's rev counter soars into the red zone. Two others, word goes round, are also for the chop.

Well, we'll soon find out. Conspicuous by his absence, Steve Gritt has left Curbs to hand out the complimentary tickets for the next match – and inform those whom it concerns to report to the foot of the guillotine. I'm concerned. As I collect my comps my heartbeat is audibly, it seems, above normal. But it's OK. This time around I'm spared the blade. Those whose heads are temporarily to roll are keeper Mike Ammann and his bosom buddy and my card school mate, Peter Garland.

For seasons Charlton's squad has been thin to skeletal. Suddenly the in-tray is full to overflowing. With the phrase 'period of adjustment' ever on the management's four lips it can only be a matter of time before the out-tray receives some attention. Whoever said there was safety in numbers?

Saturday 17 September

Pre-match aggro for today's match marginally less harassing in so far as my point of departure, Southend, is forty minutes less driving time from the Valley than home. My spirits were further lifted when, on arriving at the ground, I heard tell of Stoke's written apology to Carl for the blooper in their programme. They were abject, they had hastened to assure him, over their unseemly display of 'bare-faced cheek'.

I'd been intrigued on the way in by a radio report of a statement from Kenneth Clarke, who, as well as eating all the pies, is a lifelong Forest supporter – a misspent youth made evident by his Clough-like treatment of interviewers. He's apparently gone on record as saying that 'the introduction of all-seater stadia has not made a jot of difference to crowd safety' and, further, that in the wake of Hillsborough his erstwhile boss, the present Baroness Thatcher and mother of Mark, had not consulted at all with any of the MPs who attend football regularly.

While not knowing Best, Nanny, as ever, did know best and as in so many other instances did not want her expertise qualified, as it would seem, by informed opinion.

Reject his VAT strategies, though they might, no one, of course, would dare to eject Mr Clarke from his seat. And it may well be that he is a better fan than Chancellor. I think he may have re-opened a very worthwhile debate. I remain appalled at the attempt to sweep the catalyst for all this rebuilding upheaval, Hillsborough, under the carpet of the national conscience. Or worse, at the attempts to apportion the blame wrongly.

Now, let's take a deep breath. This is an issue requiring a clear head. Hillsborough, the plain truth is, was less a tragedy waiting to happen than one stage-managed by default by the culpably inept and negligent. Arrangements had been made to herd the by far more numerous Liverpool fans to the end with by far the smaller capacity – never mind its being still further restricted. The turnstile arrangements were stone-age. The baton-wielding mounted police only served to crank up the 'I want to get in! What's going on? Christ, they've started! We're missing it!' tension.

The deadly factor of there having been a motorway log-jam seriously delaying eastbound traffic across the Pennines was never taken into commonsense consideration. No flexibility of mind was brought to bear. Nobody from any authority had the sense, bottle and class to insist that the kick-off be delayed and *announced* as being delayed. The only initiative taken was the crass, the *fatal* one of ordering the wide gates on to the street at the Leppings Lane end to be opened. Hence the stampede forward. The deaths that ensued were overwhelmingly the product of totally incompetent, locked-off administrators and brain-dead, confrontation-obsessed policing – policing that on the matter of whether the gates were *ordered* to be opened or forced by the excluded crowd was soon to be revealed as lying.

Anyone who has ever, through no fault of their own, been late for a game, an important appointment, will understand the eruption that finally occurred. You've been delayed by bottle-neck circumstances quite beyond your control. Traffic cones. Petty officials. A missing passport. Lost keys. A knackered starting motor. It doesn't matter what. The clock has been running all the time and you've been looking at your watch with ever-increasing frequency and desperation. Now, in spite of everything, you've almost made it. Only there's one last hold-up. The impulse to freak out, to just go for it, mounts until it becomes irresistible. Impulse becomes compulsion. It's happened to all of us when the personal stakes are high. Multiply that individual reaction by the pressure of the group dynamic being generated by hundreds – 'Christ, someone'll score and we'll miss it!' – and a hysterical mass response is not only understandable but a virtual certainty.

In round figures, a hundred souls perished that afternoon in Sheffield. God alone knows how many of thousands of relatives and friends and loved ones received bruises to their hearts that will never fade. This condition is not to be confused with that of the police officer in (nominal) charge that day who, after the death toll, his unbelievable incompetence and his mendacity became public knowledge, was struck down by Post-Traumatic Stress Disorder, a condition which tragically foreshortened his burgeoning career.

Five years or so after the unspeakable events of that day, the nearest and dearest of the victims have had little more than a muttered 'Sorry 'bout that' from the fatal cluster of bungling authorities responsible.

I think it is fair to say that – at what a cost! One life would have been far too great a price – the FA has taken the lesson Hillsborough taught to heart.

But if Kenneth Clarke is correct, as I suspect he is, and all the massive structural upheaval has not materially improved safety standards; if the root cause of Hillsborough was not the terracing's configuration but incompetent planning; wouldn't it have been better to divert sufficient of that money to underwrite proper, responsible, civilised crowd management?

Life, meanwhile, goes on for those of us not directly linked to that time and place. Today at the Valley in the first of our Sod's Law ordained triple-decker against Swindon (one league match, two Coca-Cola ties), we had the sort of game that everybody was hoping that semi-final might turn out to be. A cracker.

In general we produced some of our best, flowing football of the season with Keith Jones making an outstanding ball-winning, movement-prompting debut. In particular, drawing a couple of defenders over to the right wing, I floated over a cross to David Whyte that, had he still been attached to the County Ground, Glenn Hoddle might have shed a little drool of his own over. Whytie's control of the ball and his despatching of it into the net were no less worthy of the great man. We were both on song and deserved more, I felt, from the crowd than to be distracted by chants of 'Lea – burn! Lea – burn!' every time Carl left the bench for a warm-up run.

Our cult hero was eventually sent on – a substitution (for Mark Robson) which entailed my moving to left midfield and, as a consequence, making a goal-saving tackle in our penalty area in the game's dying seconds. As Martin Ling dwelt on the ball a moment I got across him to nick it away for a corner.

'Penalty!' the Swindon fans, players and manager screamed with one voice.

'Great tackle, Nelse!' cried my team-mates.

'Play on!' called the one voice I was listening out for.

The TV replay shows that I played the ball cleanly away before making contact with Ling, but it was tight. Another time, another place, and not necessarily with another referee, and I might have been red-carded. That would have been my second set of marching orders. The first lot came as a result of dissent – the sort of muppet-like decision that in my opinion gives football a bad ... Cut!

Monday 19 September

I was offered the chance of another rest day but declined on the grounds of needing to run off the pints I got through over the weekend wetting new niece Harriet's head with brother-in-law Rodney.

Driving up I found myself killing time reflecting that with the season now settling down into its week-in, week-out stride, some of my first predictions were way off target. Oldham aren't sweeping all before them, home or away. Obvious front-runners as of now are Middlesbrough and Wolves – both managed by men with long, though differently assessed, associations with the England side. Nor is the hundred-minute match becoming the norm. The fear that red cards would become as commonplace as last year's four-letter words has not translated itself into fact. I think, on balance, there's been a reduction in clattering tackles from behind sweeping all before them. To that degree I'm guardedly beginning to think the shift of emphasis in the rules is an improvement.

Wednesday 21 September

The likely lads at Junction 9 on the M25 again and – oh! those bacon rolls. Team news highly relevant to me as we board the coach – there's no Carlo laid out like lino across the rear seat. He tweaked his calf in last night's reserve game.

76

I shook hands with Swindon manager, John Gorman, before the game – the aftermath of the (non-) penalty incident is all sweetness and light – and to his eternal credit John was shaking my hand again after the game and congratulating me on my 'match-winning performance'. (Well – only the first leg, actually, but we should be all right.) I did get two thoroughly tasty goals, dribbling the ball round the keeper for one, but the highlight as far as I was concerned was the sixty-yard ball I flighted out of defence for Whytie to run on to and – yet again – score. This was a pass Jan Molby might have put his hand up for.

The beers in Swindon tasted rather good that night.

Thursday 22 September

Back down to earth with a bump. Three hours of college. Great fun and games all round except for embarrassed me when the lecturer introduces me as the only student left over from when he taught the subject first time around two years ago. Still, as I'm always telling Curbs and Gritty: if at first you don't succeed . . .

Saturday 24 September

Another seven o'clock departure. This time for a Dartford Tunnel pick-up for the morning trip to Nottingham. No cash, word is, for a hotel stop-over last night. Jonesy had better play *really* well today.

Notts County, technically, is one of my former clubs. I went there on loan from Brighton for a two-substitution Magpie career that totalled twenty-six minutes. Not long enough to get my boots dirty. Ironically, several months later the two sides met at Wembley in the play-off final and – although thereby hangs a tale – I couldn't get on the field for either.

Meadow Lane has been totally transformed in the four years since my fleeting stay – a tremendous achievement on the part of a relatively small and indifferently supported club in the shadow of a much more glamorous one.

The managerial situation has also undergone radical change with the guv'nor of one of their youth sides during my month there now in charge of the first team. Mike Walker, the youth team coach then – *and* he lent me his car – did a tremendous job last year getting County about as close to the play-offs as is possible without, at the death, actually making it. With five minutes to go against us and 3–1 up they were, surely, there. Then we scored twice to ruin their dreams. Soccer memories are made of such charged and concentrated moments. Boardroom Alzheimer's has, apparently, eroded all recollection of the long, patient building that got County *so* close. Seven games into this year's campaign, Mike Walker has been rewarded with the sack.

Talking of transformations, my season is in danger of undergoing a major one. Two more goals in the last five minutes of *today's* game – would you believe! – took my tally to six from ten games and allowed us to come back from 1–3 down to earn a rather lucky point.

Six goals and as many goal-setting up final passes! I'm beginning to believe I'm on a roll. When it's not over before you know it, a week is a long time in football. I've just had one of my best in sixteen years.

Sunday 25 September

Got a big kick out of seeing my name up there in the leading, scorers tables in the *Sunday Express*. Quite a while since I've climbed to such dizzy heights. Enjoy it while it lasts, Nelse, 'cos it won't. No, I'm not being guilty of negative thinking. I've chapter and verse evidence the game allows very few a carefree ride at the top. After all, if last week was one of the best in my career, this coming one marks the fourth anniversary of one of its blackest periods.

It started with a call from Brighton manager Barry Lloyd to see him in his office at the Goldstone. I didn't have to hire a detective to know what was the purpose of this summons. The memory of the bonus dispute I had spearheaded on the eve of our magical mystery tour to Romania was still green – or, rather, raw – and John Byrne had newly arrived from Le Havre. I was surplus to Bazza's requirements; in his eyes a cuckoo in the Seagulls' nest.

Not to worry, Nelse. Lloydie sat me down and asked me if I was interested in moving to Bournemouth; Harry Redknapp had been in touch and was after me. Given the extent to which my relationship with Lloydie had soured over the past year or so, I needed only micro-seconds to make up my mind on that one. I may even have grinned.

'Fine,' Lloydie said, 'It's a goer. Frank McLintock will be handling the deal. He'll get in touch with you at home this afternoon after training.'

The moment I got home I was on the phone to the PFA. I knew they could tell me what I could reasonably and fairly be asking for in a Bournemouth context. Their advice, after indicating the going rate wasn't one I was very disposed to quarrel with, was that there was no point in false modesty and that at the outset I should go in at the high end and see what I could get. I was a bit taken aback by the size of the signing-on fee suggested – £60,000 – but, well, go for it. After all, this would very likely be the last move of my playing career with any money built in. The contract would be for three years and my basic salary would be £600 a week.

I'd no sooner put the phone down than it rang again and there on the line, indeed, was Frank McLintock. I told him what I was looking to get and he said that was fine: he'd merely add ten per cent on to the signing-on fee and I'd then pay this extra over to him.

Not how Bazza had explained it to me, as I now explained in turn. He had indicated, I said, that Frank's fee would be taken care of by the two clubs.

I really didn't see why I should have to pay Frank's fee. Nevertheless, I agreed that Frank should talk to Bournemouth on my behalf and also, if it seemed sensible, to Fulham whom, Frank had just revealed, were also expressing an interest in me.

The phone rang again to square the circle. Harry Redknapp said he was thoroughly willing to speak to me directly and, to be, er, frank, he could do without Frank being in on the deal. This seemed a much better way to fly. I agreed to come to Bournemouth the next day for a free and Frankless discussion.

When Harry met Garry, the new Bournemouth chairman was also present. Harry looked to be in considerable discomfort. I was genuinely unable to tell whether it was the after-effects of his recent accident or the steepness of my opening financial terms.

These were of somewhat nosebleed-inducing proportions. Add to them Brighton setting my value at £125,000, and the whole transaction was going to leave Bournemouth, already in considerable financial peril, precious little change out of £275,000 – this, mark you, for a player fast approaching his thirtieth birthday.

Harry and his chairman weren't blind to the prospect of my becoming a running financial/nasal wound if these numbers remained in the frame. They came back with an offer of an £80,000 transfer fee and, Brighton agreeing that, terms to be discussed at a future date.

The ability to compromise is a mark of the civilised. I can be civilised when it suits me. I said that I felt certain that given the good service I had rendered Brighton, Barry Lloyd would be prepared to do me a favour and drop the fee. I'd certainly think in positive terms about dropping my signing-on fee demands. So, sweetness and light. Garry left Harry and went to see Barry. The lights went out and the sweet turned sour. Lloydie made it very clear he was not at all best pleased about my venture into the DIY transfer market and no way – no way! – would he consider dropping the fee to £80,000.

On Friday I travelled with the first team to Blackburn and that evening received a pleasant surprise. On Teletext in my hotel bedroom I read that, the deal having gone through at the original £125,000 fee, I would be joining Bournemouth. How'd you like them Cherries! I inwardly chortled.

The game next day ended in a 2–1 victory. I didn't get on but, knowing I was on my way and this was probably the last chance for it, I wandered on to the pitch at full-time to give the Seagull fans a 'Thanks for everything' clap. I was very moved by the send-off they responded with. They seemed to have rated my efforts over the past three-plus years. I had a little glow inside me all the way back to the South Coast and enough scarves to open a branch of Oxfam.

But on Sunday – nothing. No phone call, no knock on the door, not even a postcard. You can't believe all you read on a cathode ray tube, I was beginning to remind myself.

Monday morning and I'm pulling Barry Lloyd aside at the training ground and asking what's going on. He responded in his usual effervescent manner. That's not to say he fizzed, but there were a lot of 'Fs' about. Yes, Harry had put something to him the previous night but, no, nothing doing. Barry had rejected it out of hand. As far as he was concerned the deal was dead.

Harry Redknapp did have the class to phone me that evening to bring me up to speed on what had happened. Even as we had been playing Blackburn, Bournemouth had been entertaining Fulham. Understandably enough, both clubs being interested in the boy Nelson, his name had surfaced over the G and Ts in the board room. Having been asked to cough up £125,000 for me the week before, the Cherries' chairman had been distinctly underwhelmed to learn that just a month earlier, in August, Fulham had been told my price tag was £80,000. So that was what they would accept! Knowing where he stood, the chairman had instructed Harry to repeat the Bournemouth offer of eighty grand. That had been the last nail in the deal coffin.

Teletext was now proclaiming to the nation's living rooms that the transfer had broken down because I couldn't agree personal terms. *Moi*!? Lloydie's PR machine working wonders there.

By now I was feeling used. A commodity regarded as of minimal value by its owners and not, finally, marketable either. End of story, maybe. For several grey, miserable no-man's-land weeks I soldiered on feeling I was perilously close to being past my 'Sell-by' date. Finally my patience and my nerves had had enough. Grabbing Martin Hinshelwood, our first team coach, I asked him what the hell was going on.

'And if you don't know, bloody well find out!'

'OK, OK, I'll have a word,' he said. 'I'll talk to Lloydie.'

He kept his word. That evening another piece in my destiny's jigsaw came down the phone. Martin told me Barry Lloyd had agreed to drop the fee and tomorrow, 24 October, the deal was going through for sure.

'Stay by the phone,' Martin rang off with.

As it happened, Brighton had a home match that next evening. No training, therefore. All I had to do was report in for the game. In that one sense, at least, I was a free agent. All morning, as the house got increasingly too familiar and oppressive, the walls closer and closer, the air heavier and heavier, Garry Nelson, father of two, wife and mortgage to support, nerves of highly strung piano wire, sat by the phone willing it to ring. It didn't. It was as diversion therapy, not in the belief that I would learn anything credible, that I picked up the remote control to access the Teletext sports pages. If they had surprised me before, what they now revealed came at me like an elbow-first aerial challenge Page 312, it was. It's burnt on my memory. There I'd been, waiting for the call to come that would confirm that, at last, I'd earned my family some decent money from the game and here I now was vainly trying to suspend the belief that I'd just read that Bournemouth had signed Andy Jones – from *Charlton*! – for £60,000.

Draw the veil. It's just as well our carpet is Antron stain-proofed.

But the night was still young. A further twist came when I reported to the ground at 6.15. Having been picked for every game, either to start or as substitute, I now discovered myself totally excluded from the squad. OK. No messing. Straight into the manager's office.

'What the hell's going on!?'

Not so much calm as glacial, Bazza told me I would no longer 'be involved' with the first team. I was on the transfer list.

'OK,' I said. 'But let's get one thing clear.'

I was very mindful of the previous performance of his PR machine.

'It's your decision,' I went on, 'not mine. I'm not asking for a transfer.'

More charity beginning at home. I was due a loyalty bonus. But if I took the initiative of *asking* for a transfer, I had as much chance of seeing it as JFK had of seeing the further side of Dallas.

Tuesday 27 September

Thrown a touch off balance on my arrival at the Valley this evening by some further remarks in the club programme from Alan Curbishley on the subject of GN. Namely:

> Garry Nelson's contribution to the team so far this season is a credit to himself. I hope and wish that some of the younger players at the club take a good look at him and the way he conducts himself on and off the field and take a little bit of what he has got on board. If they do, I am sure their careers will be enhanced. I am not just saying this because he has either scored or made goals recently. I am sure that if anyone deserves success then Garry does. After playing with him at Brighton, I knew exactly what we were getting when he came to the club and I am sure you appreciate his contribution as much as the players, myself and Steve do.

Heady stuff. Fulsome to the point of being OTT. It reads less like a eulogy than an obituary. The cynic in me wonders if he's redressing the balance after not so obliquely slagging me off a few weeks ago. The manic depressive in me wonders if he's softening me up for a killer blow: 'Nelse, I've had a tickle mentioning your name from an old mate of mine. Right now he's looking after Cowdenbeath . . .'

Thus the first defensive reaction to embarrassment at so public a compliment. But the raucous hurly-burly of the changing room, the automatic mechanics of stripping off, putting on my kit, give me not the camouflage of something to be getting on with but, paradoxically, a quiet interior moment in which to put Alan's remarks in deeper perspective. A moment's proper thought and I realise they deserve more than off-the-cuff cynicism.

It's easy to snipe at managers. Every fan, for instance, believes in his heart of hearts that he could do a better job than the X or Y who puts in sixty-plus hours a week actually running whatever team. Finally, in the classic formula, there are four ways to manage any team: the right way, the wrong way, the Curbishley/Gritt way and the Nelson way. Of course, Alan and Steve advocate some

83

strategic systems and tactical approaches with which I disagree. Of course, I'd rather not be on the end of knocking comments, deserved or undeserved, when my legs are turning to water at the end of a flat-out training session. But disregard those specifics where, because we are all human, we can agree that we disagree and I've a lot of time for both the Charlton managers.

Alan and I go back a fair way. When we were team-mates at Brighton, he established himself in my book as one of the classiest players I've ever turned out with. He was a wonderful passer of the ball – an ability crystallising his great touch, technique and vision. He was the sort of player I've always wanted and never managed to be – one whose class and finesse gave added value to his willingness to give 110 per cent week after week. When Alan graduated – if that's the right word – to managing I felt his thoughtfulness would serve him well and I actually called to mind an old Page One saying from the (mythical) *Successful Manager's Manual*: 'Your first signing is always going to be your most important – so make sure it's a good one!' When it turned out, not so long after, that Charlton's new management wanted to make me their first cash signing I was enormously gratified. I regarded it as the best accolade in my up and down career because it was, to use the word with its true force, the most meaningful.

Being an occasional opponent rather than an everyday colleague, I used to know Steve a lot less well. But we've since established that there was a deal of mutual respect behind our quick, end-of-match handshakes. Not altogether surprising, in fact. Steve's strengths and weaknesses as a player were pretty similar to my own – visibly weighted towards the commitment end of the scale rather than the subtle. But those same characteristics now serve him in very good stead as a manager, making it easy to respect and like him for his honest approach to his work.

Don't think I'm time-serving. I'm on my way out and the record shows that there have been a number of instances in my career where, confronted by what seemed to me an injustice or some downright stupidity from the 'boss' or his Board, I've dug in my heels, gone to tribunals and made life very difficult for myself. Nor am I in favour of forelock-tugging artificial respect for managers. A little surface mickey-taking is a useful safety valve in general and, if they're perceptive, can in particular cases act as a handy, unofficial early warning system. It also, quite simply, lightens the sheer slog of getting through day-to-day routines. But in a well-managed club beneath the them and us-ness will run a very real vein of mutual respect. Without it, whatever the individual talent knocking around, group potential will come nowhere near being realised.

Right now, I thought, as I surfaced in the changing room from my private thoughts, making the most of our potential, indeed, our actual advantage, wasn't going to be quite as straightforward as our fans on the terraces were probably assuming. Two goals up from the first leg and with no less than three away goals in the bank – we've got it made. We can afford to relax. Only we can't afford to relax. Not if it's going to make us complacent. But we mustn't get uptight about not being able to relax, any more than we should get uptight about getting uptight. So let's just relax. Up to a point.

We're mentally a bit rudderless. Further, several players are coughing and spluttering, and Mark Robson is looking a mite red-eyed and dishevelled after a forty-eight-hour vigil awaiting the birth of his second child. But hell, we're professionals, aren't we? We know what we've got to do. The onus is on Swindon. They've got the problem. They may go for a sweeper formation, but we run out without any special game plans or focused attitude.

In the event, Charlton versus Swindon Act III emerged as that work more generally known as *The Comedy of Errors*. It made a mockery of our 'wait and see' approach.

Prepared to try anything and everything, Swindon took to the field in Brazilian look-alike strip and, while we were still clocking the distinct lack of numbers and atmosphere in the ground, justified their pretensions by samba-dancing their way through our defence to score a goal in two minutes. The choreography, mind you, was immensely augmented by a weak-kneed, universal failure on our part to take part in the dance. We were nothing more than wallflowers – clear-cut evidence of panic. More than the pulled-back goal, it was our transparent edginess that now re-wrote the tie's script. Now it was a case of:

85

Charlton: Christ! We're going to blow our two-goal advantage.

Swindon: Hey, lads we can do this! They're here for the taking!

The black comedy of errors. We now proceeded to sleepwalk through a forty-five-minute nightmare. We hadn't had orders to attack flat out from the off and get the early goal that would make the tie tight. We really didn't do one thing or the other except gift Fjørtoft two more goals. Swindon had adapted to a sweeper system and whereas in the first tie David Whyte and I had been able to pull a flat back four every which way and get in behind, now we consistently found ourselves stymied by an intervening defender. When, that is, we got the ball. Basically that was never. We were having to come deeper and deeper into our own half to get a sniff of anything. At 0–3 down on the night, 3–4 down overall, we heard the half-time whistle and even the boos of our supporters with unalloyed relief.

We got the half-time bollocking we'd earned – but no substantial tactical insights into how to counter either Swindon's sweeper system or clamp down on Joey Beauchamp who, left entirely to his own devices, was having a (mid)field day. Swindon themselves, meanwhile, well, somebody must have put something in their half-time tea. They now opted to drop deep and do nothing but defend their lead. This strange decision now presented the fans with the tie no one wanted to win. It also gave us back the initiative.

We did carry the fight to them now – we're currently better in the second half anyway – and if we weren't fluent we were gutsy. Five minutes from time another fine example of on-the-spot opportunism from Whytie gave us an overall equaliser and the chance of doing for them in extra time.

In the brief respite before the last half-hour began, I had time retrospectively to clock a significant earlier moment. Midway through the second half Peter Garland (in because Jonesy was cup-tied) was substituted for Charlton's Under-18 England international Lee Bowyer. Lee has an old, canny head on his youthful shoulders. I had the clear feeling that for Peter this was another step backwards on the 'Up' escalator.

Extra time. For fourteen minutes we had them draped all over the ropes. They couldn't recapture their original rhythm. Then they dared to advance into our half. The defence stood off Joey Beauchamp and he compensated hugely for not fulfilling his million pound role as an Eastender by firing in the winning goal. Even that was black comedy with us the fall guys. Doing nothing wrong Andy Petterson dived to his left to cover the low shot. Had it been on target he would have saved it. But it wasn't. It hit the bottom of the upright. Hit it and rebounded back. Rebounded on to Andy's back. Rebounded and – oh, no! – re-rebounded into our net.

Given the away-goal rule we now had to score twice (a clear disadvantage, here, for teams playing at home in the second leg). We never looked like doing so. End of story. Our can of coke had lost its fizz. Sometimes only clichés will do to tell the story. Gutted was how I felt and that says it all. It had been a classic example of snatching defeat from the jaws of victory. For once I was guilty of not applauding the (non-applauding) fans. But I had one obligation to fulfil. John Gorman had been man enough to shake my hand after the first tie. I now made a point of seeking him out to shake his and congratulate him on getting his team out of gaol through his superior tactical flexibility.

In the changing room the air was appropriately funereal. No one had emerged from the night with credit and not only our short-term self-esteem, but a much-needed nice little earner of a tie in the next round had gone straight out the Valley window. On merit. I crawled down the road cheesed off and completely knackered.

Thursday 29 September

Too choked to write yesterday. In any case it was a day off. Lucky to get it, mind you. Often a 1–4 home defeat brings an all-morning running session in its sombre wake. Got through a measure of business bits and pieces as a diversion from thinking about what would inevitably be *today's* main order of business.

Which we duly got. Everyone on the staff was invited to view the video case for the prosecution in Management versus the First Team, on a charge of rank dereliction of duty, duly held at the

Valley Assizes. It was a pretty open and shut case with all parties culpable. The forwards for not closing down defenders and, when the service to them was patently in short supply, not working hard enough to make ourselves available. The midfield for operating too deeply, not maintaining shape and failing to venture into the opposition's box. The back four for granting the Swindon forwards too much time and space in which to get balls down and be creative.

A few pleas in mitigation were being advanced and the discussion growing lively when an entirely different dimension was put on the humiliation. Steve Gritt, Keith Peacock and captain Alan McLeary got to their feet. This was not in dissent but a prelude to their setting off to discharge their sad duty of representing the club at the funeral of ex-England Youth captain and former, if briefly, Charlton player, Barry Little who, after a cruel struggle, died last week at the age of thirty from a brain tumour. Thirty. A whole dozen years older than Lee Bowyer. And three years younger than Garry Nelson.

This sad downer of a moment was strangely cathartic. It put Tuesday night in its proper perspective. What does the result of a game between two indifferent football teams rate against a young life arbitrarily cut short?

Friday 30 September

Talked at length with Bob Bolder, our former first choice goalkeeper, who was forced to retire last season after a nightmare sequence of operations on a suspect knee.

Bob is still finding his feet – so to speak – while in something of a career limbo. Unwilling or unable to sever all connection with the Valley completely, he comes in two or three days a week to maintain his fitness. Totally genuine, always smiling, Bob was as brave a keeper in the six-yard box as there's ever been.

Two people not smiling at all this morning are Alan and Steve. They want to cauterise Tuesday's wound as speedily as possible by winning tomorrow. One significant transplant aimed at this has already been effected on the team sheet. Lee Bowyer keeps his place and will start his first league game. The immediate impact of this on me is that I'm late getting away from the training ground. This is because of the possibly much more far-reaching impact it may have on the career of John Robinson.

The impression that John has so far made at Charlton has been neither one thing nor the other. His chances of really making a mark have been hampered by injury and now there is the added pressure of this being the last year of his current contract. John is keenly alive to the necessity of a regular first team place if he is to consolidate and progress his career. But – enter Lee Bowyer. One man's gain is another one's probable loss. John seeks out the management to discuss his pretty apparent move down the pecking order for recall to the first team. I am left to dwell on the fragility that so often underlies all our macho huffing and puffing. There's more tears shed in private than blood and sweat out on the park and when it's going rotten you feel you're playing on glass eggshells.

When, at long last, I finally did get home, life – or, more precisely, death – once again reduced these career speculations to minor considerations. Carole told me that, after a long illness, my Nan, as I shall always think of her, had died. She was eighty-five. I felt that certain measure of relief we all experience when news of such an ending is finally given us. After a long illness she had been spared further suffering: the burden on her immediate family has been lifted. But my core emotion was sadness and a feeling of being that much more bereft in the world. Then, after a while, came gratitude as I remembered some of the wonderful times I had been lucky enough to enjoy with my grandparents in the Independent Republic of Merseyside when they and I and everyone else in the world were immortal.

OCTOBER

Saturday 1 October

Got the result we badly needed today, a 3–0 win over Watford. For all that, they had a clear edge in the first half. Then, in the second . . .

I don't know. Life's a great kidder. Just as long as it's not you on the receiving end. As sooner or later it always is.

Is it a cross? Is it a shot? In the second half, Steve Brown pumps a long ball forward from around the join of halfway and right touch lines. It's going nowhere. Then, suddenly dipping viciously, it is. It's going over the head of the off-his-line, back-peddling goalkeeper to smack against the bar. Everyone seems gobsmacked into immobility. Except me. The ball bounces back into play, sits up just nicely as I dart in and – wallop! – I've headed it in to the net with, for me, unprecedented force. Another goal! A thrill goes bubbling through me. Six now in six games. The first emotion now is getting to be not relief but glee and, almost, satisfied expectancy. Am I on a roll or am I on a roll! Let's get on with the game, lads!

Cue life the kidder.

'That's quite enough of that, young Nelson. We don't want you getting ideas above your station, do we? Time to teach you a little lesson.'

Just minutes after the strike I'm limping off the field with a hamstring strain in the leg I use for standing on. For me, the rest of the game was strictly on audio – a riddling cacophony of soaring 'oohs' and diminishing 'aahs' – as back in the depths of the changing room I iced the offending, bloody leg. In fairness, it had tried to give me a warning. Even when scoring in the last minutes of the Notts County game I had felt some twinges. Philanthropically allowing Swindon to take us into extra-time midweek had hardly been a rest cure. Now, the third hard game in eight days . . . Besides trying to supply a mental video of the ongoing game to the rise and fall of the crowd's roar, I had too much time to embroider on this last thought. Reporters might even now be penning such deathless prose as 'Current fixture schedules are plainly asking far too much of veteran Charlton striker . . .' And the management, reading this . . . You see – within minutes more eggshells and adolescent paranoia.

But no matter how bad things are, I hobbled off to find the distraction of a chat with someone with troubles of his own. Conveniently to hand was Darren Pitcher. This was Daz's first trip back to the Valley. In a totally unstreetwise travesty of PR thinking, some Charlton idiot had asked Darren to make the prize draw at half time. This is close to asking Paul Ince to take a lap of honour at Upton Park. The greeting Darren received on stepping back on to the Valley pitch was vociferous. And almost universally derogatory.

To his credit, he was now largely shrugging it off by the time I hobbled over to him. It's a drop in the ocean, he implied, compared to the hard times the papers are giving him. In their speak, speculation is rife that, after only three months at Selhurst Park, Darren is searching for the door marked 'Exit'. 'Not true,' Darren told me and said it was all a case of falsely representing the facts. The doubting Thomas in me couldn't help but wonder whether it might also be another 'load of Hall's' – a handy way of keeping an off-the-field property in the shop window.

Monday 3 October

Things may not be totally black. Jimmy Hendry's assessment of my injury has it appearing reasonably low on the Richter scale. I've torn a few fibres and strained the hamstring only slightly, he reckons. That feels about right. The spasm that was giving me real gyp has subsided to the point of my being able to get on with some strengthening weight exercises. Boring, mind you. In an effort to relieve the treatment room tedium I browsed through the litter of newspapers that always adds that little something to the pavilion's decor. Its readership in mind as ever, *The Sun* was on typically neanderthal song. Its account of the Watford game was hung entirely on Darren's reception and an alleged meeting with Palace manager Alan Smith earlier in the week. Trenchant observation there, all right. And, yes, looking hard, this alleged sports pages gossip column did print the result.

Tuesday 4 October

More of the same. Boring. And Nature is in tune with me. A chill easterly wind and a temperature drop of several degrees Centigrade give warning that winter isn't going to be backward about coming forward much longer.

Wednesday 5 October

More of the boring, necessary same. Who said R & R was fun? And tomorrow is already casting its sad shadow forward. Compassionate leave granted for me to journey north to attend the funeral of my Nan.

Thursday 6 October

The gathering of the Nelson clan to pay its respects to a wonderful old lady. A day full of the common-place remarks and small talk that do so much to blunt the immediate sharpness of grief.

Nan was buried with my grandfather in the Nelson family plot. The thing that has always surprised me about this plot is its location. It's in the one corner of the cemetery from where you can't see Goodison Park. Perhaps Grandad knew he'd be there in spirit anyway.

The wake of a reception afterwards was identical, I'm sure, for all its local differences, to the millions that have preceded and will follow it. Memories, old acquaintances, Everton games, a sudden sharp hunger – that sense of life gearing up to go on.

Friday 7 October

To play or not to play. That is the question. Has been all week. Only way to resolve it is through a Jimmy Hendry fitness test. There's nothing token about what he asks of me. He not only tests the damaged hamstring area close to destruction but comes perilously close to doing for my lungs and heart as well. But it's all worth it. A good range on the stretch, good mobility, no noticeable pain.

'Well?'

Jimmy is scrupulously careful to apply no moral pressure pro or con. The decision is mine. I hesitate a moment. A week is a short time in a hamstring convalescence. But it wasn't the full-blown variety and there's no discomfort now and with things going so well for me on the pitch it would be silly to miss a game. I declare myself fit.

Saturday 8 October

No overnight reaction to yesterday's fitness test whatsoever. Good. It's a beautiful, autumnally warm day. Winter has postponed its invasion in the face of an Indian Summer. That's got to be an omen for me. Also lightening the trip up from the coast is the presence of two good friends from Plymouth, Ken and Irene. It's their first trip to the Valley and they're more than a little impressed.

Biggish game today. We've pulled ourselves up to a current sixth place in a very tightly packed division with only Wolves and Middlesbrough, the joint leaders, winning consistently. Today we've got the early season's surprise package, Reading. Newly promoted they're sitting a couple of places above us largely on account of their mean machine of a defence. But we've got ground advantage and if we use it to win today we'll have put a big dent in their confidence.

We get off to the worst possible start. We're a goal down after five minutes. Now we've got that well-drilled defence of theirs to break down in real earnest. But right now it's yet again our own defence that's under siege. I sprint back to help out sliding and stretching to nick the ball away from a Reading forward. Good!

Done that! Now – snap, crackle and shit! I get the message instantly. A stabbing pain in the back of my right leg unequivocally announces that the hamstring hasn't stood up to the extra, straining awkwardness of an actual match situation.

Only thirteen minutes into the game. Unlucky for some. Ken and Irene won't be too impressed about *this*. Nor anyone else. There's going to be many a raised eyebrow turned in my direction.

'Gamble didn't pay off, Nelse. Why'd you risk it?'

In the too familiar cold light of the Valley changing room and that other light thrown by wisdom after the event I ponder my reply as, once again, I threaten to blow Charlton's refrigeration budget for the year.

Well, I'd come through the Friday test so well, it didn't seem like a gamble. It would have seemed unrealistic *not* to declare myself fit. Dozens of times over the past years I've been in the identical situation, said 'Yes' and been proved right. Only, at the back of my mind there's a small trap door with a question mark painted on it. I know what's waiting to spring out. All the familiar variations on the theme of my present reality. Thirty-three and in the last year of my contract. In the fight for a first team shirt, possession is nine-tenths of the law. Part of me must have been wondering whether I could afford to give somebody else the opportunity of playing well and keeping their place in the team by filling my shoes on a permanent basis. Was it *totally* a considered judgement on my part?

As the roars ebb and flow outside I go over it again and again. The changing room's walls and hooks and benches have seen it all before. They couldn't care less. Then comes a crumb of comfort to put in the 'plus' scales of my self-interrogation. The club doctor, Dr Kallend, informs me that today's strain is not entirely a repetition of last week's. There may be a knock-on connection due to an attempt at over-compensating on the hamstring's part but, essentially, I've picked up a new injury. Well, it's good news for my conscience anyway.

So. Not for the first time I'm a sadder and a (temporarily) wiser man. There's going to be no second mistake. Before I play again the leg is going to have to be stronger than it was before the first twinges developed. This will mean two or three weeks of stretching and weights. It's all been a painful and possibly costly cock-up. Certainly for me and, indirectly, arguably for the team. At half time we're still that goal down. I hobble out to watch the second half. In very short order tiny, touch-player Mark Robson, whom you instinctively expect to see taking corners, leaps like a salmon to meet one from Colin Walsh and bullets an unstoppable header past Reading's impregnable defence. One all!

One all – and at once our knee-jerk responding supporters make me uneasy by reverting to stereotype.

'You're not singing, you're not singing, you're not singing any more,' they sort of sing themselves.

Yes, I know they've been frustrated for best part of an hour now. I know they've paid their money to watch. But it's such a corny, 'me too' reaction. It makes them the same, not different, from all the fans in all the grounds this side of Casablanca and beyond. And, I know – I just know – it's asking for it. And sure enough we and they all get it. Another page one error in defence gifts Reading their second and the winning goal. So it is an all-round cock-up after all. In a day of top-of-the-table upsets, Wolves and Middlesbrough have both lost. And so have we. The exception to the rule are Reading and today's 2–1 victory has seen them emerge as today's big winners overall.

I didn't sing at all on the way home.

Monday 10 October

The leg still being able to operate the accelerator and brake pedals, I travelled to London on my own today. The nominal reason, as far as my usual fellow commuters were concerned, was that I was being selfless: taking care they didn't have to hang around after training while I had extra treatment. The probably not so hidden agenda was that I wasn't in the mood for chit-chat.

The assessment of my injury in the cold light of a Monday morning tallied with the doctor's Saturday diagnosis: the entire right hamstring is understrength and two specific areas have local damage.

Treatment today was minimal – suction pads and a small electric current passing through the affected areas. The main repair job is going to be down to good old-fashioned stretching and weights, but for the immediate moment just what the physio is ordering is rest and the state-of-the-art treatment Jimmy is lining up for me tomorrow.

Tuesday 11 October

A voyage to the bottom of the sea today for Admiral Nelson. After a fashion. Swanley is quite near the Thames but the diving tank never actually gets wet and I'm not being asked to plumb the depths in any literal way. My mission, should I choose to accept it (as if I *had* a choice), is to sit in a decompression chamber that will then be pumped out to simulate the atmosphere of a diving bell forty-five feet under water. This submarine session will last for an hour and a half. It's not a test of my ability to hold my breath. Via a mask I'll be breathing pure oxygen. The whole point of the exercise is that in this altered state the blood transports oxygen around the body far more quickly and efficiently. Recovery is accelerated.

Nice to know, because at first glance the chamber is pretty daunting – a real Captain Nemo, Apollo space capsule effort. Portholes, a door straight out of Fort Knox, (don't suppose they missed it) and the latest in Major Tom intercom systems. It's upturned kettle-drum in shape and about the capacity of a mini-bus.

Alf Rowley, the Swanley Centre's co-ordinator mainly treats MS sufferers. He's also had quite a few professional footballers, however, as the therapy is well established and known. Several Premiership clubs, in fact, have already invested in their own tanks. With Charlton, though, it's just like the team bus. Why buy when you can rent on a need basis?

Not really believing it's going to be my last, I take a deep breath and duck through the massive door. I beat off the initial feeling of intense claustrophobia. What lies ahead, I already know, is ninety minutes of end-to-end tedium.

* * *

Wednesday 12 October

A day off for fit members of the squad. Some consolation for me, though. I can trade the hike all the way up to New Eltham with a short trip down the road to Brighton. Malcolm Stuart the genial and, surprise (he must be taking his own medicine), no longer rotund physio for the Albion has never been backward in coming forward to help former Seagulls. Today he's lending me a hand.

He knows his craft. The treatment is attentive and, I sense, is doing me good. But soon it's tedium time again. The same old rehab routine of stretching and weights.

I'm not alone. Alleviating the mind-blowing boredom a touch are former team-mates Dean Wilkins (who will love you for ever if you don't introduce him as 'Ray's brother') and John Crumplin who is not only injured but in no-man's land. He's been freed by Liam Brady, but he's still got nine months of his contract to run. Short to mid-term his weight training is non-stop. He's toting a permanent ball and chain around.

Also on hand is Steve Foster – 'Fossie' to everyone in the game. He can't quite be lumped in with the rest of us. His re-hab work is restricted to his right index finger and a bicep, as from the comfort of the medical couch he works at his mobile phone. He's thirty-six, so good luck to him.

We're all making with the put-downs and the bad jokes, chuckling away, when Malcolm comes back in. He's always genial. Except now. He's got a face on him like the back of a hearse. Something we said? Our levity too undue for him?

'Nelse,' he says flatly looking straight at me. 'You've just played Swindon. How was Kevin Morris?'

Ah, I think, the job merry-go-round is creaking again. Kevin is Malcolm's opposite number at Swindon, physio there for the past twenty-five years. I'm just one of the countless players he's helped back to fitness.

'Fine,' I say a touch guardedly. 'We had our usual little chat. Why?'

'He was found dead, yesterday,' Malcolm says just like that. 'In his car. It was full of fumes and there was a hose hooked up to the exhaust.'

Jesus Christ. I feel myself grow cold under the film of sweat I've built up. I struggle not to believe what I've heard and then acknowledge that I must. His news so starkly delivered, Malcolm is like the rest of us. At a loss for words. He turns on his heel and goes.

No more gagging around now. The three of us take refuge in the familiar. We fix our minds on completing our exercises. The grunts and groans of our exertions come thick and fast to punctuate the silence as we complete our programmes in double quick time.

As I drive home I remember Kevin. In the midst of life as the Prayer Book says. A lot of suicides in sport. People who never made it to the top. People who did and then couldn't face the long littleness of the anti-climax when their time out in the middle was over. Or is that an illusion? No greater number of suicides among sportsmen than 'ordinary' people, just a higher-profiled write-up of their going? In the midst. I don't know. It seems that lately the black angel has been doing quite a bit of tip-toeing around the edges of my own life.

In the evening comes welcome diversion of a not-altogether superficial kind. I take my seat – couch potato style – to clock Robert Lee running out against Romania at Wembley in an England shirt. What gives his debut significance for me, of course, is that it's my own vicarious wish fulfilment. It's the nearest I'll ever come to realising my own dreams.

Suddenly there he was – running out with three lions on his chest on to the floodlit turf, the roars of his countrymen and, now, the national anthem. What pride he must have felt! What pride his Dad, Reg, must have been feeling! I felt the hair on the back of my head stand up as I thought how my own family would have reacted if it had been me there.

We were trailing and the game losing its spark when – wham! – it had come alight again in a way that brought me bolt upright from my slouch. Lurker's debut had progressed from dreamland to flat-out fantasy. He had scored! Latterly he's hit some blinding goals for Newcastle. This was more of a Charlton goal – one third determination, one third skill and one third luck. But it saved

Venables' bacon and underlined Lurker's very respectable overall performance against top-flight opposition.

Thursday 13 October

Thought the training ground would be buzzing today about Lurker's debut with some of the squad letting our Press Officer, Peter 'Scoop' Burrowes, in on its having taken place. Wrong, Nelse. This was another morning of tight-lipped conversations and an almost tangible sense of aggro in the air.

Source of the troubled airwaves proved to be the re-hab room which, with no less than ten bodies occupying its cramped confines, bore a close resemblance to the Atlanta square sequence in Stuart Balmer's favourite film. Jimmy Hendry certainly had the white-lipped and trembling look of a Confederate surgeon after Gettysburg. He had derived this, the world and his wife soon gathered, from being hauled over the coals by the management for seeming to allow his 'patients' to muddle along doing their own unsupervised thing. Jimmy's understandable rearguard defence had been that it was *organised* chaos, there being an unusually high number of players to treat, all with different problems and all at various stages of recovery. It's not only diving bells that exert pressure.

The general feeling that the management had been passing on some of the enhanced atmosphere they'd been experiencing themselves was confirmed to most of our satisfactions by the sudden, 'chance' appearance on the scene of the club chairman. The outcome was a decision to divide so that Jimmy could rule.

Attendance at a second, afternoon, session was enforced on half the walking wounded and both sittings were now subjected to far more specific workouts from Jimmy and his able assistant, Gary Moss.

All somewhat disquieting, though. I left the leafy lane leading out of the training ground with the immortal words of Corporal, rather than Keith, Jones ringing in my mind: 'Don't panic! ... Don't panic!'

* * *

100

Friday 14 October

The pressure today was relentless. Oxygen tank-wise, anyway. I got through it by combating density with the lightweight and read a Wilbur Smith.

Saturday 15 October

Novelty phenomenon time. What might be called a Red Letter Saturday. I'm able to take advantage of being sidelined by enjoying the luxury (as it seems) of a normal family weekend. I tried not to think about proceedings against Port Vale – I couldn't lose whatever they might turn out to be. If Charlton won, I was on a bonus – a little bit of an earner for nothing. If they lost, well, everyone would point to the obvious reason: the absence from the scene of one Garry Nelson. Either way I was on a winner.

In the event, achieving an excellent 2–0 result, so were the team. I had not been conspicuous by my absence. Good for the club and, as a couple of calls soon informed me, good for Kim Grant. I was told that Kim, who must be fairly miffed at the old man's form keeping the young gun from the team sheet, had met this opportunity head on with a thoroughly good performance.

'Thanks for letting me know. Cheers.'

I put the phone down and already those nerves in the pit of the stomach are on jangle duty. They can do without me after all.

Sunday 16 October

After the family, the relations. Public Relations. Open Day at the ground. A three-line whip out for all players to be present and show the acceptable face of Charlton Athletic plc. The non-compulsory turnout out from the public is pretty impressive. Two and a half thousand and mainly families. The efforts the club has been making with its family programme are bearing fruit.

I suspect Charlton are rather more progressive and open on this front than many clubs. Right across the country, and hence the Football League, there's both need and scope for a lot more community-relation initiatives. Not least from the players.

I can hear the groans of disbelief in the changing room as I write this. And the committed response.

'Sure, Nelse, right. Be on the case tomorrow.'

But they should. If players don't make it part of the job now, in fifteen years' time they may not have a job at all.

One player who never has trouble mixing with the public at all – particularly if the public has had the forethought to congregate at the nearest local – is Steve Cooper, a good mate of mine at Plymouth. Steve normally phones every month or so, but this time his voice is distant to the point of inaudibility.

'I know it's a long way to York, Coops,' I say. 'But either you've been ripped off on one of those el cheapo mobile deals or we've got a really bad line.'

'Could be 'cos I'm speaking from a hotel in Hamilton.'

Fuzzy snapshots of Bermuda and New Zealand and Ontario mix in and out of my envious mind. I can be sure it's not Scotland because, unlike local lad Colin Walsh, there's no way you'd describe Steve as academical. Still, better make sure.

'You've not signed on for the Accies, have you?'

'Close. Airdrie.'

My mistake. But there's no trace as yet of his native Brummie accent having been swamped by Kelvinside or, come to that, Glenfiddich.

'I've just signed a three-year deal.'

For a huge signing-on fee, it transpires, *plus* assistance with his accommodation for the duration. The green-eyed monster hovers nearer still for a moment as, fingers not quite crossed, I congratulate him. What my old manager, Dave Smith, always used to say ought to be carved in stone above the players' entrance to every ground: 'It's better to be a lucky player than a good player.'

Monday 17 October

Dropped in on Mark Barham. I'd heard over the grapevine that he'd suffered a ruptured patella and was being forced to stay at home with his leg up for the next few weeks.

Mark's league career ended two years ago and the ball hasn't run for him since. He was playing in the Sussex League for

Southwick, our friend in common Russel Bromage's side, when this last, heavy duty injury finished his career. Now his 1994/95 CV looks bleak in the extreme. Thirty-two; no job or trade; no foreseeable involvement in football on the playing side and, facing the non-existent facts, no training or qualifications for the outside world.

I tried to lift Mark's spirits but I didn't get the impression I was succeeding. An hour before I had been at a simulated depth of forty-five feet. Mark was down at a much lower level and there was nothing artificial about it at all.

When times are hard we always gravitate back towards happier early days. It seems that life without football for Mark and his wife, Max, will involve a move back to the Norwich area, scene of some of his finest moments.

Here's another one for the Christmas cracker: 'It's better to be a good player than a bloody unlucky one.'

Tuesday 18 October

Back with Charlton at New Eltham. Light training. Leg improving a lot. Mind deteriorating as rapidly on account of all the sitting around waiting for the second re-hab sitting. Performing to packed houses, The Great Jimmy and Gary Physio Show is still playing twice daily.

Wednesday 19 October

Back with Brighton as an honorary Seagull. Stepped up training with no ill effects. The leg is definitely a lot stronger.

Later I had another session in another decompression chamber. This week's big bonus – once again I do not speak literally – has been discovering another centre only eight miles from home.

At Swanley I went in at the deep end on my own. Here, where the tank is marginally smaller, the claustrophobia factor is numerically increased but psychologically lessened by the presence of four other immersees. Not fellow Football League crocks. Two in wheelchairs, two still able to manage on sticks, they are MS sufferers.

At once I feel bogus, a fraud usurping the place of somebody whose need to be here is far greater than my own. I'm a professional athlete bursting with health who could turn out in a marathon and finish in a very creditable position. My need to be here is 'serious' only for short-term, commercial reasons. I'm a prima donna with a trivial niggle that seems utterly insignificant alongside so debilitating a disease.

My co-divers all seem to be in late middle age but I suspect that the inroads of the MS have already put fifteen years on their appearance. It has also nurtured a wonderful mental resilience. They prove to be terrific company. Perceiving, I'm sure, my embarrassment, they immediately set about putting me at ease. Successfully. Their cheerfulness is catching and it is a source of genuine regret to me when, bringing me back to where we are and for what purpose, the intercom's metallic 'Masks on!' cuts short our chatting and drives me back to Wilbur Smith. God willing, I may have another half century ahead of me. As I get towards the far end of it there will be more significant milestones to look back on, I hope, than scoring for Brighton or getting mildly injured while with Charlton.

From life under pressure in more ways than one to life at the top: Man Utd v Barcelona, the pitch populated by millionaires and millionaires elect. The match itself, a 2–2 draw, was hugely enjoyable, but what caught my serious attention was a remark from Kevin Keegan that, once the European Super League had been set up, games of this quality and momentousness would be weekly commonplaces.

A slip of the tongue or Kevin's basic honesty? Either way, at last somebody had been prepared to make a public reference to the patently obvious shape of things to come. As television's influence – i.e. money – continues to call the tune, it's a natural progression.

At the moment, just within the UK, Rupert Murdoch's Sky has paid £300 million for the rights to Premiership games over five years. For the same time period, some of the ITV franchise holders have paid £11 million to screen Division One games. The pro rata division of the spoils has seen the rich clubs getting richer and, as they plough back profits by investing in star players from across the globe, the playing field becoming less and less level.

We now have a domestic elite. But with the same half-dozen clubs dominating year-in, year-out, interest in UK soccer is going to become more and more synthetic. There will be no more local heroes, no more eleven good men and true. If (when?) holders of eleven different national passports ever take the field at Old Trafford, support for 'the lads' will be totally prefabricated. Fabricated by TV. And it could well come to pass. Consider the value of the pan-European market-place to advertisers and then multiply Sky's investment in the Premiership proportionately and we're quite possibly looking, I would think, at a European League up and running by the year 2000. Watch your screen for further announcements.

Friday 21 October

A strange feeling today. A Friday morning but, for me, no game to plan for. It's very hard to motivate yourself in such a vacuum and I could tell my fellow walking-wounded were having similar difficulty in giving the session their best shot.

Moreover, my worth to the club was formally acknowledged. When in the squad you receive four complimentary tickets to a game. When you're wasting everyone's time and money being injured, two is the going rate. This week this is an annoying fact of life. Sod's law is that I've several friends in Worthing who are Burnley ex-pats. I'm obliged to indulge in some pretty serious grovelling before I can up my 'half-pay' allocation to the five tickets I'm looking for. Even then we'll have to be split up.

Saturday 22 October

Sometimes I start to despair. At a time when it can be accurately stated that eighteen clubs in Division One are in touch with relegation – so tight is the points spread – our covered end choir 'wittily' greets the visitors with choruses of 'Down with the Millwall/You're going down with the Millwall...' Burnley have only to win today to close within five points of us. And, of course, after our 'supporters' have asked for it in this way, that's precisely what they proceed to do. As for the game – draw the veil. Nelson wasn't the only Charlton player to plumb the depths this week. So

105

too, their frustration rising, did numerous other fans around me. The only lifeline to a Charlton result that I could see today was Colin Walsh, who did hit half-a-dozen defence-cracking passes in the course of the game. In various ways they came to nothing but at least the vision and intent were there. All round me, though, yells arose: 'Get stuck in Walsh!'

'Walsh, you're a waste of space!'

'Get it down the field, Walsh!'

And all the rest. It wasn't Colin's job to be a ball-winner today, thumping it forward in thoughtless hope. None of his detractors seemed able to see what he was trying to do. Not one had the intelligence to comment on the root cause of Charlton's ineptitude – that the back four were playing so deeply that the midfield, having to come right back to link with them, were allowing Burnley the freedom to waltz around the centre of the park.

After this display of bathos from the home team, my four guest-passengers were in buoyant mood on the way back to Worthing. If not submerged, I was subdued. I could be quite sure of seeing a lot more of that Burnley game next week.

Wednesday 26 October

Was I right or was I right? Today is Crime and Punishment day. Due to the poor performance against Burnley the usual midweek day off has been forfeited. In that this is my first involvement proper with the squad in over two weeks, I am almost certainly the only one genuinely pleased to be here. And from my point of view it's timely. Discussion with Jimmy Hendry is prompting the thought that, all continuing to go well, I might resume combat duty by coming on for a while in Saturday's reserve game at Highbury.

Warm-up over, I was relegated once again to the Red Cross brigade. However, I now found myself involved in a far from disabled running session, ten 200-metre runs across the training ground's entire width. It was all good news. I surprised myself by the quality of my running and then received the added bonus – no comment! – of being told to rejoin the non-malingerers.

Thursday 27 October

It would have been more romantic if it had been only twenty-four hours from Tulsa. But since I am probably the only person in the world to look upon it as a historic occasion, it is probably more appropriate that it should have been roughly three miles short of Swanley. There, in the outside lane of the M25, all but one of the zeros on the odometer of my H-reg Tempra, henceforth to be known as Old Faithful, rolled into alignment and the car had clocked its first 100,000 miles. I've had it from new. While it's happening (but against all financial logic) the symmetry of the instant is strangely satisfying. A few seconds later comes the certain knowledge that the vehicle has now completely slid off the Glass's Guide scale. Another mile or two and it seems as if all 100,000 of those miles has flashed before my eyes. Call it the agony of the long-distance commuter – countless hours of bloody-mindedness, sweat and adrenalin. Move over Damon, and go back to managing the Bates Motel. You're out of a job. After this Schumacher will be putty in my hands. The bottom line, of course, is that when Charlton approached me, the Board didn't rate my services highly enough to make subsidising my move up to the Valley's doorstep a priority. They had a more literal approach to the proposition that Garry Nelson should be accorded fast-lane treatment.

Half an hour later, the disloyal thought is chased from my mind by Mike Salmon paying me – I *think* – a compliment.

'A hundred thousand miles,' he tells me. 'That's only two K less than you've clocked playing up front for us.'

No time for pleasantries later in the day as, once again, we are kept in after school to revisit, courtesy of video, the scene of the Burnley crime. In the discussion that slowly builds afterwards, Stuart Balmer forthrightly points out our now well-established inability to play against the diamond formation and questions our unswerving adherence to a 4–4–2 line-up. This seems to me to be very much to the point; an Achilles' heel we need to do some DIY chiropody on. I do my best to support him by wondering out loud if word about this has now got round to the other clubs to such a degree that they are positively altering their formation when they

107

play us. It's beginning to look that way to me. Nobody breaks into cheers on my finishing.

Saturday 29 October

A spot on the subs' bench for the Reserve game at Highbury. I park myself there after the warm-up knowing there's faint chance today will come anywhere near to replicating the extreme goings-on of my two previous games against Arsenal.

The first, nearly a decade ago, was for Swindon Town in a Combination game. I'd actually been demoted to the reserves to teach me a disciplinary lesson. It happened thus.

In the previous first-team game I'd been subjected to a torrent of abuse from one particular fan. Even while I'd been warming up, he'd been similarly tuning his larynx at my expense and as the game proper progressed, he continuously cranked up the anti-Nelson volume knob. Then I delivered an inch-perfect cross, the despatching of which into the net, believe me, was a formality. As Colin Gordon, the scorer waved his thanks to me, I turned and despatched a no less well-directed volley of my own, two-fingered model, at the fan. Then I saw Lou Macari trotting across the pitch in my direction. He's either coming over to congratulate me or to sniff my breath, I naturally found myself thinking. Wrong on both counts. Instead, probably tongue-tied in front of the vast crowd, Lou substituted action for words and threw a couple of punches at my chin. As, in his haste, he'd neglected to detour via the touchline and bring a stool with him, these blows, fortunately for me and perhaps for him, lacked the pinpoint accuracy I had achieved thirty seconds earlier and went on to reproduce, believe me, later in the game when making our winning goal. In vain as regards preserving my first-team status.

My digital dexterity coupled with Lou's finesse in maximumly motivating his players had cost me my place. Instead, it earned me one with the Fourth Division stiffs running out against the Gunners.

Lined up against us were such luminaries as Chris Whyte, Gus Caesar, Ian Allinson, Brian Talbot, Graham Rix and Raphael

Meade. Clearly a daunting task lay before us. But we didn't allow ourselves to become overawed. Deciding to enjoy playing at a five-star ground we adopted a pragmatically mature approach and, by defending stoutly, kept the game goalless for fifteen seconds. This score against the established pattern of the game knocked us out of our rhythm. At half time we trooped back into Highbury's heated marble halls 5–0 down. A lot of people would have said that was that, but a common-sense and morale-boosting team-talk gave us a new tactical perspective on the game and consequently we were not rendered despondent by Arsenal's sixth goal just after the whistle had blown for the resumption of play. We'd been expecting it.

At this point, the Good Samaritan in Graham Rix had him tempering total all-round superiority with charity. Recognising, as he lined up a free kick on the edge of the box, that our shell-shocked goalkeeper would be grateful for assistance from any source, Graham announced loudly that he would be curling the ball into the top left-hand corner. Ah, yes, but whose left hand? Yours, Rixy or mine? Could you . . . ? Well, never mind now, doesn't matter. While the keeper had been trying to resolve this conundrum, Graham had meantime sweetly flighted the ball over the wall into one of the goal's two top left-hand corners. At this juncture all four members of the crumbled Swindon wall broke into sustained, spontaneous applause. Class! Sheer class!

They got ten in all, Raphael Meade claiming five. As he slotted the last away, I sank to my knees – I remember it distinctly – thinking that now I had arrived. This was what professional football must be all about: getting stuffed 0–10 by better players in a better stadium in front of no spectators. It must be character building. I would leave Highbury a better man.

But none the wiser. I actually entertained hopes of getting a result on my second visit there. With the luck going our way, it could be a memory to cherish in future years. The occasion was the fourth round of the FA Cup, January 1987. Arsenal were first in the First; Plymouth second in the Second. Spectators aplenty now. Some 42,000 – 12,000 of them Plymouth brethren on a day trip to the Smoke. Fever pitch stuff. The biggest game so far in my nondescript career.

It proved to be another lesson for West Country upstarts. We were put to David Rocastle's sword. He was on a totally different plane to everyone else. I'm tempted to say different planet. But let's stick to planes. We were shot down 1–6 and it was as one-sided as a set with that score at Wimbledon. We might have retained a shred of dignity if we'd held things at 0–3. But we made the presumptuous mistake of scoring. Cue for our elders and betters to put us back in our place by adding three more goals in five minutes.

Afterwards I met up with family and friends. As many as twenty had assembled to see how well the boy was doing and confirm that all those Westward Ho! reports of his career taking off had not been exaggerated. The universal post-match verdict seemed to be that he wasn't and they had. Conversation was sparse.

Seven years on, Highbury has undergone a radical facelift – if this is not a contradiction in terms – at both ends. It is now a ground of two halves. The familiar stands along the touchlines preserve the sense of tradition and the unarguably glorious past. The new construction behind the goal ends indicates Arsenal's progressive outlook (part of their historic tradition!) and how with their eye on the future they have used modern technology to ready Highbury for the next century.

When, however, sixty seconds after I'd sat on the bench this afternoon Arsenal went ahead, it seemed less a case of future shock than one of remembrance of times past. But the present Charlton first/second team is made of sterner stuff than the 1985 Swindon vintage. No further goals followed at either end. Indeed, the first-half highlight for me was when Arsenal reserve team manager, Geordie Armstrong, moved across and said to me. 'Hello, Garry. The leg coming along all right, then?'

In that moment all the comic opera humiliations of those two ancient games were obliterated. That a player of Geordie's immense stature and ability should recognise me, address me by my first name and know that I was coming back from an injury was the biggest compliment I'd received in living memory.

'Nearly back to rights, thanks,' I said and thought that even if the hamstring was not quite a hundred per cent yet, the Garry Nelson self-esteem index was close to an all-time high.

The game ended a 1–1 draw. I came on in the second half and contributed very little. I found I was much more inhibited by, far more acutely worried about, the possibility of my hamstring going 'ping' than I had anticipated. But in the end my fears were like Wimbledon. Groundless. Forty-five minutes had come and gone and I'd got through intact with no short, sharp setback.

I'd moved a few more squares upwards on soccer's great Snakes and Ladders board. But a serpent of a sort was waiting coiled at the far end of the tunnel. The result was flashed through from the Baseball Ground: Derby 2 – oh, shit! – Charlton 2. Great! Great result from a patched-up team!

'Who got our goals?'

'Kim got 'em both.'

Oh, bother! Geordie Armstrong had remembered my name but, I now mused, after three weeks would Messrs Curbishley and Gritt?

'Who? Garry who?'

Sunday 30 October

Be it of the mind or body, jaundice is something you're better off without. Kim Grant grabbing some goals and headlines clearly doesn't improve my position on the Charlton starting grid, but I didn't wake up this morning singing the blues. Taking the grown-up view, me at the end of my career and Kim hardly across the threshold of his, it's good to see him beginning to cash in on the opportunities coming his way.

And the plot is thickening. Via a personal call from a supporter who'd been at the Derby game, I learned that David Whyte has picked up quite a serious knock. Thereafter I was half expecting an official call to follow instructing me to report tomorrow, bags packed, for Wearside. Mid-afternoon the phone did ring. It was Keith Peacock, our highly respected reserve team boss. There aren't many more astute watchers of the game in current circulation – as he was about to remind me.

111

'Looked a bit nervous on the leg yesterday, Nelse,' he said.

'Didn't want to go too mad. I've not had any reaction today.'

'Hmmn. I've told Curbs and Gritty not to consider you for Tuesday. I think it's favourite you go for a full ninety minutes in the Reserves on Wednesday.'

Another trick Keith hadn't missed. As soon as I put the phone down I knew his assessment made sense. Nor could I say I was enamoured at the prospect of undergoing a 600-mile round trip, the high point of which for me would probably be feeling my bum go numb on a bench.

Because of its long-term potential, the content of a third call later this same day was of considerably more interest. It came from another supporter, Bernard Wickham, who has a slew of interests in the financial world and spends nearly as much time in America pursuing his business goals and correcting the pronunciation of his names as he does at his Bromley home. In past chats, I've let him know of my keen interest in coaching overseas, not least in the States where this summer's World Cup has clearly added to the opportunities of spreading the soccer gospel. In which regard Bernard was calling now to inform me that a Baltimore business associate of his was about to fly in to London. The relevance? The man is thinking very positively about setting up some soccer clinics next year in his home-town area. The immediate outcome was the sending off across the Atlantic of my CV. I bunged it in the post to a few bars of 'Maryland, my Maryland'.

Monday 31 October

No trick or treats on the solo trip up to the training ground today. All three other members of the Gatwick Express have booked places on the two-day excursion to Sunderland.

No chatting, either, with the managerial twosome. Keith had obviously marked their card and, in fact, as the coach carrying the more or less fit, more or less first team set off, there was a distinctly empty feel to training. Then I remembered what lay ahead of them for the next six hours and the slight pangs of left-behind, 'you're not involved' envy disappeared. This, despite the driving rain – rain which, in fact, proved a blessing in disguise. Seeping all the

112

way down to Keith's better nature, the torrents prompted this scholar and gentlemen to spare his rats a total drowning and abort the session.

NOVEMBER

Tuesday 1 November

A week is a long seven days in football when it's all going rotten. It was only a couple of months ago that I saw Spurs beat Everton in front of an ecstatic, top dollar-paying, capacity crowd. Which prompts the question: whatever happened to Everton and their nice manager, Mike Walker? Well, not *quite* unrelieved doom and gloom. Today they recorded their first win of the season. His job should be secure. For another long week. As for mine, the improvised Charlton line-up (Phil Chapple starting a game up front for the first time since he was twelve) gained an excellent draw with Sunderland. Scorer? Yup – Kim Grant.

Wednesday 2 November

Originally the fixture list had this down as a blank week for the deadwood stiffs. Now, though, a re-arranged home Combination game against Bristol City has turned it into a first-rate opportunity to subject the healing Nelson hamstring to its severest test yet. Moreover, should we win, we'll be top of the league, sir. Heady stuff. Good news for some. Those unfortunates who travelled to Roker Park for the sole purpose of making the bus seem less empty had the metabolism-destroying duty of playing their coach-lagged hearts out a mere ten hours after getting back home in the wee small hours.

As well as by me, they were also joined by Carl Leaburn and Mike Salmon, both coming back from long-term injury, and by Stuart Balmer who these days – difficult to under-stand, this – finds himself rather nearer to the frozen wastes of Outer Siberia rather than the warmth of the first-team changing room.

Show time! We ran out to the deafening roar of the crowd in the West Stand's sold-out row H and I cast up mine eyes unto the visitors' section to see whether my pals from Bristol had mustered enough solidarity to turn up and applaud their erstwhile travelling companion. Dream on, Nelse. This is footballing reality: £10 for the win, a fiver for the draw; two hundred spectators and twenty-two wannabees and has-beens.

Meanwhile, a seething Nou Camp had collected 124,800 more specimens of football-crazy humanity than we attracted to witness Manchester United execute a nightmare performance in the Barcelona away game. It's not what you don't do, it's the way you don't do it. It wasn't just the 0–4 scoreline. It was the humiliating totality of the defeat. Barcelona were a class apart. When Stoitchkov and Romario (Barcelona's Nelse and Whytie as they're becoming affectionately known down Las Ramblas) weren't leaving the United defenders lumbering in their wakes like Frankensteinian dinosaurs, they had them running around like headless chickens. It did my old heart good to see so many of the English game's plutocrats reduced to technical bankruptcy. United are now third in their four-team European group. We, by contrast and following today's collection of a tenner each, sit proudly on top of the Avon Insurance Combination League. There is a measure of difference, I concede. But it can only be measured in light years. United may yet show enough character to qualify for the knockout stage of their little dooflip next Spring. Right now, however, our Mr Peacock is to be seen preening his feathers a wee bit.

Friday 4 November

A moment of sadistic serendipity today for Colin Walsh and myself. We were tasked with awarding the yellow jersey to this week's winning loser. We prolonged the pleasure as we scanned dossiers on several players, but in the end it had to be Shaun Newton. He took the dubious honours not only for a catastrophic performance in yesterday's five-a-side but also for a quote that

116

earned him a £2 fine on the spot and possibly a place in Charlton folklore.

'Remember when we went to Spain for the Anglo-Italian?'

Meanwhile, with Carl and me both declaring ourselves fit for tomorrow's game, Curbs and Gritty had a marginally less cut and dried selection process to tackle. They didn't hang about, however, and in short order Big Carl and I were both despatched to train with the reserves as the starting eleven were put through their paces against the Youth Team. The two of us seem to be fighting it out for the honour of a place on the bench tomorrow.

A player certain not to be on the bench tomorrow is our S.E. Eskimo, Stuart Balmer. A player who less than a year ago was being half-seriously recommended to Craig Brown as worthy of investigation, he's been frozen out again. Hypothermia has not, however, penetrated to two of the fingers on his right hand. He has, alas, used them to pen two transfer requests – one to the management duo and one to the chairman.

Late in the morning I was given a clear indication of where I'll be playing tomorrow – nowhere – by an involuntary, *I think*, slip of the tongue from Keith Peacock.

It's all a bit convoluted but against the background of a new initiative/regime whereby Saturday's non-combatants are being asked to put in a training session *after* the home game, Keith told me I wouldn't need to participate anyway. Emphasis on the anyway. Not quite as unequivocal as the classic formula 'You can have chips with your lunch today' (i.e. you've not been picked), but I still caught the drift. Chips never feature in my pre-match diet whatever my role. If I'm playing it's peaches and cornflakes – and, yes, Kelloggs, I am available for commercials.

Saturday 5 November

Fireworks night tonight. But *pro tem* I've ceased to be a nice little sparkler in the eyes of the dynamic duo. They let me down gently on my arrival in the manager's changing room office with a script I could have written for them myself: 'Can't afford for you to break down again, Nelse, we've got to go with Carlo. Give it another week and another game in the Reserves.' I can see their point of view. They took a fair bit of flak over my marginal appearance against Reading. On the other hand, though, omitting me for my own good gives them a very easy out.

Come three o'clock, then, I was taking my seat in the stands while Carl was being eased back into the real thing via a seat on the bench. Whatever our 'two into one won't go' career rivalry, both of us, I reckon, had identical feelings at seeing stopper centre back Phil Chapple pushed up front alongside Kim Grant as a makeshift target-man. Must drop the management a memo, I thought: size isn't everything.

Ironically, the partly unavoidable, partly tactical, reshuffle resulted in minimally visible difference to our play and none whatsoever to the game's outcome. With our defence still far too deep, two consecutive defeats at home stretched to three in a carbon copy of the Burnley game. Beware Lancastrians. Bolton, clearly a bigger, more physically developed side – and one that hasn't had to sell any of its very gifted squad to make short-term ends meet – were clearly more complete technically as well. Despite injury/selection problems of their own, they outplayed us with a good deal to spare on the way to a 2–1 win. I wouldn't mind a little money on them right now to end the season as champions.

The impact on our league position is significant and worrying. Our hold on top half of the table is of fingertips-only precariousness. We're now tenth overall – a position, so tight is the grouping, that leaves us only four points clear of the relegation zone. But always look on the bright side. We're only five points adrift from the band of play-off contenders just below the top. If we can prise the ice-pick out of Stuart Balmer's frozen mitts we should be able not only to halt our slide but start chipping our way back towards the summit.

As for this narrowest of points spreads, I think it's easily explained. There's an unarguable lack of distinctive quality in Division One of the Endsleigh Football League.

Monday 7 November

How long is a piece of string or a short time in football? I forget. But it was only a week ago that my three fellow commuters were off to Sunderland while this little piggy stayed at home. This morning Robbo and Steve Brown joined the never diminishing queue for the treatment room and only Kim and I are able to train.

In their wisdom – but it's probably quite sensible – the dynamic duo have given the first team a two-day break/rest period commencing tomorrow. But no rest for the wicked or the stiffs. We have a Reserve game tomorrow to prepare for. A further jolt to my day is that, still under pressure from above, Jimmy Hendry is continuing to divide and heal. His second re-hab session kicks off at 2 p.m. Now that I'm fully fit, the frustration of having to twiddle my thumbs for an hour and a half while Robbo and Brownie are waiting in line for their ten minutes of electro-suction – to their injuries – is getting the better even of my habitually unfailing, sunny disposition. It's as well Jim's acupuncture needles are under lock and key. His rear end might otherwise become the butt of a sharply fundamental reminder that time waits for no man. Normally I would be more forbearing but today I have a 3.30 appointment in Worthing I'm very anxious to keep – the once-a-term governors' meeting at the George Pringle School.

Encompassing the five- to sixteen-year-old band, the school is dedicated (in every sense) to children with learning difficulties, behavioural problems and, in some cases, physical handicaps. Although not nearly to the extent that I would wish, I've been involved with the school since 1988 when I received an invitation to join the governing body from the then headmaster, a fellow Old Boy of Southend High School. My role when I visit is mainly to figure as a local hero (third class). As a footballer I'm less obviously one of 'them' (an adult authority figure) and that much easier for the kids to relax with and relate to. Since few groups are so cruel as 'normal' kids can often be, life outside of George Pringle is sometimes very hard for its variously handicapped and so soft-target pupils. If nothing else, my occasional visits and careful dropping of a few items of inside soccer info do give the kids a bit of ammunition in their battle for street cred and, beyond that, self-belief.

As ever, working their daily miracles, all concerned are coping admirably to get an unbelievable most out of the wholesale shortage of space, materials and resources. Each day is a necessary but needless triumph of the concerned over adversity. It is necessary because the kids need all the help going. It's needless because the uphill struggle should never have come into being.

George Pringle School is shoe-horned into the cramped quarters of a former RAF Signals Station. The Gatwick Hilton caters to high flyers. After the school, the hotel's seemingly computer-designed interior seemed absurdly opulent. In a rags to riches, asbestos to formica, end to my day, Carole and I found ourselves dining in the restaurant with Bernard Wickham and Baltimore resident Jeff Carrington. On the table, the viability of running some soccer clinics next summer on Jeff's home turf. The discussion began positively and got better. There would seem to be a real opportunity in Maryland for quality coaching. Kids in the sub-twelve bracket in the area participate in soccer far more than in the traditional American sports. Given any sort of marketing, the clinics are likely to be hugely over-subscribed. The opportunity seemed to be bristling with more and more possibilities as we left Bernard and Jeff to catch the original Gatwick Express and steered the Tempra back towards Worthing. My long day had begun tediously but it was ending on a note of excitement. Time will tell how justified.

Tuesday 8 November

For this relief much thanks – a bit of a lie-in possible this morning. Having gone to bed with my brain still in overdrive as it tried umpteen variations of the clinic on for size, modified, rejected, thought of the first number again, I scarcely enjoyed the best night's sleep in the world. But tonight it's QPR's second string up in Harrow and no need to report for training. Somebody else with no need to report for same – although I doubt if he was allowed a lie-in – is Mike Walker. When I gave him at least another week in his job I wasn't very far out. But he is. Peter Johnson and the Everton Board have finally shown him the red card.

Mike is raising his eyebrow over the precise timing of his going –

at a moment when, having gone three games without defeat Everton could be said to have turned a tiny corner – but I think I can hear a hidden agenda in his ironic tone of voice. The message I'm getting pretty loud and clear is that his successor has already been approached and agreed terms and there now only wants a diplomatic delay to ensue before an announcement can be made with a modicum – but not a lot – of seemliness. That's how it's done these days. You don't give the incumbent the push until you've nailed down his replacement. Mike's hurt feelings will be soothed by the Evertonian mint of severance pay he now has to trundle to the bank.

As to the identity of that successor, all manner of names, some plausible, some silly, are being noised abroad on the airwaves: Steve Coppell, Howard Kendall, Gerry Francis (known to be at odds with tonight's opponents' Board over its contortionist wooing of Rodney Marsh over his head and behind his back), Peter Reid, Butch Wilkins, Joe Royle.

As a Blues supporter I would like to see it be Joe Royle. I can still see the hat trick he scored against Leeds in the 1969–70 championship season. In front of a 50,000 Goodison crowd, me on my milk-crate at the Park End, Everton won 3–2.

But from the sublime to – Harrow Borough. I know where I'd rather be, but today the real world is a pitch, of sorts, in the north-west of London. Obviously a good time was had by all at the firework party here last night – not least by the igniter. To complement the rich strewing of empty shells scattered across the playing area, his car tracks had inscribed exquisite patterns all over the midfield. If only I'd been able to repay him in kind.

Help, however, was at hand. Having recently taken delivery of several yards of sand, the groundsman appreciated that there could be few better ways of off-loading them than by covering over these Fawkesian tracks. This was clocked and bemoaned in the pre-match team talk but only in passing. Perhaps more than the first team encounters before capacity crowds, games like this are all about attitude and (self) motivation. We know that with both Curbs and Gritty sitting on the bench (surely the most ancient in the seventy-two-year-old Avon Insurance League) this is no time,

121

either in team or individual terms, to start musing on the charms of a quiet stroll in the park.

Fired up or not, I got off to a good personal start slamming a free kick in from twenty-five yards. I struck it low and hard just outside the wall, just inside the post. In the stiffs the old man occasionally gets to take one.

Playing virtually all the game in midfield, I was in constant touch with Harrow's mint-new beach. I'm sure it says something in the Bible, somewhere, about not executing your build-ups on shifting sands. As the game wore on, so did my hamstring and by the latter stages it was zinging out a nagging ache. QPR managed an equaliser, but I came up off the beach a happy man. In very severe conditions my leg had held out and the point was enough to keep the stiffs 'top the league, sir'.

Wednesday 9 November

After yesterday's exertions the blessing of another long lie-in. Consequently it was only by mid-morning that it came home to me that this may be a watershed day for English soccer. And a totally bad one at that. Today *The Sun* moved soccer off its back page and on to its front by putting Bruce Grobbelaar in the tabloid dock. The implications, and my immediate personal reactions, are complex, to the point of gobsmacking bewilderment. They spiral away towards, if not infinity, vastly more pages and words than a few paragraphs in a diary. It's tempting not to try summarising my feelings. On the other hand if not here, where else? This is the most obvious means at my disposal for trying to work out what I do feel.

The urge not to comment in any way is due, I'm sure, to my knowing I'd be heartsick should the allegations that Bruce has been a party to fixing matches prove true. My gut reaction is that they're not true. Which is to say, of course, that I don't want them to be.

I've always been a huge Grobbelaar fan. He's always seemed to me to play football in just the right spirit – a smile on his face more often than not and a 'go for it' attitude whenever a heart-stopping crisis has asked him to choose between spectacular commitment or safely anonymous buck-passing. As a result his career has been punctuated by some of the grossest clangers in the history of goalkeeping. But for every howler, he's pulled off a string of mind-blowing, match-saving, match-winning saves. However, reading *The Sun*'s case for the prosecution – or, rather, circulation – a literally sickening (in my case) weight of evidence seems to swing the scales down on the side of the head rather than the heart.

The verbatim, four-letter-word transcript of the video recorded by secret camera – hang about: is there no concept of entrapment in British law? – seems damningly explicit and confessional.

I find myself trying to shy away from the face meaning of the transcript and devising near fantastic alternative scenarios. Well aware of what was going on, Bruce was winding up his little shit of a friend and ex-business partner. He was fabricating a long list of 'crimes' so as to allow *The Sun* to dig its own grave. As for his ex-comrade in arms, the loser businessman Chris Vincent – well, vomit is not the word. Party to the planting of a hidden video camera, what did he feel like while sitting there listening to his mate (!) apparently condemning himself out of his own mouth? How could remorse not have him breaking down and declaring: 'Look, Brucie, it's no good. I've got to tell you. I've set you up.' Alternatively, how could bloody-minded greed not have had him visibly hugging himself in glee as, on camera, he bunged Bruce an envelope containing an alleged two grand 'weekly retainer'? Well, we don't need to hazard too much of a guess. With friends like Chris Vincent, who needs a Judas? No doubt *The Sun* paid him off in silver.

If, though, there's a measure of truth in the allegations, then there's no getting away from another utterly unpleasant train of thought. The feeling that, not so obliquely, I've been spat upon. How many others, you have to start asking. What does it do for my career if maybe – just maybe – I've been out there on the park alongside bought, bent players?

Well, at the risk of seeming hopelessly naive and squeaky-clean, I can't bring myself to believe I ever have been. Certainly I've never been approached. I've no idea how deeply into the English Football League the 'book' run by the Mr Short-arses of the Far

Eastern gambling houses extends, but in my days with Southend, Swindon, Plymouth and the like, the nearest we ever got to an inducement to influence a game's result was via the Swindon Board member who was in the habit of putting his head round the door and dazzling us with: 'Win today, lads, and you're all on a free chicken.' I always declared mine to the Inland Revenue.

But if I ever discovered that I'd run myself into the ground in a match which, because fixed (either way), had always been a foregone conclusion, I would be furious. I may be a run-of-the-mill player, but winning, losing or drawing I've always tried to give it my best shot. To have been a patsy in a fixed game would make a mockery of all that blood, sweat and tears; it would cheapen all my endeavours and so me. I don't want to learn that I've ever been an unwitting pawn in some sleazeball's dirty little scam.

The FA's reaction to what I suppose is going to get labelled as 'The Grobbelaar Affair' has been predictable – unswerving commitment to playing it safe. Graham Kelly has rigorously declared there will be an all-out, no punches pulled investigation. Or in *Sun*-speak, probe. So there needs to be. For everyone's sake.

Thursday 10 November

I think the tabloids are protesting too much. 'I SAVED GOAL BY MISTAKE AND LOST £125,000!' *The Sun*'s front page screams today. (For those of us with black and white sets the figure is in red.) Well now, years of perusing *The Sun* in passing – it can take whole seconds – has demonstrated to me that its perception of what happens on a soccer field, and its consequent perceptiveness in reporting any game, are of the same quality as a Matabele's mastery of the giant slalom. I simply don't believe that a keeper can pull off 'two blinding' saves, as *The Sun* describes them, by accident.

This highlights what both yesterday and today was the topic all conversation at the training ground kept coming back to: *How was he supposed to do it?* If what the bad guys were after was a definite scoreline (3–1, 2–0, whatever) what were supposed to be the *mechanics* of contriving that precise result? For a goalkeeper of all positions!

As I'm sure every fan in every pub in the country has pointed out, a keeper can deliberately miss a cross or dive the wrong way to concede a goal. But what control does he have allowing him to prevent a team-mate turning on a scintillating twenty minutes that radically alters the score? (Grobbelaar plays for the same side as Le Tissier, for God's sake!) How can he prevent a referee who's having a 'mare of a game awarding the biggest joke of a penalty in the history of the game? At either end. Grobbelaar's alleged career as a 'fixer' seems to have been a very hit-and-miss affair indeed. Of the five matches *The Sun* cites as intended wrong 'uns, only one, the game against Newcastle produced a result in the Arthur Daley sense of the term. The others all finished with the wrong scoreline – partly due to a number of brilliant or, as that's expressed in *The Sun*, accidental saves from Bruce. Against Newcastle the entire Liverpool team were as much swept off their feet in the first half hour as had been Royal Antwerp. Bruce Grobbelaar had no more chance of saving their three strikes than, well, a Matabele on skis.

If you're a little match-fixer, and in the business of getting just one man to fix not only a match's overall result but its precise final scoreline, logic overwhelmingly dictates that you bribe an outfield player, a Roy Paul, say, or a Tony Kay. Total logic states that you bribe all twenty-two men on the field or, if your bung budget is small, find yourself a bent referee. If such existed.

No question there is now a case to answer. For the moment Bruce has gone walkabout as far as Fleet Street is concerned (would you believe he's got an international in Zimbabwe this weekend!) but through solicitors he's issued a writ for libel against *The Sun*. Not that the tabloid can lose. Whatever the final verdict of the courts, its circulation, Merseyside always excepted, will be boosted everywhere. The monies to fund *The Sun*'s defence and, as necessary, pay any damages and costs will be as a drop in the ocean to a Murdoch empire which has half the media world as its fish finger.

Meanwhile, an event which would have been front-page news itself most days of the year has been relegated to 'other item' status. Perhaps choosing this moment to make a blind-side run, 'Deadly' Doug Ellis has added the name of Ron Atkinson to the long list of managers sacked by Aston Villa in short order. It's a bit like elbowing Captain Kirk off the *Enterprise*.

Everywhere you look these days it is fear of failure rather than the hope of success that drives Board, managerial and even on-the-field decisions. In Villa's case it is fear of commercial failure.

One managerial door shuts, another opens to reveal Joe Royle walking through it to the rapturous applause of a hero's welcome at the Everton AGM. The manifest stage-managing of this tends to confirm my theories as to why Mike Walker was given his cards despite his then team seeming to have turned the corner. The nicety of a small interval elapsing before the new appointment had to be observed. It's fair to assume a long-term game-plan has been carefully adhered to.

In their various ways Messrs Royle, Atkinson and Grobbelaar are men of the moment. Mike Walker, for the present, is very much yesterday's.

Friday 11 November

A photo of Graham Kelly is everywhere to be seen today. It shows him standing, slightly smirking (but what else is new?) flanked by the two *Sun* reporters who are delivering their organ's anti-Grobbelaar dossier into his hands. Don't they have a tradesman's entrance at Lancaster Gate?

In the meantime, the managers' Magic Roundabout has cranked out another revolution. Gerry Francis has resolved his acrimonious relationship with the QPR Board by resigning. I'm much reminded of the old Manchu proverb: never dismount from a good saddle until you are certain fresh spurs are to hand.

At the end of the day, a ray of light cutting through all the murk of this scandal, sleaze and opportunistic speculation. I returned home to find my son, Chris, positively fizzing over with the excitement of being kitted out for the first time in his life in top-to-toe proper football kit. His first pair of boots. First shin-pads. First strip. He was so proud he wouldn't change back to 'civvies'. The carpet ended up looking like a giant waffle from all the stud marks.

Just one fly in the ointment. The strip makes me a turncoat! Albeit an out-of-date one, it's a Man United outfit. I bought it there before our losing Cup game as an indirect souvenir of the one and only time I'll ever play at Old Trafford. Perhaps it'll change Charlton's luck if Chris runs out in it as a Valley mascot.

Tomorrow he's got proper football training too! I'd love to be there sharing it all at one remove. But like so many other fathers, I've got to go to work tomorrow . . . Football training! Therein, of course, lie several potential problems. Because I am (or was) a professional player, others may expect a great deal from him on the field. Too much, maybe. (He can always say: 'My dad's only Garry Nelson, not Peter Beardsley', mind you). Then again, I may be tempted to put too much pressure on him – try to have him realise my unfulfilled fantasies for me. I don't think I'll be that silly or selfish, though. If he wants to grow up to be a chef or a trombonist or a doctor, I hope I'll be the first to enjoy the sight of him becoming his own man in his own way. (I'll only disinherit him if he takes up a position with *The Sun*.) That, alas, will all happen the day after tomorrow. But right now, tonight, Chris is, yes, over the moon because of football and, bless him, through him some of my affection for the game has been restored. Their feet of clay crumbling, stars may topple from their pedestals; teams may be discredited; leagues may wither away. The game will endure.

Saturday 12 November

Dad off to work, then. But to train, not to play. It might be Saturday, but we aren't involved. With their flair for anticipating the season's quality highspots and their desire to deliver maximum possible viewing figures to their advertisers, LWT's *Big Match* decision-makers have opted to zoom in on slipping

Charlton's star-studded glamour clash with almost bottom-of-the-table West Brom. To suit their scheduling, the game's been switched to tomorrow. Traffic-thinned motorways and Grobbelaar fall-out apart, today feels to me like an ordinary weekday. But for a lot it won't: it is the first round of the FA Cup.

Which is why I find myself feeling displaced today. Having spent most of my early days in the lower reaches of the League, I'm largely conditioned to being involved in the Cup starting this weekend. And ending. In my very first season at Southend I shared in the shattering experience of elimination at the hands of non-League Harlow Town.

To be honest, it wasn't too much of a personal downer. I still hadn't adjusted to the never-never land fact of actually being paid to play football. To receive £50 for coming on for fifteen minutes in the first game and as much again for merely being a sub in the lost replay was both too unreal and significant for me to be inconsolable in defeat. I wouldn't have said 'no' to a whole string of similar non-appearance bonuses.

A few seasons later and I did feel properly, professionally gutted. This was during my 'happy days' at Swindon under Lou 'Sting Like a Bee' Macari and, once again, the underdogs inflicting humiliation upon us were a bunch of my fellow Essex lads. Away at Dagenham, not overawed by the lush and picturesque surroundings, we scrambled a 0–0 draw. A good result to come away with from such an awkward tie. But it was all we came away with.

During the game some changing-room thief was able to unlock the tightest of defences and cleaned out the pockets of each and every one of us. We took it like men. Listing for the benefit of the insurance company the Rolexes, Nikons, gold ID tags, Bugatti wallets and Waterman pens which the members of this Swindon generation had all come to regard as mandatory good luck charms, we all consoled ourselves by looking forward to the fruits of our inventiveness. Then we fell victims to a second mugging. We lost 1–2 in the County Ground replay and there was absolutely nothing any loss adjustor could do about that.

* * *

128

Sunday 13 November

The thirteenth. Maybe bad news for Charlton that today's game is being televised. There's a TV jinx on us. In our last eleven 'live' appearances on the box we've not recorded a single win. The last time we won under the glassy-eyed stare of a live camera may have been the 1947 Cup final. I'll have to ask Steve Gritt if his Wembley memories confirm this. My own most memorable contribution to a televised game was earning my one and only sending off. It was for extending to an official a free and frank appraisal of his competence – all from entertaining a civilised desire to indicate how he might best further his career. Salt is still rubbed in my wound nearly every week by Yellow Pages featuring the incident in one of their commercials. Thankfully my comments – of a somewhat technical nature, you'll appreciate – have been over-dubbed to save my blushes. Then again, neither LWT or Abbot Mead Vickers (the Millwall-oriented ad agency) have coughed up so much as a brass farthing by way of residuals for a performance even Kenneth Branagh would be hard pressed to equal.

West Brom always give me bad vibes. They remind me of my first ever trip to Wembley when, aged seven, I was taken by my dad and grandad to the 1968 Everton v West Brom final. It all started badly when we found ourselves marooned among Baggies' supporters and it got worse when Jeff Astle, hero of the Jalisco Stadium, rifled in an extra-time screamer. For me disaster went to tragedy when in the sardine-tin unfamiliarity of the tube I was visited by the sort of fierce call of nature that all seven-year-olds have at the most inopportune times. I could only relieve myself – but not my feelings – in the most humiliating of ways.

But today, surely, a quarter of a century and more on, revenge! Well, not actually. Make that an even dozen. The glassy-eyed jinx continues. Like Lord Chatterley we had a lot of possession, and not much penetration. The game ended in a 1–1 draw. My own role was pretty much a return to the full-time flanks. Kim Grant's form preventing anyone nicking the first team shirt from off his back, I was slotted in to the conveniently vacant left-sided berth in midfield. My efforts there were pretty marginal in the other sense too. The game turned five minutes after the re-start when a well-struck Mark Robson 'goal' that would have given us a 2–0 lead was ruled offside. A goal did follow immediately. At the other end for West Brom's very impressive target man, Bob Taylor. In a way, of course, I'd already put the mouth on Charlton today by extolling the virtues of Grimsby's then manager, Alan Buckley, in this very diary. Now he's moved to The Hawthorns, his intelligence at work on this wider stage should see his new side making steady headway up the table.

Monday 14 November

Another manager's bit the dust. Bristol City have asked Russell Osman to sling his (Butcher's) hook.

Zimbabwe won over the weekend. Grobbelaar, reports say, played badly. I wonder why.

Tuesday 15 November

Training a low-key affair on account of our long list of injuries. Praise be I'm not on it. Chief interest today derives from the teletext revelation that there's been another spasm from the Magic Roundabout. Gerry Francis is going – surprise, surprise – to Tottenham (score one for the Manchus) and Dean Wilkins' brother, Raymond, is taking over at QPR. Joe Jordan who never sold his house in Bristol, where he has lots of ship-shape and fashionable friends (not least City's chairman), is resuming occupancy not only of his former domicile but his former desk chair too. Time to go home, said Zebedee.

Wednesday 16 November

Wednesday is normally a day off, but a Sunday game throws the best laid schedules of mice and Addicks all to cock so once more I take on the 150-mile round trip.

Today, though, the journey seemed a positive intellectual cornucopia compared with the mind-numbing monotony of training. Keeping fit and sharp are vital, of course, as is the specific planning for the next Saturday, but it's not easy, familiarity breeding sterility, to keep injecting into practice sessions that touch of novelty which keeps tedium at arm's length. Today should have been declared a non-runner in the enthusiasm stakes. It didn't begin to get off the ground. Unfortunately, rather than cut their losses, the management gritted their teeth and persevered. I don't think they had much to show for our efforts at the end of the two-hour stint, although the running exercises did keep the caustic comments down to acceptable levels.

You wonder how the England coaches keep things buzzing. In the pre-match TV sequences it all seems fun, fun, fun. Perhaps there's a prize for the player who remembers most of his teammates' names. If I bump into Robert Lee again, I must ask him all about it. Somebody certainly bumped into him this evening – a rather thick-set Nigerian who, trampling Lurker's hand into the Wembley turf, curtailed his second appearance for England very early into the proceedings.

The game overall had a lot of points of interest. The exciting breaking ability of the Nigerians; the professionalism of the English players; the naivety of the West Africans in overall tactical terms. This failing is a big minus at such a level and England capitalised sufficiently upon it to squeak out a narrow 1–0 victory.

No Evertonian graced the team in white shirts, but there was one very visibly out there in green. Amokachi is Everton's first black international and, many would say, their first black player. This latter piece of folklore isn't strictly true: Cliff Marshall was a previous non-white on the Everton books. But the fact that I can so readily remember him as the past exception underlines the possibility (and certainly street-talk conviction) that there was an apartheid rule at Goodison. Everton, essentially, have lagged at least a decade behind other clubs in taking on black players and it's hard to believe that this is all down to signing the right man for the job in every specific instance and him always turning out to be white. As a true-blue who is now involved with very much a multi-racial club – one with vigorously enforced anti-racist stewarding – I would very much like to believe that the *prima facie* case for the club's pre-Amokachi profile is misleading. Now, after the arrival of chairman, Peter Thomson and, credit where credit is due, Mike

Walker, the old, bad rumours can be conclusively scotched. Certainly, Amokachi ran out for his first home game to the warmest of welcomes. The Everton fans will judge him in terms of only one criterion. His footballing skills.

Friday 18 November

A very early start to the morning to accommodate a change in routine. Today it's a short train journey to Shoreham, a taxi to Kim Grant's place and then a chauffeured ride up to the training ground. The purpose behind all this cross-country scramble is to allow me an extended stay with my extended Liverpool family after the Tranmere game.

And I do mean extended. I am forced into another sort of scramble, grovelling and outright begging my way to securing a total of no less than eighteen complimentary tickets for the clan.

After this, the morning session comes as light relief. It takes the form of many such on a Friday morning, namely a practice workout against the Youth Team. The name of the game is not winning (we'd be in with a bit of a shout there, I think), but being in the right place at the right time for all set pieces, for or against.

From coaching to the coach. And I find I've not been very clever. This is my first trip since the Notts County game way back in the dim, dead days of September and I've forgotten how it all goes. I've come aboard with no book or magazine and my absence has cost me a place as of right in any of the card schools. It's full house time even in the Chase the Lady game. I'm left in a solo school. Why, I've had more fun than this in a diving bell! Of course, there's always the video which today is: Charlton v WBA. Ah well, every cloud has its silver lining. I'll have no trouble getting off to sleep.

The five-and-a-half-hour trip is over in a matter of aeons. Amazingly, when we finally arrive, it's still the twentieth century and I'm looking at the familiar vista of Lord Lever's Port Sunlight works and, across from it, thank God, the oasis of the Village Hotel. I'd forgotten all I'd been missing. Injuries spoil you.

132

Saturday 19 November

Passed the agreeable time of day with a Championship medal-owning former Evertonian, Gary Stevens. Since his move to Tranmere from Glasgow Rangers, he's become a temporary permanent resident at the Village Hotel. I'll be seeing quite a bit more of him later today so I'm hoping he's gone back a bit on his England cap-winning form of those heady, mid-eighties Goodison days.

John Aldridge has lost all his form. A foot injury has ruled him out for today. What bad luck! Grief-stricken is not the word to describe our back four. They've also all measurably put on two inches in height. Just because in 162 games he's scored 113 goals – 22 of them in this still early days season. What do statistics signify, I ask myself. I'm sure that if I were a defender the man would be as much putty in my hands as Schumacher.

Almost as impressive as John Aldridge these days is Prenton Park. Tranmere have effected an almost complete transformation of three sides of their ground. Over the summer they also invested a cool half million in re-laying their pitch. To excellent purpose. Despite the last couple of days' torrential rain we'll be going out on to a perfect playing surface. The hamstring won't be sorely tested by the sort of glue-pot that in days of yore, once the fixture list had you going to the Wirral in November, you could guarantee would be lying in wait to trap your soles.

The new, improved surface suited our game and, doubtless inspired by the serried ranks of Nelson supporters, Charlton totally dominated the first half. Ironically, the pleasure of scoring their opening goal fell to their most ineffectual player. Me. For forty-four minutes the game had virtually passed me by. Or vice versa. When I did have the occasional close encounter with the ball it was basically of the wrong kind – a misplaced pass, a bumbling first touch, a woeful shot. But who needs feet when you can use your head? Just on the interval I ran on to a Steve Brown flick-on for a cranial tap-in from a yard or so out. It was a strike you could describe as positively Plattitudinous.

As we sat in the changing room at half time, we could sense, almost feel, the heat of the lambasting the Tranmere players were getting. We had every reason to believe we'd be in for a radically different second half. And correctly. Pat Nevin came in off the wing to drop into the hole – when have we seen that before, Alan and Steve? – and proceeded to create havoc. Despite our counter-measures an equaliser seemed, and in due course proved, inevitable. Now we were hanging on grimly for the draw. It was all against the run of play that we forced a corner. Carlo flicked on, I gave a volley everything including direction and for a split second thought I had hit goal number nine and the match decider. Not so, alas. Eric Nixon produced yet another wonder save and we had now gone six games without a win. But justice had been served. A second goal would have been more than I deserved, a win more than Charlton. And 1–1 away at Tranmere will do most teams nicely, thank you.

Off the hook for the tedious coach ride south, I joined my personal fan club – relative values being thicker than judgement – in the Merseyside Clipper next to Prenton Park. One slap on the back was delivered with rather more clout than the rest and, turning, I was delighted to see Tranmere defender Dave Higgins whom I'd last encountered in Birkenhead's spiritual twin town, Orlando. We had a chat. It became clear that his season was turning out very much how during that last meeting I had been envisaging mine would be: a sustained string of appearances in the Rovers reserves being punctuated by just the occasional first-team game. Dave felt well able to diagnose why.

'When you're thirty-three, Nelse, they put a bad game down to your age. You know what I mean, like?'

Indeed I do, Dave. Indeed I do.

The main topic of general conversation inside the Clipper was Bruce Grobbelaar's return to between the Southampton posts and to a welcome from the crowd befitting a Saint. Reports told of his having had a fine, shut-out game for Southampton in their win over Arsenal. Must rush out first thing on Monday and buy a *Sun* (if I can find one in these parts) to see if they have sacked or suspended Brian Woolnough, who on 10 November unequivocally trumpeted forth: 'Bruce Grobbelaar has played his last game of football in this country.'

Even with a glass in my hand I can tell when I'm indulging in wishful thinking. If my shooting were so horrendously wide of the mark as Woolnough's, I would expect to be dropped immediately. As, after today, may well be the case. The truth is that our attention spans are so short, so distracted by the next force-fed diet of headlines, that we forget the most outrageous assertions overnight. In one ear and out the other. We get, in short, the newspapers we deserve.

But enough of tabloiditis. It was time to relax back into the comforts of my almost native town. My Uncle Don at the wheel, I forsook the pub for a brief, pulse-quickening game of Liverpool Roulette. We set off through the twists and turns of the Mersey Tunnel.

Sunday 20 November

An immensely enjoyable day of family visits with just one contrasting public note underlining the deeper, private pleasures. To a man and a woman, my relatives were incensed by the fresh pile of sodium chloride newly rubbed into the unhealing wound of Hillsborough. Application of these grains of salt, but scarcely wisdom, have come discourtesy of an old managerial foe of Merseyside, Brian Clough.

Lecturing from the pulpit of his just published memoirs the ex-Forest (and Brighton!) boss has deployed his omniscience in assuring the world that the people responsible for the Hillsborough disaster were those from whom its victims were exclusively drawn, the Liverpool supporters. Further, pressed by questions at one of the book's launch beanfeasts as to whether he was worried that expressing such a view would have the same negative impact on his book-of-revelations' sales in Liverpool as did *The Sun*'s anti-Reds stance, our Brian (a scrambled form of 'brain') is quoted as replying that he wasn't concerned as: 'One half of the people in Liverpool can't read and the other half are out stealing hub caps.' Sic.

If this is accurate reporting, my first reaction is that Brian Clough lags even further behind Stein as a man and Shankly as a wit than he did as a manager. The remark comes over not so much as a cheap shot as a cheapskate's shot. It's unworthy. It is unworthy of a once fine manager and serves only to remind us that while Cloughie might once have walked on water, today he is in very real danger of drowning. The members of the Nelson family who tend that plot in the Walton cemetery are neither illiterate nor thieves. Nor, much more to the point, are they at all unique. Clough should apologise.

Monday 21 November

If only! The management's special dispensation to the old git once again allowed me the luxury of an extra day off along with an easy ride south by train. But if only the demands of my own team's scheduling had allowed me to delay the leaving of Liverpool those few extra hours! I could have been there reliving Joe Royle's hat trick as I bore witness to the rebirth. Tonight Everton defeated the Reds 2–0. Joy, sheer joy! Instead, once again I had fallen victim to striker's syndrome – being in the wrong place at the wrong time.

Tuesday 22 November

Back in harness at New Eltham. No one remarking on, or seeming to have noticed, my absence for an extra day. Business very much as usual except that with the 'dead wood' playing West Ham tonight, there was less safety in training numbers. As I was soon to find to my cost.

It's a fact of working life, hard learned by many, that you're much better off not being a smart-mouth at Alan Curbishley's expense. However apt, witty or justified your put-down, you can be sure that, once past your lips, it will be returned unto you tenfold – and over a period of days rather than hours. Crack wise at Alan's expense and he's quite unable to roll with the punch. Give him any jibe and he'll jab back and back and back. At Brighton he earned the nickname (one of the respectable few!) of 'Counter-jag'. The image is of a serrated-edged knife. And you can throw in a goodly coating of curare too.

It was with actions rather than words, but today I made the mistake of getting too clever by half and reaped the full dividend.

It happened during one of our keep-ball sessions. These are regular training pass/pastimes wherein two poor sods at the centre of a ring try to prevent all those around them from clocking up twenty first-time passes. If this target is reached the piggies in the middle have to stump up a fine. Those of us who are long in the tooth at this particular game like to relieve our tedium and practise fiscal risk management by throwing dummies and difficult passes that will ensure our more youthful colleagues stay rooted to the centre spot. Being the beautiful passer of the ball he is, Curbs can't abide this hoking up of the exercise. Today, after I had successfully duped several of the younger set, he felt enough was enough. I found myself on the receiving end of that jagged tongue's full force. The reprintable translation and bottom line were that, although I'd fluked a goal, he was in no way pleased with my contribution on the field at Tranmere. As if he could think I was either!

I decided silent discretion was the better part of answer-back valour but found it harder and harder to bite my tongue as the public tirade continued close to non-stop for the next three and a half hours. It was a tough way to earn tomorrow's day off. Profoundly motivating, of course.

Brian Little, on the other hand, was profoundly motivated by something today. Whatever it was, it impelled him to resign from the manager's job at Leicester. Perhaps he's looking forward to putting his feet up in some nice labour-free retirement villa.

Friday 25 November

In another PR disaster for professional football, the *Daily Mirror* has punted its own 'World Exclusive' soccer scandal on to the front page.

It becomes clearer and clearer that football has ceased to be a subject the tabloids want to cover for its own sake. Indeed, unless a manager spells out in a debriefing press conference what has just happened on the pitch to make them wise after the event, their soccer pundits are largely incapable of writing a grown-up analysis of a game. Their ears are more important to them than their eyes. The tabloids' exploitation of soccer reduces the beautiful game to no more than the raw material from which they can extrude the 'human interest' story: the nightclub punch-up; the adulterous fling; the drunk-driving write-off; the bung.

Now it's the superstar druggy. The name of the game for the tabloids isn't soccer. It's sleaze. And in this latest example of their art, a particularly nasty tackiness soon makes itself apparent. Entwined around Paul Merson's drug habit, like poison ivy around a diseased elm tree, is gambling addiction. The heavy-duty bookies are in to him for over a hundred grand. Were. I wonder what the figure was for which he sold his own, his wife's, his family's privacy to the *Mirror*'s caring exclusivity.

In fact, though it may have hit the bar, I don't think the *Mirror* has got its equaliser. It seems to me the shock of the new exposé will peter out far sooner than those triggered by allegations of match-rigging. Doing drugs, however many players could hypo-thetically be involved, is first and last an individual problem. Fixing results clearly goes to the heart of the game.

I find it interesting, if saddening, that the revelation that a hugely talented player (as Merson is) has a drugs problem doesn't greatly surprise me. Why should it? For those with more quick money than long-term sense – actors, pop stars, commodity brokers, prospective peers of the realm – the drug scene has long been a commonplace: an ultimate form of social recreation that is the God-given perk of high flyers.

When I was sixteen it was an against-the-system thrill to get served in a pub and puff on the odd fag. Now, when the latter phrase has rather different connotations, the going norm seems to be slipping an 'E' that, costing no more than a few quid, gives you an energising high for several hours. Footballers are not immune to such short-cuts when seeking a stairway to heaven. The nature of this book is to inform rather than inform on, about playing on the grass rather than grassing on the players, but the answer to your question is: 'Yes, I know of several players who, to pump themselves up for their clubbing and bird-pulling, regularly pop pills.'

It's stage two. Alcohol is the first and, as we all know, has been quite sufficient of itself to destroy some careers. But if you can take booze in your short-term stride, then the coloured pills and the white powders are waiting up ahead. When you're half-cut, there they are – probably in the identical state. Perhaps you'll have recourse to them out of a genuine need to ease the ever-present pressure of feeling obliged to deliver performances matching an annual salary of two hundred grand plus. Perhaps you move on to drugs because you're an empty-headed idiot who thinks (by default) you're going to be young and fit and rich forever. Either way there will be some friend standing at your elbow to guide you on your way: 'Go on – it'll make you feel good.' The motive may be money or the reflected glory the 'good mate' feels is to be had hanging out with the star. Contempt is far too weak a word to describe what we should feel about either specimen. Respect is what we should feel for the person, footballer or non-footballer, who, when promised all the kingdoms of the earth in a line of coke, is unfashionably grown-up enough to turn around and say: 'Go forth and multiply, scumbag.'

Paul Merson, it seems reasonably safe to assume, is no Einstein. I'm sure he's not by nature vicious but, to an unbelievable extent, has been a fool to himself. He's this week's example of too much too soon; that more money (once!) than sense syndrome. The FA's decision – since the drugs were 'recreational' and not performance-enhancing – to take no action and allow him space to get sorted seems to me exactly right. Coming from them it appears extraordinarily enlightened and humane. I would hope to see Paul Merson back playing at the highest level. I would hope that he is man enough to manage it.

Saturday 26 November

SE7 at its miserably dank, autumnal worst. The Valley floodlights had to be switched on as early as 2.30. Unfortunately, this only served to illuminate the play of our visitors, Middlesbrough, as they stole an almost instant lead. Whatever was being asked of us at the kick-off had seemed steep. Now, just four minutes later, we were confronting something that made the North Face of the Eiger look like a bowling green. Mr Robson's fielding of three Herculean centre halves was already a palpable master-stroke.

The machinery was already there in place to cancel out our own lone giant, Carlo, and stifle our attempts to get on terms by crowding out the midfield. We huffed and puffed and even threatened a bit before half time but we couldn't knock Boro off the firm foundations of their formation and their early goal. Their second score after sixty minutes condemned us to a long half-hour of surround-sound audio experience. Over there the Teesside Operatic Society in bravura, victorious voice. Everywhere else our own supporters giving out with the moans and groans and boos that are not associated with any river but with pissed-off fans the world over.

My contribution to the festivities was another below-par performance. It seems I no longer have it to do well in the position, on the left flank, that I occupied so often in my first eight seasons. In three games on the trot I haven't delivered a telling cross. I don't have the tricky feet of a Mark Robson and, talking of on the trot, it would seem that *pro rata* there's nothing to choose between the nought to sixty of my ageing Tempra and myself. We've both got a few too many miles on the clock. Despondent is how I felt inside as I shook hands with the Boro players on the final whistle. I was hurting in mind as well as body. I came off already anticipating Counter-jags remarks and feeling that my season might well have reached a crossroads. A few weeks back and I was knocking on averaging close to a goal a game while featuring in nearly as many assists. Then a run-of-the-mill injury, a lost place, lost momentum and now . . . ? Three steps forward and three back. I'm back to the also-ran scenarios I was foreseeing out in Orlando.

I got into our starting line-up thanks to injuries to others. But now it's a whole fortnight before we have our next game. By then all hands will be reporting fit for active service. Curbs and Gritty will be able to select from 'their optimum squad' – something which also in their own *so* motivating words, they have 'not yet been able to do'.

I drove back home depressed by a sense of *déjà vu* and visions of running out for Bournemouth. Get a grip, Nelse, get a grip, I told myself. But it was hard to take in the message. I never did like listening to whingers.

Sunday 27 November

A milestone first in the career of a footballer called Nelson. No, not participation in a televised win by Charlton, even though today is Sunday. And not Garry but Christopher Nelson, younger by some twenty-seven years. Debut day. Wick Dynamos versus Worthing Dynamos and Chris running out to represent the latter in his first match proper.

He's a chip off the old block, all right. His commitment and enthusiasm are commendable. The skill element, however – well, time is on his side! All in all, given that he'd only had the benefit of a couple of sixty-minute training sessions and that his first game was against a side a good year or so further down the nursery slopes, he didn't do at all badly. He had nothing to apologise for when he came off. The score? Well, who was counting? I mean, at that age it doesn't really matter, does it and – oh, well, OK – not only did they lose but I lost track of by how many.

Monday 28 November

There is a destiny that shapes our diaries, rough notebooks though they be. Yesterday I watched Chris participating in an event that could be of profound or negligible significance in his life. Today is the anniversary of a clear-cut turning point in mine: my debut at Roots Hall for Southend United Reserves against Brighton and Hove Albion Reserves in the London Mid-week League. Delving back through the mists of indifferent time even further, I can record that I had already put in eighteen months of regular training with Southend when I was a fourteen and fifteen year old. But I'd drifted away. The sessions were very heavily weighted towards stamina and body-building rather than on-the-ball technique. In time, this unchanging emphasis disheartened me. Instead, still fifteen, I took my first step into competitive men's football playing with my father, Ron, in the Southend and District League for Crouch Nomads second team. Although young, I was a big fish in a little pool. I quickly progressed to the League's Premier Division by joining Stambridge United. In my first season, the team pulled off the League and Cup double and I had started to carve out a reputation as a prolific goalscorer.

Not everywhere. No approaches from Football League clubs came my way in the summer of 1978 and I wasn't really expecting any. I certainly didn't have sufficient self-belief or motivation to take the initiative myself and write off asking for trials. Come the autumn, I continued to play for Stambridge – and the goals continued to flood in as a matter of casual course. That October I was selected for the County side. On my debut against Inner London at the no-longer-in-existence ground of the legendary Walthamstow Avenue I scored a hat trick. And now there were indications of jungle drums beating in the heart of deepest Essex.

A native-born local hero always makes for a good feature article. The local paper, the *Evening Echo*, wrote me up as a whizz-kid in the making. People told me that Ipswich and Colchester were getting interested. I still wasn't. When, out of nowhere, the Southend physio and coach *volunteered* his services as sponge man for the next County game free of charge I naively didn't give it a second thought. What did I know about undercover scouting? On 25 November, however, I played for Colchester United's reserves against Wisbech. We lost 1–2 but obviously, as I realised, I had caught somebody's eye. Roy Massey, the second string's manager, was desperate for me to sign something – anything! – right after the game. It was probably no more than associate schoolboy forms, but I did myself a big unwitting favour when the streak of wariness in my nature made me reply I'd like to think about it. An instant autograph then would have signed away my freedom. The slant of this particular form gives all the advantages to the club and none to the individual lad.

Re-enter the *Evening Echo*. Mining this minor story for all it was worth, they were now working up a fine head of indignant steam against Southend's allowing yet another catch to slip through their shrimping net – escaping, heinously, into the maws of their immediate Essex rivals. It was literally while I was reading this article that our doorbell rang. Answering it I found the threshold filled by our one-night-stand County sponge man, Brian Beckett. He had a favour to ask of me: would I consider – 'it would be really helping us out' – playing for Southend the following night against Brighton? Tricky question, eh?

Honest as the day is green, I did actually mumble something about having an understanding with Colchester and shouldn't I speak to them first and see whether it would be OK?

'Have you signed anything for them?' asked kindly Uncle Brian.

'No.'

What a pro! Not a muscle on his face twitched.

'Then leave it to us. We'll have a word with them and tie up all that side of things. All us league clubs work on a share-and-share alike basis when it comes to schoolboy talent.'

It was only years later that Brian, now sadly no longer with us, told me that no call to Colchester was ever made.

They put me in a Number 11 shirt and my mum and my step-dad, Trevor, in the Directors' Box close to the Courvoisier and the VIP treatment. I don't remember much about the game except that my literally opposite number in the Brighton Number 11 shirt was one Gary Stevens destined for Tottenham medals, England caps and, after many adventures, being crippled out of the game. Oh, and we won 3–0. I couldn't have been rubbish. Straight after the game came the invitation-summons to the boardroom where I was re-united with a beaming mother (highly appreciative of the five-star hospitality lavished upon her) and introduced to Southend manager Dave Smith, his assistant John Latimer and Board member Frank Walton. No, I hadn't been rubbish. Yes, I had impressed them. They were going to make me an offer I couldn't refuse. Except I did.

Not completely. What I actually replied was, yes, well, thanks a lot, but I still had my 'A' Levels to complete. After I'd got them out of the way I'd probably be more than happy to sign. They weren't best pleased.

Looking back I can see that it was a pretty brave, even mature, move. I was putting a Boy's Own Paper dream come true – schoolboy to pro footballer in less than a week! – at very considerable risk. None of the discussion, bear in mind, was going on the record. Nothing was in writing. If I'd been injured, suffered a catastrophic loss of form, my career might never have got off the ground. (All right! That's quite enough from you in the

North Stand!) It wasn't that I was playing hard to get. I wasn't that canny. What it was, I think, is that I've always been resistant to overt 'it's now or never' pressuring from figures in authority. Also there was another strand in all of this.

Just the previous week I had travelled up to Loughborough University for an interview. The same week as the game against Brighton I'd received a letter offering me, subject to my gaining acceptable 'A' Level grades, a place there to read Geography, Physical Education and Sports Science. An entirely different path into the future had now become an option.

Now I don't want to over-romanticise my situation that night in the Directors' Box. I can't honestly pretend that, as in one of those terrific ninety-mile-an-hour 1940s movies, I was faced with choosing between becoming a classical violinist or middleweight champion of the world. In my case the dice always were loaded towards football. I had drifted into the sixth form at my grammar school mainly through inertia and on the strength of being competent enough at the curriculum subjects. The staff had sort of assumed that I would, so I had sort of assumed that I should.

Somewhere in the family background were those folklore assertions that: 'You can't beat a good education.' On the same drift I could have, I'm sure, like hundreds of thousands of others from the 1950s onwards, proceeded to Loughborough (my grades were good enough) got an undergraduate degree and . . . Or could I?

I'm not sure it was ever quite there in my genes. I'm not academic at heart and none of my working-class family had ever got closer to higher education than watching the Oxford and Cambridge boat race. Further, we were pretty poor. OK. Those hundreds of thousands of other teenagers broke the mould and went on to degrees, but few of them were presented with so immediate and comparatively glittering foreground alternatives.

Record on file or not of that Directors' Box evening, Southend kept their faith in and with me. I got my three 'A' Levels but they came back with an offer not only firm but generous and forward-looking. It offered me £60 a week (as against the going rate for new pros of £35) and a three-year contract. Sixty pounds to an eighteen-year-old in 1979 was the stuff of overnight rags to riches. Three years was eternity. I realised (accurately, I think) that I'd had enough of book bashing to keep me going for quite a while. Except for fairy tales, maybe. Inevitably there were dreams of 'glory, glory', Goodison and Wembley. Putting two and two together you'll have gathered that it cannot really be said that there now ensued dark agonising nights of the decision-making Nelson soul. Delighted to do so, I signed on the dotted line and swapped my Billy Bunter costume for a Billy Bigtime career.

No shining pedigree, you see. No England Schools, England Youth, you name it. No apprenticeship. Just a raw talent who got a break at the right time and was prepared to work hard to improve. On the strength of that last characteristic, I've managed to construct a career of sorts. Twice the age now of the boy who signed that first contract, I'm still working hard to improve. But this morning, as so often, hard work and good intentions weren't enough. Our team were given the run around in a small-sided game. There is still no substitute for skill.

And in my career precious little glory. No Goodison. No Wembley. Today, yelled at by a manager still going on about my Tranmere performance, pretty certain I'm going to see most of the rest of the season from the subs' bench, it's inevitable I should ask: 'Nelse, if you had it all to do again, would you still?'

You tell me. Every one of us, the businessman who was a brilliant schoolboy Macbeth, the teacher who might have trained as an opera singer, the housewife who is cleverer than her bread-winning husband, the Sheffield lad who might have been Albert Quixall but had to settle for being deputy leader of the Labour Party – all of us have looked back over our shoulder in the direction of the road not taken and wondered: 'What if . . .?'

Well, those moments of choice are like half-chances in the six-yard box, aren't they? Miss one and it doesn't do to dwell on it too long. Learn the lesson, if any, and wait for the next one to come along. If, that is . . .

'Nelse!'

'OK, Curbs, just coming!'

DECEMBER

Friday 2 December

December already and not a trace of Jack Frost nipping at our toes. Goldfish are jumping and, betrayed by the spring-like weather, time-warped daffs and crocuses are flirting with blossoming. Oblivious, it seems to our just having come through the warmest November on record and going by the calendar alone, the more wimpish members of the playing staff have already taken to donning tracksuit bottoms, gloves and hats for training. I've been biding my time. When we have a real cold snap – as we will – I want to be feeling the difference.

There's even more point to rejecting extra layers today. We're not working towards any game tomorrow. We can enjoy the delightful, rare prospect of a weekend off. But up front the delight is severely qualified by the sure-fire knowledge that today we'll be asked to run our butts into the ground. As we push our bodies up into overdrive, and temperatures zoom up the scale, winter woollies is the last thing we'll be wanting.

I can write worthy words in this tome about working hard to improve. More true than not. It doesn't prevent me, truth be told, joining the old lags doing their best to get through the regulatory five-a-side game at as close to walking pace as we can manage. We're all shrewdly aware of the physical demands that are going to be asked of us the moment play-time is over.

Sure enough, here comes the call to arms. We're despatched on a twelve-minute run whose minimum requirement is that we complete eight laps of the full pitch within that span.

The going is not to the liking of two of our thoroughbreds. With back and hamstring twinges respectively, Carlo and Paul Sturgess pull themselves up. Well, it's an ill wind, I find myself thinking – especially as we are now being asked to do a full lap in better than sixty seconds (two repetitions), half laps in under thirty seconds (four repetitions) and six box-to-box runs in as quick a time as we're individually capable of. Greetings suckers, climb aboard and grab a piece of the action.

Knackered? We hardly had breath left with which to discuss Vinnie Jones' latest instance of bringing the game into disrepute by accepting the invitation to represent Wales in their forth-coming European qualifier. We found ourselves somewhat divided as to the basis of his own qualification. Was it Lloyd George knowing his grandmother? A career-long association with leaked goals? The fact that after a game Mark Hughes once found him in his pocket? I'm not sure about the Valley but he'll probably find a welcome in Cambria – just so long as Mike Smith remembers to send him a route map.

Saturday 3 December

Not having a fixture today due to Burnley's involvement in the second round of the Cup has not deprived Charlton of momentum in the league table. With other sides winning we continue downwardly mobile. We've now slid to an alarming sixteenth. It's something of an irony that, with the strongest squad overall on the books in my time at the club, Charlton are now in the lowest league position. Part of our problem, I think, is an embarrassment not of riches but of equals. If our 'first' team played head-to-head with our table-topping reserve side few would be brave enough to put their mortgage on the outcome. The ongoing result, I think, is that it's never been that obvious to the management what is the optimum combination. I'm far from being the only one made jittery by an element of revolving door selection.

But there's always the Cup. Briefly, anyway. This evening the traditional televised coverage of those sprightly lads down at Lancaster Gate playing with their balls climaxed for Charlton with the revelation of a third round London derby game away to

148

Chelsea. Despite our abysmal home form, I don't think having to travel across London is a blessing in disguise. You always want to be at home in the Cup. Especially against opposition from a higher echelon. There's always hope, I suppose. A gross amount of injuries have prevented Glenn Hoddle's side doing him and itself complete justice in the first half of the season. All the same, given the elegant way they stroked and strolled past us this pre-season, we're going to need the luck of the Cascarinos to progress to the fourth round.

Sunday 4 December

Amidst all the sleaze a gathering of genuine good guys and one of soccer's most heart-warming success stories. This weekend marks the second anniversary of Charlton Athletic's return to their traditional ground and spiritual home, the Valley. I had the privilege of playing in that game. By the skin of my teeth. My sole red card had been earned thirteen days earlier. A further twenty-four hours would have seen me automatically banned but, because the date of our game had been put forward a day for Sunday televising, I had that vital period of grace.

To run out on to that gorgeous playing surface and to that red and white spick and span newness was quite something. But the setting was as nothing compared to the warm sense of human 'rightness' that the crowd's cheering seemed to float on. This was a simultaneous homecoming for thousands, a distillation of every positive emotion. Along with the red and white balloons, there were lumps in throats and tear-tracks streaking the red and white painted faces of 'tough' street-wise teenagers. It was all the climax to a remarkable story.

By the mid-1980s, a long, sorry saga of mediocre results and gates, complicated fiscal and legal relationships and some simple greed had led to Charlton, then under a totally different Board, to within hours of official bankruptcy and extinction. Frantic last-ditch fire-fighting kept the club alive as an organisation, but access to and use of its ground, the famous Valley, was lost. The acreage was too juicy a real-estate morsel, the smart money said, to continue to be monopolised by a middling soccer team you'd never put down as a banker and these days couldn't introduce to one either. Get the right planning permission and buyer and it would provide a much more tangible result than – to pick one at random – Charlton 8, Millwall 0.

From October 1985 Charlton entered upon a sad, sustained period of playing all games 'away' in perpetual exile. They first camped out at Selhurst Park (whose remoteness and inadequacies generated a keenly felt loathing on the part of Charlton fans for all things Palatial), and then at Upton Park (which generated nothing: West Ham, winners of the 1966 World Cup, are the one London side whose plus half-time scores get a cheer at the Valley). It was during this time, and the management of Lennie Lawrence, that for four years, incredibly, they maintained a place in the top division. It remains a perfect proof of what shoestrings, sellotape and selling off all your best players can achieve.

Relegation inevitably came in due course, but by then the new Board had achieved nodding acquaintance with financial stability. And the Valley, though now a tip in every sense, still stood empty. It was time to stem the running financial haemorrhage of paying rent for every 'home' game and return to Floyd Road.

'Not so fast my fine Addick friend!' The guys in the black hats suddenly rode out of the woodwork to litter Charlton's way back home with obstacles and objections. Planning permission to restore the ground was opposed not only by local residents (some of whom had nipped in to buy neighbouring properties on the assumption that they would rise in value on the ground's final demise) with a No Soccer Hooligans In My Back Yard Campaign but, as well, by Greenwich Borough councillors still seeing the site as an opportunity to put up a parking lot, blocks of flats or yet another south-east London 'pile it high, sell it cheap' temple of Thatcherism. It was formidable opposition that had its fingers on many of the levers of power and certainly controlled the one labelled 'delaying tactics'. Local government elections were by now, 1990, looming but there was no possibility of any significant . . .

'Wait a minute, guys. We can always do it in the barn. What if we formed a party to fight the election too?'

'You've got to be kidding.'

'Yes, I was just joking. Hang about! No I bloody wasn't!'

Formed as a 'Single Issue' party, the Valley Party was immediately derided with unique unanimity by the established parties (that curiously illogical mirroring of national alignments that bedevils local British politics). This was no more than a bunch of thicko soccer hooligans doing a Screaming Lord Sutch. The Valley Party would be a nine-day wonder.

Wrong. The Social Dems and the Libs and the Tories and the incumbent Socialists had all overlooked that the Valley Party already had in place a far more extensive and committed grass-roots organisation, the CASC, than they themselves could individually command. Not to mention an almost certainly higher collective IQ. The Valley Party could field an electioneering team of all the talents.

Spearheaded by brilliant poster advertising and well-argued, genuinely literate, campaign literature, the Valley Party put its case to the electorate with tremendous verve, even as it put up candidates in every single ward in the borough. It remained a wild card, unknown quantity as a vote-taker, but now the attitude of the established groups was: 'Gentlemen – oh, and, of course, ladies – we can't afford to ignore this unlooked-for element.' The simple end result was that, in the Borough of Greenwich, the return of Charlton to the Valley became *the* number one issue of the 1990 local government elections and virtually every traditional candidate was declaring that he/she had been in favour of their going back for, well, ever such a long time, really. Now, I don't imagine that, lined up against a wall by a firing squad, any but the most rabid of Charlton fans would continue to insist that the return of their club to its ground was of more fundamental importance than improved schooling, better hospital services, enhanced community care. But these issues were constants, anyway. And, as the Valley Party profile rose higher and higher, the stirrings of change could be detected in those council offices where the incumbent Labour Party had most to lose. Opposition to the return began to wither; planning difficulties eased; compromises began to emerge.

In the end, while polling a hugely creditable 13 per cent from its standing start, the Valley Party failed to win a single council seat. The pressure it had exerted, however, was incontestably influential to the way being opened for the contractors to move in and begin building the new all-seater stadium.

I've dwelt on this four-year-old series of events because I think two of their chief implications have never been sufficiently absorbed by the British public at large. The first is the total sophistication of the Valley Party's putting the democratic process to practical use. Protestors on the verge of riot are always being urged by the smug likes of Sir Kenneth Baker to 'use the proper democratic means at their disposal'. Indeed. Where there is a Sellafield issue, an M11 extension controversy, a Post Office privatisation dispute, there too should be a Sellafield, an anti-MWE, a Friends of the PO party. Let's be sensible. The chances of an outright win are zilch going on zero. But, no two ways about it, the Valley Party experience makes very clear, whatever the one-off issue, *that's* going to be the one rocketing to the top of every contestant's agenda.

The second truth to be drawn from the Valley Party campaign is surely that every general member of the public needs to guard against thinking the mandatory way to qualify 'hooligan' is with the adjective 'soccer'. Charlton fans did not go on the rampage through Woolwich town centre; they did not trash Greenwich town hall. Instead, with intelligence, persistence, lucidity and style, they made their point in an eminently civilised fashion. It surely earned them a place in the history of supporters' clubs that in its trail-blazing uniqueness, they can be proud of.

In that sense the first game back at the Valley was always going to be a day for the supporters rather than for us the players. But to make their day absolutely complete, we were as desperate to win as if it had been the Cup final. We knew it was a special, even a unique, occasion and that the result wasn't irrelevant. A defeat couldn't but be a downer. If it was a privilege, an honour, to be taking part in this rebirth match, there was an obligation to give the occasion our very best shot. We ran out nervous as hell but determined to give the fans the best of all salutes. A performance worthy of their own.

You don't always get what you want. That's what football is all about. And Portsmouth certainly had no intention of rolling over. But sometimes you do. Sometimes they let you have the story-book ending. The Charlton supporters did not have to wait for Heaven to get their reward. The clocks had not yet reached 3.20 p.m. on the afternoon of 5 December 1992 when a pass from a player of 'limited ability' (and described as such in a subsequent television interview by the recipient) found Colin Walsh in space. That cultured left foot earned Walshie his own little guarantee of immortality as it directed the ball sweet and low into the Portsmouth goal and for a wonderful while it seemed as if Heaven and the Valley were one and the same place.

Tuesday 6 December

For the playing staff it's business as usual and the depressing reality is that we're back on the training treadmill. Any pack of laboratory rats watching us would laugh their tails off, particularly at my expense.

In the course of the three mini-matches I found myself moved from the left side of midfield to up-front and then to the Eastern front, frozen right out of the side altogether by the end of the third session. Well, worry about that later. Priority now, having got the extra running successfully under my belt, was to pull Curbs aside and establish exactly how I would be getting to Barnsley hard on the heels of the ultra-inconveniently scheduled (Friday afternoon) exam. Curbs responded in scholarly and gentlemanly fashion. I could have his car. Not only that, but a chauffeur, Peter Burrowes, our PR man.

With a shrug of one shoulder and a faint shimmy of the hips, Curbs skilfully dummies the conversation. Now we're discussing left-wing issues. Not Clause 4 but my seemingly ill-at-ease performances out wide in the last three games. Forget the 'seemingly'. Curbs is just being diplomatic. He's going on to say he enjoyed (sic) my little twenty-minute up-front training run out alongside Carlo and asking me – ever so nicely – to put in a whole ninety minutes in that forward position in the reserves tomorrow night.

'After all, it's been two months since you played there,' he ends by saying.

I feel the threat of Alzheimer's hovering. I'm all but thirty-four and, it seems, in danger of forgetting over two months what I've done for two decades.

'OK, Curbs,' I say.

The unspoken implication looks ominous. This weekend Charlton can put into the field the 'dream ticket' up-front pairing everyone's been waiting for: Big Carl and Whytie. Their selection looks a cast-iron bet from where I'm standing. Or, more to the point, going to be sitting. Those World Cup cushions are about to come into their own.

Wednesday 7 December

Heavy session of cramming for most of the morning for Friday's important exam. 'Don't panic, Mr Nelson, sir,' I hear Corporal Jones declaiming. Who's he trying to confuse? I know when it's time to panic.

More dense cramming on the motorways this afternoon. Truly horrendous conditions. Wind and driving rain, the day turning to night by four o'clock and nose-to-tail traffic almost all the way. Just two Gatwickers for this glamour clash against Tottenham Hotspur reserves. Myself and John Robinson. It's my honour at the wheel. There would be major consolation for this chore if we knew we were heading for White Hart Lane, but Spurs are another Premiership outfit quite happy to risk their millions of quids-worth of reserve assets at St Albans FC's ground. The turf may be hallowed but it dates from about the same time as the martyrdom.

On the subject of possessing assets by the million, Ian Rush must be a substantial tad closer to membership of that club following his testimonial match last night against Celtic. The bottom line, the car radio now tells us, was £250,000. A nice little earner and then some. I'm green with envy, of course, but not in the least begrudging. For ten years plus, Rushy has been right at the top always working very hard at his game and for his team-mates. Three hundred-odd goals is an exceptional total in the modern game so hold your hand up you deserve it, Rushy.

But life for us connoisseurs is made up of more subtle constituents than talent and rich rewards. In spite of the appalling conditions we arrive safely at the training ground to learn that the torrential rain has waterlogged off any prospects of a nice little Home Counties footy match. *Our* reward after seventy-five miles of fifty-yard visibility, putting life and limb at risk, is a half-time cup of tea and a Mars Bar. Now, turning round, we have, as they say, got it all to do again.

Thursday 8 December

A 'day off' for some of us, then, yesterday. But as today got into its stride I received firm, if unofficial, indication others had been active enough. The gossip-machine was up to full revs and one item it threw out hit me right where it hurts. A 'Charlton insider' as the tabloids would put it, told me that the team for Barnsley was picked yesterday and I'm out. On the bench at best. Hearing you've been given the elbow from a third party or learning about it first in the papers is a nasty – the worst – way of finding out. Every manager knows as much. Each should be man enough, diplomat, long-term planner and personal psychologist enough, to break the news in person. When you know the real 'why' it's a lot easier to take.

I received official confirmation of my down-grading when training got around to a First Team versus Driftwood game. I was handed a white bib and it wasn't to keep the Cow and Gate off my shirt. 'Driftwood' is very much the right expression, Brian, as following the unremitting heavy rain the New Eltham training ground resembled the Serpentine. The dynamic duo persisted in soldiering on, but only into a farce in which the conditions had the last laugh. Rain stopped play. But not work. Balls away, kiddies,

155

it's time to run again. So we ran and we ran right up to the dam. And lots of other words too.

Rescue from a watery grave came in the form of a first-team squad meeting in which, as probable substitute, I was included. After a quick session with Jimmy Hendry to have the webbing between my toes removed, I found myself sitting next to Johnny Reb himself, Stuart Balmer. He's still on the transfer list but back in the first-team frame and in a consequently good mood. He much prefers the pelting English rain to the frozen Siberian wastes of soccer exile. Soon he's positively amused. It seems that to counter Barnsley's 3–5–2 formation, we will take the field at Oakwell with a five man midfield of our own. Stuart catches my eye and I can see that the irony is not lost on him. For the first time this season a tactical approach I've been advocating quite strongly is going to be adopted. Minus my own participating contribution.

It strikes me that it's time for a little off-line chat with the dynamic duo. They make time for me straight away. My gripe, I let them know, isn't that I've been dropped – fair enough, it's their decision; I can't quarrel on recent form – but the way in which I've come to learn about it. I don't come on too heavy. Raising the roof rows aren't my style. Discussion beats argument every time. If you stay rational there's a chance that logic will develop the exchange along useful lines and even suggest solutions. Flat-out shouting matches might temporarily relieve feelings, but the dust they raise seldom settles in the memory. They thicken the air. On this occasion, Alan and Steve, as they are occasionally called, were quick to express their regret that I'd heard about my being dropped on the grapevine; it hadn't been what they intended, nor was it a controlled leak. I accepted that at once and the conversation broadened. We talked strategy and tactics for a good hour. My experience does mean that I have views that aren't entirely to be disregarded. In cricketing terms, after all, I'm the senior pro. I think the official Charlton managers appreciate that they can do worse than pick my brains from time to time to gain a third opinion and possibly, thereby, a different perspective. Perhaps today they were just doing their job to diplomatic effect, but I came out of the meeting feeling considerably more valued than when I went in.

Friday 9 December

An avenue straight back to the worst part of those happiest days of your life. Millions of adults who've passed through the British educational system (whichever one it happened to be at the time) have that nightmare where they're sitting taking an exam on a subject they haven't revised and know nothing about. Today I had the waking version. The real thing. The three-hour paper proved every bit as daunting as I had feared. The thing is that within the confines of the time limit, there's little scope for dwelling on the ball. Too much analysis eats into basic writing time. The urge to get *something* down is well nigh irresistible. I just hope I didn't succumb to it too quickly.

The mental agony over, there was no time to unwind. It was straight home for a quick bite, a quicker kiss and hug for Carole and the kids and then a five-hour slog up to the team hotel in Rotherham. Forewarned is forearmed. I've shared trips with Pete Burrowes in the past. Knowing my nerves wouldn't hold up to his species-endangering style of driving the whole way, I took the sensible step of volunteering to handle the Worthing–Toddington leg of our trek. When, at around ten, we finally reached our hotel the 'It's Time For Britain To Shut Down For A Month' pre-Christmas parties were in full swing. I was drained and in a club tracksuit. Party? Who needed it? I had a job to go to next day. I went straight to bed.

Saturday 10 December

When the fixture list throws up a December visit to Oakwell, your fancies not so lightly turn to thoughts of quagmires. To wind, rain and sleet and eleven Northern Bastards, as the song so charmingly expresses it, burning to turn over the visiting Southern Softies. Today's fixture demonstrated that fancy and fact aren't always a million miles apart. The weather lived up to expectation. Teeming. As a result the pitch soon cut up rough. As did its owners. The impact of some of the Barnsley challenges would have made

157

Ronnie and Reggie wince (the brothers Kray, that is, not Messrs Noades and Burr). Entering into the spirit of the occasion we battled toe to toe, and over the early rounds the scorecards were pretty even. Then a complete miscue from Shaun Newton made Barnsley an offer they couldn't refuse. Once again we were a goal down and on the ropes.

In the second half we had the Yorkshire Mistral in our favour and came more into the game. But the minutes ticked on with us still scoreless. With a quarter of an hour to go, I got the nod. I stripped off thinking that, with time running out, we'd go to three up-front and an all-out long-ball bombardment. Wrong again, Nelse. I went on as a straight swap for Carl Leaburn. But it seemed to be decisive. Any ambitions I might have had of doing a David Fairclough impersonation faded into the darkening night as Barnsley promptly added a second goal. One of our own from Paul Mortimer was nothing but a too-late consolation. Our romantic sojourn amid the dreaming chimneys of South Yorkshire had ended in another defeat. Our league position was plummeting as rapidly as the ambient temperature. We were looking at a winter ahead longer and bleaker than the road back to London.

We tackled the lesser of these two evils in sombre mood that easily prevailed over the half-hearted attempts at whistling in the dark. The fish and chips stuck in our throats that little bit greasily more than usual. Then came diversion of a sort. Grapevine news spread that Spurs' chairman had received a standing ovation when taking his seat at White Hart Lane today. Coach consensus was that the crowd had mistaken him for Steve McQueen.

As the archetypal Swindon fan, Chris Carter, I know, will be fuming at Spurs' great escape. The original twelve-point penalty has been totally wiped off the slate, entry into this year's FA Cup is also permitted. 'Why them and not us?' Chris will be baying at the moon.

Sunday 11 December

Another 'Don't watch the game, just feel the sleaze' day for the press. And once again their righteously indignant spotlight is focused on Highbury. Exit 'The Merse'; stroll on George Graham.

For some time the tabloids have been looking askance at the influx into the British game of so many Scandinavian players. The question has been: they're good but are they *that* good? There's certainly a case for answering: 'Yes, pretty good.' Denmark, after all, were European Champions in 1992 and Norway and Sweden both made it to the World Cup finals – the latter to finish third. Clearly you don't have to go to Minnesota to find Viking talent.

Arsenal obviously thought so. After the European competition they bought final goalscorer John Jensen. A snip, some would say, at £1.7 million. Particularly so, then, at £900,000, the amount which his former club Brondby insist is all they received for him. It's not quite a question of a fluctuating pound–krone exchange rate discrepancy. A trifling £800,000 seems to have gone walkabout. In whose direction, it seems reasonable to ask. And, indeed, how?

The transfer market operates differently on the Continent. In Europe the role of the agent is far more formalised and accepted. In many instances clubs directly employ agents to negotiate on their behalf.

Scandinavia, in particular, is an agent's paradise. There is no internal market so the prices of good players are low. The way for any interested party to cash in on them is to sell them abroad to the rich Italian, Spanish, German or, failing that, British clubs. Apparently along these lines . . .

An agent, smooth, let us suppose, as his talk, offers to act on behalf of a relatively naive Scandinavian club. In the course of very pleasant preliminary discussions he gathers they would be happy to let Gunner Garbo, shall we say – sorry, that should be Gunnar – go for £300,000. The agent then lifts a phone and courteously informs various overseas clubs that Gunnar is about to come on the market at a rock-bottom, bargain-basement snip at £500,000. What's the difference? At a rough guess £200,000. Where does it go to? The marginal discrepancy is, in fact, at the agent's disposal to do with as he best deems appropriate. He can shove it in his Swiss bank account. He can disburse it for services rendered. If, of course, the buying manager were to say '£500,000 is my unlucky number, let's make £600,000 but I don't want it to get around that I'm superstitious' the disposable petty cash will become even more divisible.

Thus, while Scandinavian players can be pretty tasty on the pitch, there may be other factors influencing the enthusiasm of agents to sell and managers to buy them at such (inflated) bargain-basement prices.

The highest profile among the Scandinavian agents at the moment belongs to Guernsey-based Norwegian Rune Hauge, who is alleged to have set up twenty-three deals in Britain along the lines of the hypothetical Gunnar transaction. Following a measure of northern exposure, Hauge now faces investigation for possible tax evasion in Norway as football authorities everywhere look closely at his MO.

Which brings us back to Arsenal. George Graham, hitherto one of the most respected figures in the game, appears to have received a £286,000 'gift' from Rune for – what? – facilitating the Jensen transfer. But not for keeps. In the nick of time, and with Caledonian cool of the highest order, George has nobly toe-poked the pot of Norwegian gold out of the path of the British taxman beating a full speed path to his door and into the touch of the Arsenal FC account. It gives you the feeling that he's got more in common with Eddie than with Charlie George.

Tuesday 13 December

From the murk of high soccer finance to the murk of New Eltham and the routine professional sharp end. A grey day in every sense. An almost visible cloud of doom and gloom hung over the training ground. Training was a real despondent slog. If Andy Petterson had been one of our number and not off on loan to Bradford City he would have received proof positive that it is the Pom's basic nature to whinge. Morale is sinking. The entire squad need uplifting. Right now our twin managers need to be earning their money by virtue of their man management and motivating skills. The team needs to come in for its mid-season full service. Let's hope it's not a complete rebuild we're looking at here.

Wednesday 14 December

A boost for my morale. I was delighted to find a Christmas card from my former manager at Southend and Plymouth, Dave Smith, in this morning's post. We still keep in touch and it's always a pleasure to spend a few hours listening to his silver-tongued, quotation-laden observations when we visit the West Country.

Over the years I've had a lot to thank Dave for. He was the one who saw enough in that raw, skinny schoolboy to sign him as a professional. Then, during some of my darkest days when choosing football was beginning to seem the worst possible career move and I was on the verge of giving up, it was Dave who got me back on track. Somehow he managed to persuade the then Plymouth chairman, Peter Bloom, to lash out a whole £15,000, the price of buying me from Swindon.

I'm pleased to be able to record that I justified the astronomic outlay. Believing in myself again, I put in arguably my most consistent season, playing a full part in Plymouth's gaining promotion to the old Division Two. But nothing has ever run smoothly for too long in my career. Even that euphoric promotion campaign had a nasty sting in its tail for me.

Towards the end of the season I found that I – a top rate 'trainer', whatever else – was literally exhausted at the end of every training session. It wasn't old age. Basic tests showed I'd picked up some kind of a virus. Somehow, by only playing – resting during the week and not training, hoping our opponents wouldn't suss my condition – I made it through the last weeks of the season. The incredible promotion-deciding game against Bristol City will always be a treasured memory. But just as abiding will be the dark counterpart memories of the nightmare weeks that now followed.

The rest of the Pilgrims progressed on to their holiday breaks conscious of a job well done and looking forward to proving themselves at the higher level. I took it easy. Rest was what I needed, everyone assured me; by the time we reassembled I'd be feeling my old self. Rest, though, did nothing for me. Some days what I felt like was a very old man. It was an effort to get up the stairs. I went back to pre-season training in no better shape than I'd been weeks before and the pattern of breaking down, inexplicably exhausted, continued.

A crunch of sorts came when, still gambling I could get through a Saturday on automatic pilot and adrenalin, Dave picked me for a game against Leeds. I lasted twenty minutes. Twice I threw up on the pitch and when they hauled me off I was on the point of collapse. In the physio's room they found I had lost eight pounds in weight since the kick-off.

Whatever I'd got, it needed more than rest. Dave put me on the next train to Harley Street. For five months I'd been wallowing in a grey limbo of uncertainty, speculation, hope and depression. Now, within two minutes I was told the exact score. The consultant informed me that I was suffering a mild form of ME. Contrary to all outward appearance I was a yuppie. Well, at least Yuppie Flu made me an associate member of the club.

There was, straight off, a clear-cut sense of relief at finally getting a precise diagnosis. But the secondary reaction was devastating. It went far deeper, was far longer lasting. Indeed, it threatened to last forever.

Consider. I was twenty-five with a wife and two young children to support. Earning my living depended on my being what six months earlier I had been – super-fit. Now, just when I should be hitting my peak as an athlete, I had entered this nightmare world where there seemed no way of my being able to control my body and no time limit set as to how long the condition would last. I might be obliged, it seemed at the lowest moments, to go through the rest of my life moving as if I were under water. Football would be out. So might any other sort of employment. The thing is, when you're in the middle of something like this, you just don't *know*, you can't *feel*, that you'll ever come out of it. There's no rule that you ever will. As you're coming up to your twenty-sixth birthday that's a heavy load to have to take on board and live with day after day.

I don't like to think about this black time. (And there's a cupboard in the back of my mind in which the knowledge the condition could return is under lock and key. How securely, I'm not sure.) I go into it only as background to writing into the record that throughout this quite long (or, as it seemed at the time, endless) period, Smithy steadfastly stuck by me. Perhaps acknowledging my earlier efforts to put mind over what was the matter with me, he consistently resisted what must have been the very strong temptation whispering in his ear day after day – go out and sign a left-sided player. He never did; not even a loan signing. When, three months after seeing the consultant I was at last fit and well again, he put me straight back into the side. He knew then and knows now that I was eternally grateful. But I never had a sporting chance to demonstrate this on the field.

Plymouth's promotion was followed by a year in which they finished comfortably in the top half of the Second Division. By this season's end my two-year contract was on the point of expiring. The club proposed offering me basically the same deal again – I'd be on a basic wage of £250 a week – but only in respect of a contract for one year. There'd be a sweetener, though. And would you believe the generosity – a signing-on fee running into five figures! £1000. Five if you count the pound sign.

OK, they may have seen me as a potential invalid again. But on my side I wasn't best pleased to be offered these terms by a club for whom in my last two seasons I'd scored over twenty goals from the wing and on whose behalf I'd semi-literally played my guts out for. Then, as I was hesitating, quite out of the blue, Brighton came in for me. They were willing to more than double my annual salary.

No contest, you might think. But I still hesitated. I felt I owed Dave one and, on a selfish note, Carole and I simply loved living down in the West Country. In many ways I didn't want to move. I went to see the Plymouth chairman to ask whether he could make it worth my while to stay. Mr Bloom thought long and hard.

'Tell you what,' he said, 'I'll put you on the same rate as the rest of the first team.'

The bloom went off the mayflower very rapidly at that point. I no longer felt I would be acting as a mercenary bastard if I put my family first. And when I reported as much to Dave, the man who'd found me and twice rescued me, he didn't begin to try talking me into staying.

'You've got a family and a career to think of,' he said. 'And we both know there's no way in the world Plymouth are going to get near matching Brighton's offer. Go to the Goldstone and good luck.'

Well, I've had a bit here and there since, but not much to match knowing Dave.

Not that I've any complaints about tonight. This evening I skippered the Reserves to a fine 5–1 Combination win over a strong Portsmouth outfit.

A yellow mark for me, though. My first booking in two years. It was the quite justifiable sequel to a clumsy late tackle. Not malice, I swear, but ineptitude. I got there as quickly as I could.

Simultaneously, Bulgaria were toying with Wales in cruising past them 3–0 and effectively eliminating them from the European Nations' competition. After the match, debut boyo Vinnie Jones said that it hadn't been as hard as many league games he'd played in. He didn't comment on how the skill levels compared. Perhaps he didn't notice.

Friday 16 December

Another Friday, bloody Friday. The dustbins stood around while the first team practised their set pieces and patterns of play. The pressure cooker atmosphere is still palpable. My guess is that it had a lot to do with the management's decision to drop Mike Ammann for a fit-again Mike Salmon. Salmsy has all but worn out his patience and I'd have had to put money on his non-involvement tomorrow causing him to reach for Stuart Balmer's pen and paper. The last thing the Charlton camp needs right now is further discord and awareness of just that has, I'm sure, no little to do with Mike Salmon repossessing the goalkeeper's jersey for tomorrow.

For me it's more of the same. Let's hope the cushion is made of sterner stuffing than our recent performances.

Saturday 17 December

Charlton v Oldham today – not a game to feature that high on the list of contenders for 'Match of the Century' but for us the most important fixture so far on our season's schedule. Just one point out of a possible fifteen from our last five home matches is Exhibit A in explaining our depressing slide down the table. Failing to win today will probably see us descending all the way to the basement. Four, bear in mind, go down this season.

Ensconced in Charlton's subterranean bus shelter (aka the home dugout) I have a chance to clock the response that being under pressure draws from our management duo. Grace is not the most obvious characteristic on display.

Gritty seems to have delivered himself into the hands of one of the currently trendy showbiz hypnotists. Every time he sits down he seems convinced it's upon a red-hot poker. He's up and down more times to the minute than a yo-yo on fast forward. It's not only his bum that's been brainwashed. He's also got a Pavlovian reflex to the linesman's flag as well. Each time it waves Gritty goes into Nixon speak. Record him and then delete the expletives and you'd end up with white noise.

Curbs endeavours to show that he's unruffably above such behaviour by taking a seat in the main stand. He's been known to stay there for minutes. Usually, though, the seat has had no chance to warm up before he's joined us in the ref-baiting pit. Then he returns to his cold seat for a cool appraisal. Then he's back down to earth again. He's another yo-yo on a longer string. Come the second half and the string snaps. Permanent squatters' rights are established on the bench.

Nobody, let me add, blinks over-much at these manic performances. They're managers, aren't they?

Today the antics are largely justified. A first-half exhibition of jittery edginess on our part and a lack of any interest on Oldham's in venturing forward condemns everyone in the stadium to a quite atrocious three-quarters of an hour.

Perhaps suffering a delayed trauma from Joe Royle's defection, Oldham opted to defend even deeper on the resumption. Their manifest lack of confidence eventually helped us to steady our own nerves. Suddenly Mark Robson was doing a very acceptable minor key impersonation of Tom Finney down the right wing and crossing to feed the on-the-spot David Whyte's killer touch. Still a few wobbles, but then the rare spectacle of a Charlton midfielder bursting through to join the attack and Keith Jones had headed not only his first goal in a Charlton shirt but the game's clincher.

A corner turned? Perhaps. It's difficult to tell given Oldham's dreadful and surely untypical performance. But for the moment, anyway, there was the sound of laughter, a sense of relief in the home team changing room.

Monday 19 December

An appalling night's sleep – or, rather, lack of it. There were moments when I thought the grim reaper was calling my name. Certainly it seemed as if his scythe was between my ribs. By dawn the dull ache of the previous evening had risen up the scale into the excruciating band.

I somehow managed to make it to the training ground, but it was only ever going to be for diagnosis. Driving was quite physical effort enough, thank you very much, given this, as an examination soon showed, inter-costal strain. Inter-costal is Jimmy Hendry talk for the muscles between the ribs. This particular one plays a major part in the breathing process. Hence, I suppose, my feeling that I'd just furnished the raw material to create Eve. Packing me off homewards, Jimmy told me to delay reporting back to the training ground until Friday but to clock in at the Brighton treatment room for the next three days. He also slapped a ban on me. I am not to attend the players' Christmas social in Croydon. I think I can live with this. I've never felt there was anything the least sociable about Croydon.

Thursday 22 December

As so often, Malcolm Stuart's handiwork at Brighton has worked a minor miracle. The pain is gone. The injury seems to have cleared up. It would be silly, though, to invite its return by volunteering to resume training. Much better to spend the third day of my convalescence relaxing and taking a gentle stroll through the papers.

Inevitably the sports pages first. Two items – both good news – leap out at me. Our Youth Team has achieved a 1–1 draw up at Old Trafford in their FA Youth Cup match. A fine performance that offers hope for the club's long-term future whatever the replay's result. Would the old men had managed as well last March. No less satisfying is the announcement that John Gorman is back in business. He's joined Bristol City as assistant to Joe Jordan.

Pleased on both counts I now turned to the *Telegraph* to clock its Fantasy Football page. This, of course, has been a hugely popular initiative. Initially I was interested in the valuation given to the roster of Premiership players. But as I dawdled over a cup of coffee I began to fantasise on my own account. I wonder if the *Telegraph* is missing a trick. Perhaps the better game to have set in motion would have been The Make-Believe Managers' League.

Let us presuppose that the rules of the Fantasy Football League positively encourage managers, all with notional millions to spend, to traffic for players by means of backhanders and bungs. How would it work? Musing thus I found myself embarking on a fact-finding investigative tour of my own fantasy scenario in the Land of Let's Pretend.

First I journeyed to the Make-Believe Midlands and spoke to the manager of a struggling club whose consistently indifferent form has long been trying its fans' patience. This manager had a long history of buying players from still lower leagues. It didn't seem to bother him that this policy had not bought success. I asked him why not.

'It's like this, Nelse,' he replied. 'If I bought a Cantona or a Ferdinand it would blow my entire budget. And I couldn't afford their wages and the agent's commission. But with these lower league boys it's all different. I can get 'em on the cheap, double their wages and give 'em signing-on fees that are way over the top. It's only natural they'll then want to express their gratitude to me. As this is only a fantasy situation, I can suggest – well, insist, actually – that they do this by slipping me a whack out of the aforementioned signing-on fee. Strictly cash, of course. On my level of buying and with my budget I can do this over and over again.'

'Yeah. But in the meantime your results are awful. Don't you care?'

'No. Why should I? I'll create a new fantasy football team next season and do it all over. It's a lot better than working.'

Somewhat bemused, I followed the yellow brick road south to London. Perhaps if I spoke to the manager of a consistently successful side I would receive more encouraging and enlightening answers.

'What's the secret of your success?' I asked him.

'It's obvious,' he said. 'I employ a Fantasy Football-approved agent.'

'But won't he represent thousands of other fantasy managers and players?'

'That's the point. It all works very well. Those managers who try to play by the book and don't use fantasy agents are going to miss out every time. They're living in a world of their own. There's too much money at stake to do it any other way.'

'Fantasy money?'

'Naturally. But in the Land of Let's Pretend that's the accepted currency.'

'Of course. Silly me. So – what *are* the benefits of using a fantasy agent?'

'Well, I've bought a lot of players from outside the UK. Now, then – once you go abroad, it's the agent and not the selling club who sets the price. But, guess what else besides?'

'What?'

'The agent will be working for the selling club as well as for me, the manager of the buying club.'

'Working both sides of the fantasy street.'

'Yes. A typical Fantasy League fee right now is half a million. Now – if the lad's any good he'll help the team go on collecting points and everyone's happy.'

'But, what if he turns out to be a unicorn?'

'Eh?'

'A fantasy donkey.'

'Oh, well, not a problem. Not for me. The fantasy agent's already sorted me out for buying the lad in the first place and when we've settled on his signing-on fee, I get some more fantasy money – strictly cash in hand, you understand – for being like a Dutch godfather to him. Another plus is that at the start of the year we get fast lane updates on all the best up-and-coming fantasy talent. We clock all these. They might be in the non-fantasy lower divisions right now, but sooner or later they'll come on stream as Fantasy League commodities. The fantasy agent offers his services to the non-fantasy clubs explaining he's a flexible friend with fantastic access to thousands of managers in the FFL.'

'Fantasy Football League.'

'Got it in one. He tells them he can secure top prices for their players. Once he's got these players in his stable, the agent procures the players favourable press coverage – among other things – or, failing that, and since any news is better than no news, unfavourable coverage, by using his many contacts in the fantasy press to pitch in. Finally, when the price is right, he lets all of us fantasy managers know that the player is up for grabs.'

'Through his fantasy manipulation of the player's reputation, the agent has now hugely inflated the price you could originally have picked him up for.'

'I'm more than happy if he has.'

'Why?'

'Because I'll then be getting some more fantasy money back from the fantasy agent because he's now earned extra fantasy commission from the selling club for pushing up the transfer fee. Clever, innit?'

'Fan-bloody-tastic.'

As I sat nursing my coffee, it seemed to me that The Make-Believe Managers' League would be overwhelmingly fuelled by greed.

It's a blessing that it's only in the Fantasy League that corruption is a problem. We know this because back in the real world the Commission probing transfer fee irregularities is audibly struggling to find any evidence thereof. What a relief! All together now: '*Cos it's hoe-honely make-bee-leehee-heave.*'

Heave indeed.

Friday 23 December

From fantasy land to winter wonderland. My drive north this morning was through a Sussex magically transformed by hoar frost. Then the Wicked Witch of the West did her stuff. She abruptly surrounded me with freezing fog that made the final approach to the suburbs a white-knuckled nightmare.

But every London fog has its lining. The light at the end of the motorway for me was that, with visibility at New Eltham too limited to permit any structured work, it was a case of this morning we improvise. We were divided into four teams of six, viz: The Old Gits; The East London Mafia; Five Star Plus One; and, as expressed with political correctness, The Brighton Belles. A morning of fun and games had been devised.

Geography rather than chronology operating in my case, I was included in the last rather than the first of these elite cadres as we all prepared to contest a tournament made up of various skill tests. Dribbling through cones, keeping the ball off the ground, pinpoint accuracy in passing were three of the typical events. With pride very much at competitive stake, battle royal was joined.

Largely on account of the wrong sort of ringer, the Belles, far from going like the clappers, distinctly failed to chime. With logic as dense as the fog, we had been assigned David Whyte. Largely unacquainted with us South Coast folk, he looked well out of sorts. And, for once, touch. We finished last in the first three events. As we completed the successive bouts of penalty press-ups our sorry performance had earned us, we could only console ourselves with the thought that things could only get better.

Or, as that's sometimes put, worse. Another show of petulance from Whytie suddenly saw him being red-carded from the exercise. Furious, he chose to demonstrate as much by volleying a ball straight at the pavilion. For a moment I saw a 'paned'

170

expression flit across Alan Pardew's face. But today our shooting star could do nothing right and, the strike missing any glass, Pards was not required to revive the glazing skills of his non-League days.

The Belles' performance improved dramatically with the Gritty old git substituting for the prima donna. But the incident left me pondering a soccer question as old as the game. Whytie can do things on and with the ball I couldn't master in a thousand years. He's in a very select band in that respect. But why is it that it is precisely these kissed-by-genius skill players who most commonly seem to be beset by flawed temperaments? Why do their dazzling, ball-players' feet so often turn out being the ones with Achilles' heels? Is it that it's all come so freely and easily to them that they grow impatient when subjected to discipline? Are they so often winners they haven't had time enough to learn not to be a sore loser? Does awareness of their skill overlap in their minds with the sense they are invaluable and so have licence to do what they like? Certainly, out-and-out thugs apart, it's almost always the flair player who will give his manager personality problem headaches.

Saturday 24 December

Christmas Eve in the workhouse. A normal training day geared to our holiday fixture list. Managed it back to home, though, in time to savour and share some of the children's excitement and to welcome our guests for Christmas – Carole's sister Melanie, her husband Rodney and their already unwrapped prize gift of the year, their now four-month-old daughter, Harriet.

Christmas Day, Sunday 25 December

A performance of amazing restraint this morning from Carly and Christopher. The Nelson family were woken not by a pre-dawn chorus of gleeful yells as they ripped open their Christmas sack, but by the everyday sound of my alarm noising off at seven (landlubbers') bells. I was able to spend an all-too-brief three-quarters of an hour watching them open their stocking fillers; then I had to curtail their fun and set them a patience test. Our prior family agreement was that we would leave all our major presents unopened until my safe return from the pleasures of Christmas morn training.

This has been the pattern of my day for the past sixteen Christmases milestoning my pro career. With my previous clubs it has meant only a two-hour separation or so. With Charlton, most annoyingly, I have to write off half a day.

My only consolation today was the total absence of any other poor sod on the road. My immediate present for being a nice, obedient little player was a private race-track.

The training itself was short and sharp. Perhaps for that very reason, I spent it mainly wondering whether my journey had been really necessary. The rationale of the powers that be seemed to have been: we're all professionals; this is just another working day; we have four important games coming up; if we don't have everybody in for training somebody somewhere will be pointing the finger. All very well and good. But no marks for guessing which consideration has really driven the decision. Why else is this invariably the shortest session of the year? Let's be honest about this: today's exertions are token at best.

The biggest effort put in today, being honest in return, was the sprint to the showers. Collective speed saw the Gatwick Express rolling back out at 11.30. The management's farewell message – 'Don't eat or drink too much' – struck me as unnecessary and unseasonal, but by 12.45 as I crossed back over my own threshold I was also entering into the holiday spirit.

'Let the festivities begin.'

Monday 26 December

For virtually everyone else in the country today is Boxing Day. In the Nelson household, however, that awareness is beaten well into second place by its being our son's birthday. It shouldn't have been. His arrival eight years ago was premature by a matter of several weeks.

As Christmas Day 1986 was drawing to its close, Carole, heavily pregnant and in considerable discomfort, thought she might be experiencing contractions. I, the ice-cool diagnostician, safe in the knowledge of the mid-January ETA, was able to tell at a glance that she was mistaken. Overdoing it on the Christmas spread had obviously induced only indigestion. I wasn't having my pre-Boxing Day match beauty sleep ruined. Sympathetic to a fault, I fled to the sanctuary of the spare room.

I was hauled back to the real world by a 3 a.m. hand on my shoulder. One glance told me that the Rennies had been asked to accomplish a little more than they'd been designed to do. What a blessing I had never felt the call to pursue a career in medicine. Our second child was insisting we got on with it.

We did our best. I flogged what speed I could out of our ancient Volvo. As in a cliché film sequence we skidded to a halt outside Plymouth's Freedom Fields Hospital.

'Try to get on with it,' I urged. 'I'm supposed to be trotting out at Home Park six hours from now.'

Aren't men little dears? It's as well looks don't kill. And it's a shame Carole is not always so co-operative. Her obedience on this occasion was total. We never made it past the Admissions Room. Christopher put in a complete and healthy appearance at 4.56, surprising everyone by the speed of his delivery.

Honourably released, proud as punch, I didn't trot, I floated out at Home Park. The high Christopher's birth had given me inspired me to a high on the pitch. But not quite enough rubbed off on to the rest of the lads. Portsmouth beat us 2–3. But who cared! Mother and child were both doing well and the male missing from the bottom line on the Nelson family tree had now arrived to carry the clan name forward.

Today, eight lightning-fast years on, the Nelson standard bearer is strutting his stuff in full Charlton strip, complete with name on the back. The associated number caused a problem or two. The old man's current '12' seemed rather a liability to load on his back and '111', though witty, a bit far-fetched. In the end we settled for a topical '8'. I'm fairly confident that in a pinch I'll be able to tell him apart from Stuart Balmer.

Parting is such sweet sorrow. For a while. Then it becomes a routine drag. Today, not even the slightly later setting-off time of 8.30 could offset the tiresomeness of having to earn a crust entertaining 10,000 holiday-makers.

Nobody had bothered to decorate the dugout, but I don't believe it was that which caused Gritty to launch into a marvellous impersonation of Victor Meldrew – 'I don't believe it!' – once the game got under way. Southend totally dominated the first half and should have had two or three goals to add to their single penalty strike as reflection of their superiority. Playing with one foot in the grave, we were very lucky to go in just one goal down.

Curbs' stocking filler must have been a manual on the art of full-frontal verbal assault. He launched into a bravura dressing-room dressing down that would have put life back into an Egyptian mummy. Drooping heads began to lift.

Within five minutes, courtesy of a now re-gruntled (and who else?) David Whyte, we had equalised. Ten minutes from time Carlo rose to the occasion of a Mark Robson cross to score our second goal of the game and his first of the season. By this time I had been given a token canter. I was in danger of playing out time without getting a touch. Then our midfield recalled that we are supposed to operate with a left side to our attack as well. I was fed a ball, returned it to General Walsh and we zig-zagged our way down the wing. Walshie found me, finally, on the edge of the penalty area and, taking it round a defender to the byline, I clipped it low and fast to Carlo for a tap-in at the far post. He got the cheers but I got a handshake from an appreciative Mark Robson.

Well now. A winning run. Two straight wins. All together everyone: *'So here it is, Merry Christmas, everybody's having fun.'*

But don't get too excited. We're playing Slade's home side on Wednesday.

Tuesday 27 December

It's been victory at a price. The 'No Vacancies' sign was up on the treatment room door today and, as Jimmy and Mossie worked overtime to earn their Christmas bonuses, the one conspicuous absentee was Florence Nightingale. Richard Rufus and Paul Sturgess are definitely out for tomorrow. Steve Brown, Keith Jones and Mike Salmon all face late fitness tests. The relative size of our squad this year is making sense right now.

But not the fixture list. After just three games in four weeks we are now required to reel off four in eight days. It's curious how the game's administrators never seem able to bring a playing background to their decision-making. Still, I suppose they're happy in their work and it would only get in the way of their seeing the big picture.

Wednesday 28 December

Wolves away and a long day in prospect. Boarding the team coach at Junction 9, I find it as crowded as the treatment room. Taking no chances Curbs and Gritty are still in the process of perming eleven from a travelling squad of eighteen (nineteen if you count that strange lady in the corner with a lamp) which includes three goalkeepers. Andy Petterson has been forcibly brought back from Bradford in case Salmsy has a relapse.

After a tortuous series of tedious detours, we arrive at Molineux just an hour before the evening kick-off. But from this point on there's no question that we are travelling first class.

Nobody with a memory can fail to be anything other than impressed, awe-struck even, by the transformation Molineux has undergone. It seems another era – it was actually only nine years ago – when, in front of a meagre crowd of 3,000 spread sparsely about the two sides of the dilapidated ground that had not been condemned, I played a part in Plymouth's 3–0 thumping of Wolves, so helping to shovel them down to Division Four at the end of the season. That they have since risen from the ashes of those grey days to challenge for a Premiership place can be attributed to two men above all others.

Off the pitch, Wolves are indebted beyond calculation to Jack Hayward, the elderly multi-millionaire property dealer (Peter Shilton apart, is there any other sort?) who has underwritten the reconstruction of Molineux. If nine years ago the ground, like the team, was largely condemned, today it is the best stadium in the Endsleigh League. Bar none. All it now lacks is the spiritual 'topping out' of the club's entry into the Premiership.

On the field, Wolves are arguably as much in debt to the best striker in the contemporary game to have pursued his career outside of that top flight. Throughout their climb back, Steve Bull has been a leader in more senses than the obvious. Without him, Wolves hardly bare their fangs. He has all the primary qualities you look for in a striker – enthusiasm, bravery, an insatiable appetite for goals and the ceaseless determination to be an all-round bloody nuisance to defenders. Right now, the need to emulate Bully's attitude seems to be putting extra pressure on the rest of the team. Their recent record of just two wins from eight starts no more than mirrors our own. Awareness of this will be exerting the greatest pressure of all on Graham Taylor, their manager.

Life in the hot seat is scarcely a new experience for the much (and perhaps over-)derided former England boss. But he could possibly win a few more friends, influence a few more people positively, if he paid just a bit more attention to detail. Certainly, he less than endeared himself to Alan Curbishley as managers and captains swapped teamsheets in the referee's room. Turning to his aptly named captain, John de Wolf, Graham suavely said: 'John, I don't believe you've met Charlton's co-manager, Steve Gritt.'

Curbs – for it *was* he – commendably rolled with the punch at this juncture to let the moment pass. But on his return to the changing room, where a delighted Alan McLeary was revealing all, the counter-jag was a foregone conclusion.

'No wonder he couldn't pick an England team!'

Steve Gritt wasn't smiling much, either.

The game kicked off in torrential rain and gale-force winds. As unnerving was the gate of 27,500. This all but capacity crowd had hardly had time to focus in on the action when, with extraordinary courage (it's very much the exception rather than the rule), the referee awarded us, the away team, a first-minute penalty. Up stepped a far from hundred per cent fit Steve Brown to convert it into a precious second-minute goal. Alas, he wasn't fully focused either. His weakish shot was saved.

That was about as good as it got for us. From this early peak, we went into a terminal eighty-nine-minute decline. Steve Bull, rampaging all over the field, added another goal to his long list and a few minutes later Phil Chapple, returning from a month's exile in the stiffs, submitted his personal entry for the Grosser Than Danny Baker Own Goal Of The Month Award. Losing possession in midfield he praiseworthily raced back to cover as Wolves worked the ball to the wing. His anticipation was exemplary. As the dangerous cross did, indeed, come arrowing in, he was there to cut it out. His intercepting leg shot out to play a lightning one-two with the post. Rick O'Shea cannoned the ball back into Phil's knee-caps – thence to rocket into our net. The Wolves fans went into a knees-up of their own.

By now the ability to predict the shape of results to come was utterly dampening my usual eagerness to get involved. We were struggling to put two passes together. The Wolves were rampant. Nothing to do with me, guv. I couldn't see how my introduction into the game would alter a thing. As so often, the management had other views. With half an hour to go they played that last desperate card of a losing team – the old double substitution ploy. Go out and work a miracle, lads. Well, it may have all been happening like that around Christmas knocking on two thousand years ago, but times and locations change. Soundly beaten, we trooped off the Molineux pitch to lick our self-inflicted wounds. We went home by another way.

Thursday 29 December

After the off-day, a day off. My Christmas has at last arrived. My new mountain-bike was proudly wheeled out of the garage to join Carly and Christopher's new models. Some two hours later when we returned home I had rediscovered my childhood. Outwardly we were caked in mud. Inwardly we were glowing.

Saturday 31 December

No peace for the wicked, no chimes at midnight revelry (and that iffy moment of having your own mortality underlined) for those at the Charlton sharp end. We have got it all to do tomorrow. We all ken there'll be no Auld Lang Syne for us tonight.

Virtually every other pro side have their league games today. Not us. Mark up another mindless victory for soccer violence.

At the start of every season the football authorities ask each club what opponents it would prefer to face over the Christmas and Easter holiday periods. First choice is almost invariably a local derby. It's a certainty the gate will be bigger and travelling for away fans minimised.

Charlton's obvious local derby opposition are Millwall. Last year, however, there was a minority of fans indulging in the rare spectacle of crowd violence at the Valley. It was localised and quickly snuffed out but, a Sunday fixture being easier to police, it caused Charlton to request that this year's fixture be put back twenty-four hours. The computer initially confirming a New Year's Eve clash we thus found the game being postponed into next year and ourselves ending up as two-time losers. No New Year's Eve bash. Two games in two days.

A year ago the holiday fixture boot was completely on the other foot. Away to Nottingham Forest we *were* in a hotel – and certainly being monitored. As the old year began its last hour the entire, and entirely dry, Charlton squad were to be seen milling around the foyer area sourly watching everybody else easing into a great time. Then came a concerted move towards the lifts. To hell with it! Out of sight and out of mind. It was less galling to turn in for the night.

But gall, it is well documented, is often made up of more than one part. Extreme insult added to our injured feelings was the sight of our management duo (both still registered players) propping up the hotel's magnetically attractive bar. Scarcely an example of solidarity. Hardly a case of all for one and two for all. It would have worked wonders for team morale if they'd postponed their quaffing until later and invited all the players wanting to see in the New Year formally to rendez-vous with them in the bar a few minutes before midnight for a couple of token drinks. No harm but considerable goodwill would have been done.

But that never happened. Tweedle-Dee and Tweedle-Dum are, in fact, particularly strict on the alcohol front. They don't object to us having a drink at other times, but during the last twenty-four hours of countdown to a game alcohol is strictly *verboten*.

I can live with this. But equally I've never had problems with easier regimes. At Brighton, for instance, where I not only played alongside but drank alongside Curbs, enjoying a bit of a session on the eve of a game was par for the Goldstone course. We didn't, for the most part, abuse this easygoing approach. Some players do.

On the other hand, if you bottle up a team too tightly with a drinking ban, you're likely to find Prohibition blowing up in your face. An earlier New Year's Eve in Nottingham, this time 1991, points the moral. Three weeks earlier I had completed my twenty-six-minute month with Notts County and returned to Brighton. Now I was back for the famous Trent–South Coast holiday derby game. We were staying at a hotel in the heart of the city centre and any local will tell you that is where it all happens in Nottingham.

Suddenly I was the most popular man in the squad. The reason, though bad for my ego, wasn't hard to deduce. My recent stay, everyone was reckoning (correctly enough) must have taken me through the thinking footballer's 'What's On In Nottingham?' form book.

Knowing I wouldn't be involved next day, I didn't think twice. My personal position, after all, was much more out than in and I didn't feel I owed Lloydie any more favours. A quick fiver was passed to the night porter to ensure his turning a Horatian eye to our return through the side door he'd left open and, here we go, here we go, here we go, the city was our lobster as we joined the throbbing masses.

'We' was myself and five others – four of whom were definite starters for the morrow's noonday kick-off. With this date with destiny in mind, we did nothing very wicked or silly. We were back in the hotel within a quarter of an hour of having heard the bells ringing out in the main square. Only, having tiptoed down the corridor to my own room, I found my knock getting no response from my obviously AWOL room-mate Steve Gatting. Hmnn. A pass-key job called for here. I retraced my tiptoes back to reception. It was not deserted. Who should I there bump into but yet another of the lads committed to tomorrow's battle. He beckoned me mysteriously. Who was I not to follow – all the way to the bar. Lo and behold! There, before my very eyes, was the rest of the squad doing a serious demolition job on the hotel's supply of Becks. It would have appeared churlishly anti-social to have spurned their kind invitation to assist them. Breakfast next morning was poorly attended. Black coffee was the big seller. Mark Barham was one conspicuous by his absence both over the cornflakes and, later, on the pitch. He had travelled with the need to run a fitness test, but liberal applications of German beer had not speeded his recovery. At literally the eleventh hour I was told that I would be, yes, involved.

We lost 1–2. I put it down to ground advantage.

JANUARY

Sunday 1 January

The year 1995 came in with the thermometer struggling to rise above zero and a biting wind straight out of Stuart Balmer's freezer. As I again put my World Cup cushion to practical use in the dugout, I speedily clocked that the Charlton sections of the stands looked to be surprisingly thinly populated. That guaranteed bonanza gate was well below expectation. I think this went beyond Charlton fans waking up with a sore head and deciding there was more to life than paying to flirt with hypothermia for a couple of hours down by the Thames. Remembrance of last year's unpleasantness and the negative edge to the day that a heavy police presence and all the concomitant hassle – 'You're not going down that road, *sir*, if you haven't got a ticket' – will have played their forbidding part in keeping numbers down.

Ironically, footing the bill for the heavy and on double-time Bill will have left the club out of pocket on this crowd-puller. Policing has got to be tapered off if the nuts-and-bolts games of the Endsleigh League are to be events to enjoy rather than officious gauntlets to run. As Newton, Isaac not Shaun, pointed out reactions, by definition, are secondary. Policing generates and does not ease tension.

On two counts the Charlton Board must have been grateful for the excellent showing from the Millwall supporters. They filled the South Stand to capacity. And, to a man and woman, they behaved in exemplary fashion. Possibly there is a collective New Year New Den resolution to behave properly at football matches.

Possibly their hangovers had not inhibited their attendance but only their aggro.

The Lions' fans had first cause to roar in the first half of a mediocre but exciting game when Alex Rae ran unimpeded through the deserts of the Charlton midfield to fire a stunning long-range shot past Salmsy. Yep, tell me the old, old story. Once again we went in at half time a goal down.

I have a tendency to make a rod for my own back when on the bench. I'm congenitally unable to refrain from voicing the occasional comment on the play going on in front of me. I'll broadcast the odd little pearl of tactical wisdom into the vacant air. I'm not sure this does me any long-term favours. You could make a good case out for Curbs and Gritty putting a youngster in the Number 12 shirt to blood him and allow him to acquire experience gradually. But I think the managers quite like my occasional observations and the alternate view they sometimes offer. During today's first half I made three comments. It could be sheer coincidence but it was the self-same three that Gritty threw in to our half-time team talk. As we trotted back out, sub goalkeeper Mike Ammann tapped me on the shoulder.

'Nice going, coach,' he said.

Be that as it may, after the interval we had the edge. When the recalled John Robinson got in between defenders to head yet another Mark Robson cross past yet another American goalkeeper, justice was probably done. Honours even. Pride still intact.

Happy New Year, Charlton and Millwall.

Monday 2 January

It didn't snow enough. The game at Luton is still on. In fact the Kenilworth Road staff ought to be in the New Year's Honours List. Mid-range forecasting on their part has kept the length and breadth of the pitch covered these past five days. Removal of this protection revealed a surface that, despite the steadily dropping temperature, was relatively soft and certainly playable. It may have been ignorance of this that caused club chairman Roger Alwen to put himself in pole position for the next yellow jersey award. On his motivating pre-match visit to the dressing room he left us with a real morale-booster.

'Rather you than me out there tonight, lads,' he said.

'Cheers, Rog.'

Our high-frequency fixture schedule is now causing high anxiety about our casualty rate. Missing tonight are Stuart Balmer, Richard Rufus, Paul Sturgess, Keith Jones and Peter Garland. But five men's loss is another man's gain. Who do we spy stepping in from the cold but Alan Pardew?

The Silver Fox has not exactly been revelling in exclusion from the first team. Never one to keep his feelings to himself and blessed-cum-cursed with the sharpest tongue in the club, he has embarrassed the management to the point of synchronised squirming during various exchanges. Now, if only by default, he's back in the frame with the pressure to perform very much on. A good game tonight and he could find himself running out against his favourite team in next Saturday's Cup game.

Despite the conditions, Luton tried to play an elaborate passing game. Some of what they did began to look pretty, but too many pleats spoil the Chanels. We, by contrast, cut out the frills and competed very well. Pards as effectively as anyone. The night's only class bit of play was a flowing four-man build-up to yet another lethal David Whyte finish from six yards.

We should have had two more to ward off any anxieties but sadly, perhaps typically, the chances weren't taken. David Pleat now executed a few chess moves. Curbs instantly discerned a fell motive that I was completely blind to. With just fourteen minutes left on the clock, he told me to get stripped.

It took me another two minutes to cross the line. The cold had got to my fingers so much I was fumbling with my kit that long. Think about that the next time a sub comes on in Arctic conditions and you expect him to go from 0–60 with his first touch. My first touch now was hand-to-hand with a Mark Robson rightly no more best pleased at being taken off than I was to be sent on. I was mightily relieved the score stayed 1–0 until the end. If Luton had got anything towards the death, questions might have been asked in the houses of a lot of Charlton fans as to the point of mending a machine that hadn't been broken.

Another win! Hot diggitty! And cold baths. Never mind. We were too happy to mind very much. But a word to the Luton wise might be in order. After seven home defeats this season it's surely worth them updating their gamesmanship ploys. I know the ground looks like something out of the Ark, but the roasting hot dressing rooms, the differently pressured kick-in balls, the half-time teapot that's oversugared to a Tottenhamesque extent, the icy cold baths – we've all been there, seen it and come away with three points. Aren't there any twentieth-century ways of loading the Luton dice before 2001 is upon us?

Tuesday 3 January

An incoming call this afternoon makes it seem that I can look forward to a hot, labour-intensive summer break that's not going to have too much 'holiday' built in. It was Jeff Carrington phoning to update me on developments in Baltimore over the proposed soccer clinics. Good news, too. Interest, it seems, is running very high and filling the places on the courses should be no problem. As far as everyone at their end is concerned, the project has a green light.

That puts the ball back in my court. I need to put together a course programme/timetable and, obviously, a team of coaches that will give us a sensible teacher–pupil ratio.

There's also the fundamental question of how long to plan on having the clinic open for business. My gut feeling is to just dip a toe in the water, this time. Come the summer, I could well be in soccer's no-man's land with no need to report back for training. But let's stay balanced and resist the temptation to create a new lifetime's career overnight. Let's walk before we run. What's surely called for here is a short pilot study. *Next* year can be 'Tomorrow the world!' time.

One thing – I've no worries about recruiting coaches. A wee whisper in the changing room – 'Anyone fancy a couple of weeks' work in the States, all expenses paid?' – should make me a very popular man.

Friday 6 January

The mercury has climbed a few wary degrees upward overnight. Enough to dispel the tundra and allow us to prepare for tomorrow's third round Cup tie on our dirty green training ground grass. Our road to Wembley starts tomorrow away at Stamford Bridge. Taking a line of form from our pre-season friendly with Chelsea, it will most probably end there too. Yes, the Cup's a great leveller, Des. Allegedly. The growing gulf between Premiership 'haves' and Endsleigh also-rans is steadily diluting that old cliché. It's true, too, that Charlton's form against top teams these past few seasons has been very respectable. But we're falling way short of that level in our bread and butter games and I don't see us transforming ourselves overnight.

The slight thaw is the only change I am able to detect at New Eltham today. We've certainly not had an away-from-it-all, let's-get-focused break in Spain. We're not even having any special kind of build-up here, either. There's no break in routine at all as, just as on any other Friday bloody Friday, the first team and dustbins spar with each other at three-quarter pace. I suppose this is an effort to appear super-cool – 'it's just another game, lads. They're only eleven names on a piece of paper, same as you' – but my own instinct would have been to make a big, big thing of the tie in an attempt to psyche everybody up to the top of their potential.

As things were, nobody got the least excited. The going through motions ran its mind-numbing ninety minutes and that had been that. I hope both sides can serve up something a bit less mundane tomorrow.

Far more interesting to me was the newspaper report that my mate, Tommy Johnson, is the beneficiary of yet another million pounds and over transfer. This time from Derby to Aston Villa. He's still only twenty-three and unless he blows it, he's already financially made for life. As will be his agent.

Saturday 7 January

Even though it's increasingly coupled with the name 'Littlewoods' these days, playing in the FA Cup still sets the blood pulsing that little bit faster through my ageing arteries. I still get the goose-bumps on the back of my neck. The Cup is still special. However flat I felt yesterday, today I know it can still be the short cut to glory. It's asking a lot of us to match last year's achievement of reaching the quarter-finals but, let's look on the bright side, Brian. We've turned a bit of a corner coming in to 1995 and, yes, our Saturday morning spirits are high.

As with so many grounds today, redevelopment is changing the face of Stamford Bridge. New stands are shooting steeply up. But this is no place to bring a sufferer from claustrophobia. The new layout is eroding yards from the width of the broad playing surface once at the centre of the vast Valley-like bowl of an amphi-theatre. If there's a 'pile 'em high, sell 'em dear' policy being implemented here, Chelsea fans may have to pay for it not only with their cash but by enduring a future of slugging matches on a traffic-jammed pitch where, denied space, flair and vision are the infrequent exceptions. It's hardly the ideal canvas for Glenn Hoddle to create patterns on.

Scott Minto, good on him, was there to meet us prior to the serious business of the day. He's a real West Londoner now. Not only is he totally at home in Premier company, his dedicated follower of fashion turnout proclaims he's having no trouble adapting to a legend of the King's Road lifestyle. He's always been the most dapper of full-backs.

Nothing dapper about our changing room, mind you. It was strictly school of 1960s nuclear bunker minimalist. This is a part the rebuilding funds haven't reached. The 'Nothing to lose, lads!' shouts of encouragement echoed off its concrete walls with a hollow ring. I clutched my cushion to me as I clattered out. The starting eleven began well. But within nine minutes this confident 'We're here to play' opening was no longer very relevant. Under pressure Mickey Bennett committed a pretty palpable foul in our penalty area. The ball ran Chelsea's way. The 'play on' gesture from referee Terry Holbrook was hopelessly ambiguous. His out-stretched arms pointed straight at the penalty spot. To a man, red-and blue-shirted players ground to a halt. Almost to a man. No whistle had gone. Next to me on the bench Keith Peacock showed admirable restraint as his multi-talented, quick-thinking-and-footed son, Gavin, rapped a perfectly judged chip-cum-shot into our net. It was fairly rough justice but justice. It had been a foul.

Chelsea now retreated into a calculated shell. They conceded us plenty of possession but, with ominous ease, denied us any clear-cut scoring chance. We were all foreplay and nothing more. Then came a dugout sensation. Just before the interval, most uncharacteristically, Glenn Hoddle was heard uttering the F-word. The shock waves this generated had immediate impact on the game. Chelsea swept forward and won a corner. Scott Minto's immaculate left foot hung the ball up short of the crowded box for Frank Sinclair arriving late and like a train to plant the ball in the far corner of our goal. It was a perfectly worked set piece. The expletives were now coming from our dugout. In stereo.

Curbs' assessment of the game's pattern during the interval was exactly my own. We needed better quality, faster reactions in the final third of the field. More inventiveness. It was perhaps to throw a joker into the pack that just two minutes after the interval Curbs substituted an off-song and bemused ('Why give me *two minutes*? Why not take me off at half time!?') John Robinson. On to face his boyhood heroes came Alan Pardew who, in my opinion, had been very hard done-by in not being allowed to start the game. Meanwhile, Chelsea and I had something in common. We both had a comfortable cushion.

As my ongoing role of not going on was prolonged, Chelsea more than ever sat on their two-goal lead. Their surrender of the midfield allowed a largely unchallenged Colin Walsh to ignore the pain in his knee and, rolling back the years, deliver the sort of performance that took him as far as the Scottish bench. But all his canny promptings were dribbled into the sands as our front men dallied on the ball and continually refused to take responsibility for a strike. Edginess begat confusion. When Carlo and Whytie, the dream ticket, tripped over each other on the penalty spot I began to feel hard done-by too.

By now the Charlton fans were chanting my name. At Brighton this was usually the kiss of death. Lloydie would rather have foregone his post-match drink than be seen to be influenced by a supporter. Today, though, the message got through. I got the nod with a whole twenty-five minutes to go.

I was up for it. At 0–2 this was almost certainly going to be my last Cup tie and I was going out there to enjoy myself. I did. Out wide on the left I several times went past an international right back to cross dangerously. My best effort created the rare spectacle of Dimitri Kharine wasting his neatness on the empty air.

But still no goal. Then, ten minutes from time my moment came. Boring down the inside-left channel I had a window on the goal. I gave the left-foot drive my best shot and knew then and there we'd pulled one – DAMN! Bloody foreign imports! Who opened that Iron Curtain! Not flapping at all, Kharine had homed in on the ball like a graceful Exocet and, demonstrating his status as a World Cup keeper, made the save look ridiculously easy. In that nano-second my hopes of adding a Stamford Bridge goal to my FA Cup collection died a final (well, third round) death.

In the last minute, as fine a save from Mike Salmon summed up our day. Going through the motions of throwing everything forward we cleverly lost possession anyway. Mike was left exposed one-on-one against John Spencer. There was nothing wrong with the short-range slammer of a shot but, defying the laws of physics, Mike got down to beat it out – straight back to John Spencer. With goalkeepers still on the ground, international strikers aren't in the habit of missing out twice in a row.

A 0–3 defeat. The scoreline flattered Chelsea but, easily soaking up our soft-centred pressure and counter-attacking at will, they always had something comfortably in hand. They won on merit. We in time-honoured tradition were left to concentrate on strengthening our position in the league.

Monday 9 January

No time for 'might have been' musing on who we'd be playing in the next round (Chelsea have got either Millwall or Arsenal) or how much 'bonus' dosh the club would be making.

Life, as they say, goes on. Business as usual. And then bloody some. Re-arranged from early December, a trip north to Burnley. Once again it was the road to Wigan Pier writ slow.

Tuesday 10 January

Overnight the rain has poured down non-stop. By morning it let up enough to allow us a session on a sodden (and other such adjectives) training pitch in which to stretch our legs. In the afternoon I headed straight to bed for some pre-match shut-eye. I didn't get to journey far into the land of Nod, however. Several phone calls, all suspiciously pointless but all in pointed Lancastrian accents, made sure I kept having to return to the borderline with consciousness. Just good old Burnley hospitality, I expect. Then, via an approved source, an old friend, my room-mate Phil Chapple, received some news that kept us fully awake for the rest of the afternoon. Andy Cole has moved from Newcastle to Man U for a fee of £6 million plus the £1 million-rated Keith Gillespie.

My instant reaction is that this is good business on Keegan's part. Although Cole is still a relative youngster, I think Kevin has had the best out of him. I suspect that, although getting an *English* striker for his European campaigns, Ferguson won't be benefiting from anything like so sensationally sustained a scoring purple patch as St James' Park witnessed. The Newcastle fans clearly feel otherwise. At any rate the knee-jerk reaction of many of them was to mill about outside their ground in semi-formal protest. I much admire that Kevin Keegan went out to meet them one on many, man to men – a lot of managers wouldn't have had either the bottle or the sense. But my guess is that the fans' indignation is unnecessary. I don't know any of the behind-the-scenes issues contributing to the deal (even when Cole's goalscoring was in full spate there seemed to be a certain reserve between him and his manager) but I do know that with this millstone of a price-tag around his neck Andy Cole will be under intense pressure every time he runs out in any of the United shirts.

If I can compare small things to great, I would like to point to the season I had after my thirty-two-goal year with Brighton. Playing for a relatively weak side against the better players of a

189

higher division, I scored sixteen goals. I thought that wasn't bad going. General opinion seemed to be that I'd let the side – and myself – down. And that was without the millstone. Part of the problem is that it's worse for a striker. When you play up-front, people measure your contribution by the number of goals you knock in. You can play a blinder, make three or four goals, pull the crucial defender all over the place and create gaps an army could pour through but, if you haven't scored yourself, you won't get a mention on *Match of the Day* and the Sunday newspaper fan will reckon you were off song. Andy Cole is obviously too useful not to give Ferguson *some* return on his money but I wouldn't be that surprised if three years from now the clearly very gifted Gillespie turns out to be commanding the higher transfer fee. One immediate deduction to be made from the level of the transfer very much suggests I should reconsider my start of the season remark that Chris Sutton was way over-priced when bought by Blackburn. By comparison he's beginning to look like the boot fair bargain of the season.

Taking a more general view, the transfer has to be regarded as bad news. It's bad in that it points to the shape of things to come. The gulf between divisions has just distinctly widened. Sooner rather than later, it could be a case not of the playing field no longer being level but of only a handful of clubs being allowed to play on it. The rest will be told to bugger off.

Which, returning to the real world, is essentially what we were told to do this wet afternoon in Burnley. At 5.45 a fully in flow Gritty was holding us spellbound with his anticipatory breakdown of all Burnley's set pieces when a basic weakness in the Turf Moor scheme of things was officially confirmed. The turf couldn't handle any more water. The game was off. We'd sacrificed virtually two days going miles out of our way for this non-event.

Most distracted member of our squad was YTS trainee Jamie Stuart, who would definitely have made his league debut at left-back if the game had gone ahead. Rated as a potential Scott Minto-plus, he'll find his time will come soon enough, no doubt of that. But short term he now had economic injury added to disappointment. An unheralded stop on the way home from our fools' errand saw the entire travelling squad lining up for a fish-and-chip supper in no-man's land. I refer not only to the Watford Gap service station (although it's that, all right) but to the fact that, no game having been played, it was not clear to anyone whether club or individual should be picking up the tab. This may seem incredible, given we had several millionaire Board members in our midst, but either they were all busy on their mobiles arguing with their Burnley counterparts as to who should pay for our stay at the Hotel Sleepnot or else they timorously feared buying us all fish and chips might be construed as an illegal gift bringing in its wake a plenary session at Lancaster Gate. Whatever, far from making his debut, Jamie, whose weekly wages run into the thirty-somethings (that's pounds, Andy, not thousands), found himself lighter by the fiver he had to fork out to fork in well. Which may have been his summing up of the gastro-economic experience.

One player who wouldn't pass the till at his own expense (he's not much given to passing in most situations, actually) was David Whyte. Sheer bloody-mindedness on his part finally compelled one of the Board to stand him his supper. It was the principle of the thing, Whytie could have argued with justification. All the same, we had a nice variation on the fans' chant for the rest of the way home: 'David Tight, Tight! Tight!'

Wednesday 11 January

Still no peace for the wicked – for those, anyway, hovering between first team and stiffs. Tonight the treadmill brought a Combination-topping Reserve game at Welling against Crystal Palace.

My route to the game took me via Shoreham, to say farewell to Mark Barham who is returning to Norwich. The place, that is, not, alas, the Canaries. The truth is that what he's really returning to is a great deal of uncertainty.

Thursday 12 January

Got a better result this morning than last night (a 2–2 draw with Palace Reserves). A quiet word with Curbs and another day off.

'Free' day for me meant tying up a few business ends in the course of a trip to London and then a trip back to the Valley for an evening kick-off. Two games in twenty-four hours, then? Rested? Dropped? None of these. This is an FA Youth Cup game against Manchester United.

The big name and a sense, I think, that Charlton are building rather a tasty squad for the future pulls an unbelievably big crowd. Like most Charlton fans, I time my arrival too close to the last minute and the narrow approach roads are clogged chaos.

'Just where do you think you are going, sir?'

He must watch a lot of television. I flash my Charlton player's pass and now we – I'm smuggling four SE likely lads in with me – gain access to the blocked-off Floyd Road and thence the ground's car park. Chaos is still all around us. Charlton were simply not expecting a crowd of 3,500 for a Youth game. They've only made provision for the opening of one stand.

Old age has its privileges. I pull rank again and the five of us end up in the directors' box about fifteen feet from one Alex Ferguson. I'm impressed. Wherever you've looked these past two days, he's been there in the papers and on the box being berated or applauded for his madness or shrewdness in spending a royal ransom on young king Cole. Right now he seems totally oblivious to all of that. He's here keeping an eye on his own 'babes'.

Nor is the evening without its sour little joke. Seated just behind Ferguson is former Charlton hero Mike Flanagan. What irony! Mike is now manager of Gillingham, who this week called in the receivers. Owing a few hundred thousand has really put them on the financial ropes. Never mind the seven million. The agent's nice little earner from the Cole deal would go a long way to keeping them in the game. They're the club that produced Steve Bruce, of course. What's he up to these days?

The game begins. It's great entertainment. The youngsters are all prepared to play positively, risking the possibility of mistakes if they think there's a better chance of pulling something off. Such a politically incorrect attitude will doubtless be drummed out of them soon enough. By half time the crowd are purring. The Charlton lads are 2–0 up. With Lee Bowyer, the best man on the pitch, running the game they are doing an Italian job on the cream of Manchester's youth crop who, reduced to a crude long-ball game, are being made to look very ordinary.

At the interval Alex Ferguson dives below – presumably to boost morale by chanting the magic motivating incantation 'Seven million, seven million.'

Come the second half, the cream rises to the top with a vengeance. The sorcerer's spell on his apprentices really is magic. Suddenly looking twice as big, Man Utd shorten their game and score five – count them – goals in thirty-five minutes. They march off the field to a generous ovation and on, on, on towards the flock of agents circling above Old Trafford.

Talk about your game of two halves, Brian.

Friday 13 January

With exquisite regard for the calendar, it's been made public today that Charlton are 'putting' (sic) four of the current squad on the transfer list to join the already disaffected Stuart Balmer. The way the announcement has been made gives the clear impression that it is the club taking the initiative here because the 'In Tray' is too cluttered and it's the right moment to adjust.

Oh yes? The last two observations may be more true than not, but there's no question there's an image-preserving, damage limitation exercise going on here. Of Messrs Balmer, Grant, Pardew, Petterson and Robinson, no less than four have actively asked to leave. The Board and management, though, are plainly trying to play down any suggestion of a winter of discontent. Cost-cutting and squad-trimming are clearly high on the current Board agenda.

Saturday 14 January

I avoided a rather large fine today by allowing myself two hours in which to do the Worthing to Valley journey. At the death I needed every last minute of it. Some Ministry of Transport jack in office who works only Monday to Friday and never consults a fixture list had ordained that this weekend, when Charlton are at home to Derby and West Ham are entertaining Tottenham, would be rather a good time to conduct major roadworks in the Blackwall Tunnel. The build-up to the tunnel's approach had spread out on to the surface streets in every direction. We had to dispute every inch of the last two miles to the ground with the bedecked cars of Irons and Spurs fans.

We made it just inside the witching hour for what has to be a crunch fixture. A win will leave us sitting very comfortably in mid-table with even the possibility of some end-of-season play-off chasing frivolities should we stumble upon the consistency that has so far eluded us since, er, August.

The immediate hurdle is Derby County. Their 'Buy! Buy! Buy!' policy has failed to purchase a triumphant move up to the Premiership, close as they came in last year's play-off final. That policy, in fact, has recently gone into spectacular reverse. The team's indifferent start to the season provoked a radical shift in the thinking of the Rams' Board. 'Sell! Sell! Sell!' came from the floor of the Baseball Ground and several star names moved on. Not only my pal Tommy Johnson, but both Paul Kitson and Gary Charles have gone and the word is that soon Craig Short will follow. Financial consolidation seems the Board's goal for this season. It leaves manager Roy McFarland selecting from a diminished squad.

But not by too much. From my now customary seat on the bench, it was clear, the game under way, that some very keen and talented youngsters were filling the shoes of the dear departed. Charlton, by contrast, were neither one thing nor the other but somehow, with both defences occasionally turning to jelly, the interval curtain came down on a 3–1 home lead. Flattering in the extreme, but never look a gift horse in the mouth when it's bearing three points.

With a 3–1 lead Charlton are, of course, at their most threatening. To themselves. Just ask Swindon. And now Derby. Five minutes into the second half some woefully negligent defending of a set piece saw them getting to 2–3 and putting the pressure fully back on. Twenty-five minutes then ensued in which the game could have gone either way – ours if our dillying and dallying attack had accepted responsibility for a series of possible strikes. Then, in a moment of pure farce, the game swerved closer still to a complete reversal of fortune. Derby keeper Steve Sutton plucked down a too generous corner and cleared over-long to downfield defender Paul Mortimer. Casual to a total fault, Morts judged his deft header (as opposed to an 'anywhere will do' clearance) to the inch. It ran straight into the path of Marco Gabbiadini. Mike Salmon found himself in a one against two Derby forwards situation: 3–3.

The managers were spare. The natives were restless. Another three home points were ebbing away faster than the nearby Thames tide and as inexorably. You folks want the course of the season changed? The ghost of relegation busted? Who you gonna call? No problem. Send for Nelson. He's got nine whole minutes left to sort it in.

I actually did go from 0–60 in nothing flat. Within seconds of coming on I made a good run past defenders to lay the ball back from the right wing. Then, two minutes later, the real chance to do the duty expected of me. Anticipating and latching on to a channel ball down the right, I had a run on goal, albeit at an angle, with a defender ahead and the ball on my club foot. I didn't reckon beating the odds with a swing from that dodgy implement so – hey, presto! – I sold the sweetest of dummies to leave the defender for dead as I worked the ball on to my left foot. Now! DAMN! From high in the rigging that sniper had taken aim and, lacking a fraction of momentum from the dummy, the ball was stuck under my feet. All I could do was lay it off. No ecstatic embraces for the match winner. Suddenly no one, not even Hardy, wanted to kiss Nelson. The chance had gone. The victory was sunk.

So, too, any point at all. Moments later our defence horrendously retreating all the way back to Plumstead Common, gave Gabbiadini a long run on our goal. Marco made full use of the hole in the middle. So 3–1 had become 3–4 and, gutted beyond anything we had previously experienced, we trooped off with our heads on our chests. Better they had been under our arms.

Heartsick at my own miss – *If I could just have it to do once more!* – I didn't have spirit to raise my arms in a 'thank you' clap. But what need to a booing crowd?

We sat about the changing room as if it were a lethal chamber. Wishing it were. The emotional temperature was sub-zero. Then abruptly it was screaming upwards. I do mean screaming. Curbs announced he was going to conduct a post-match analysis which would step through the team from attack to midfield to back four. But his journey foundered with its first steps. A knock-down, drag-out, four-lettered verbal battle between Curbs and a Carlo who had had a particularly languid game was suddenly blistering the changing room's paintwork and everyone's ears. Rational analysis was as out of the question as demanding a replay. Grace under pressure was again out to lunch.

I could understand why. In the space of fifteen minutes we had been relegated from the comfort to the danger zone. It's a potentially season-shattering result. There's little prospect of 'bounce-back' relief in the two tough away fixtures and the blank Saturday in the next three weeks ahead.

Sunday 15 January

Not so much an away day as a 'get away from it all' day. A family trip to Hayling Island visiting former Southampton goalkeeper Ally Sperring and his wife Paula. Ally lodged (and put up with) Carole and me when he spent a month on loan at Swindon during Super Lou's reign. Very sensibly he decided at an early age that pro football wasn't his game and fashioned a new career for himself running his own motor factor business. But he's still finely tuned in to what goes on in a player's mind. We were strolling along the front. The breeze was cold and the grey January sea looked the way I felt. Throughout a night of fitful sleeping and waking my mind had insisted on constantly replaying my non-moment of glory. *If I could just have it to do once more!* Ally was not blind to my symptoms.

'You know,' he said, 'I don't regret quitting one little bit. What is it that keeps you going?'

'Because it's there, Ally,' I pretend to joke. 'It's what I do.'

Monday 16 January

My birthday. Thirty-four. Only one year to go before I become a footballing pensioner. If I'd had a breakfast drink to celebrate it would be a sobering thought. Not, though, as sobering as the prospect of today's training session. I'm not expecting any icing on the cake. I'm not expecting a cake.

The meeting we all dread is convened. It kicks off with a public apology to Carlo from Curbs for the tone and content of his Saturday evening remarks. I'm not sure myself whether this is a positive or negative step in CAFC terms, but person-to-person it's civilised. It prefaces one and a half hours of breast-beating. As we warm up, contributions follow hard on each other's heels from all sources. What is the road to Hell paved with? As is so often the case with group therapy sessions, only a few issues – too general to help much – emerge from the welter of input. For the record they are:

- As a team we're not defending well.
- We seem confused as to which pattern of play best suits us (a confusion compounded by the injury/loss of form/revolving door team selection. Virtually everyone party to the discussion has some right to feel miffed at having been dropped at some time or another.).
- We're unprofessional at set pieces.

My contribution to the meeting was mainly directed at this last point. In the three years-plus that I've been with Charlton Steve and Alan have always made absolutely sure that their teams are given detailed information about the opposition – the make-up of their side, their formation, likely style of play, collective and individual weaknesses, what side of his shorts each player tucks it down. These pre-match analyses usually take place on a Friday at the training ground or on a board at a pre-match meeting in the overnight hotel.

Nobody can accuse our co-managers of not preparing their players thoroughly. But, given that the concentration span of most footballers lasts only a few minutes, the question has to be asked: how much of this wealth of detail do we actually retain? I know I'm often guilty of letting my thoughts stray and, once you stop meeting him halfway, Gritty's sessions can make the Ancient Mariner seem like Ceefax.

But my point now was a more subtle and serious one. I suggested that, to a degree, our weakness at set pieces was the paradoxical outcome of overkill: that, by spending so much time on what the opposition were likely to do, we were electing to bat on the back foot all the time. Surrendering the initiative we were choosing to *react*. OK, yes, we all knew what positions we should take up given this or that situation. But what if our opponents worked a variation? What if they proved particularly inventive? The time it takes to realise that something different is being worked can often be that vital split second that makes the difference – that vital second too late. Hence, I argued, a large part of our propensity to leak goals at set pieces.

While appreciating that I wasn't criticising him personally (the decision to give us so much information is a joint policy) Gritty, no great surprise, didn't agree with my comments. The detailed briefing on the opposition, he and Alan feel, should be the basis from which we anticipate local situations. But, joint policy though it may be, it's Gritty who actually has to take us through the other team's set pieces week after week – a pretty thankless task given its mundane nature and inevitable unpopularity with easily bored professionals.

One positive Charlton initiative that was announced today certainly had my undivided attention. We're going to try to take some of the strain off the midfield and attempt to give ourselves more attacking momentum and direction by reverting to hitting balls into the channels. Channel balls, of course, are what I'm all about and today's news that they will figure more in our scheme of things now produces the most ambivalent compliment I can remember ever having received.

'That's good news for Nelse,' Alan Pardew chips in with. 'He's the best channel runner in the club. As a matter of fact he's made a whole bloody career out of it.'

Gee thanks, Pards.

It's only a passing moment of light relief. Ninety minutes and, truth to tell, lids are drooping. Then, hooray! The bell goes and it's playtime. We launch into an enthusiastically contested, high quality, small-sided game.

The air seemed to have been cleared, the players lifted. The meeting, in its fashion, had worked. We were nicely set up for – Oh, no! Mercy! Mercy! – another meeting.

No nodding off here. The content had its built-in benzedrine. CAFC had undergone a bloodless boardroom coup. Roger Alwen was still on the Board, but we now had a new chairman and a new managing director – Messrs Martin Simons and Richard Murray respectively.

The new order starts with a moment ominously close to yellow shirt status.

'I didn't realise we had so many players,' says Richard Murray.

'Why not?' I felt like responding. 'Aren't you supposed to?'

Discretion being the better part of contract renewal, I held my peace. But I could sense that the remark had done nothing to put a bridge over the troubled waters that exist between players and directors. Players know that first and last they are the directors' chattels (dictionary definition of which is *a moveable article of property*). We are their stocks and shares, their commodities. Perhaps worst of all, we are their playthings – their Lego blocks. When it suits them, they buy. When your job has been done or you don't perform to expectation or they just get bored with you, they divest. Nothing personal, you understand, business is business. What does it matter whether you're one hell of a nice guy, a complete arsehole or someways in between? You're their puppet and their attitude is that they have paid for the right to pull the strings.

That said, the Charlton Board probably stack up better than most. They're clearly not in it for a quick buck – they'd be running a privatised utility if that was their game. They're certainly well regarded by Charlton fans, who recognise that the Board's financial commitment was central to the club returning to its spiritual home. More immediately, there's no doubt the low-key readiness with which the club's directors make themselves accessible to fans is well appreciated.

Their interest, mark you, in making a long-term buck is

something else again. The heart of today's statement of new intent was that the Board had based their entire commitment upon Charlton securing a place in the Second Division – of the Premier League. Such an extension of the Premiership remains, at present, hypothetical. Nobody has declared it will happen. But there isn't a director, manager, player or fan in the country who believes it's a Fantasy Football concept. As our meeting casually but completely presupposed, it's going to happen. And, the explicit message was, the price of not being there would be too awful to contemplate. The almost explicit message was: pull your finger out or else.

You're only a small club, anyway, so why should anyone care about you? The chances of a minnow pulling itself up by the scruff of its gills to become a shark will be about the same as Garry Nelson picking up a Golden Boot award at the next World Cup.

For Charlton this has to be the key issue. We're rapidly becoming a borderline case in terms of a rating in the 'Top Forty' charts. Having a neat ground with adequate capacity won't gain us 'Serie B' Premiership status if we haven't earned it by our points total come the season's end. We're going to have our work cut out to do that.

There's a final straw in the wind as the meeting breaks up.

'How would you like us to address you?' someone asks the two new top Board executives.

'Martin's fine by me,' says Martin Simons.

'Address me as Mr Murray,' says Mr Murray.

Tuesday 17 January

One of those days. I spent a good part of it psyching myself up for the highly charged tie in the Kent Facit Cup against Gravesend and Northfleet. My heroics in battling against a puncture, gale force winds and driving rain again prove predictably futile. Forty-five minutes before the 7.00 p.m. kick-off the pitch is declared the 'no-go' area it so obviously is.

I'm so pissed off I just can't face the return journey. Yet again I stay over. The thing is, I really needed this game under my belt. Two ninety minutes in two months. Nine successive substitute spots. Whatever happened to that season that started so well?

Wednesday 18 January

Things can only get better. Carlo is complaining of a slight hamstring strain and is doubtful for Saturday's game. And the bad news? It's possibly our most difficult match of the season. Bolton, away. Training ground gossip is that Carlo may have fallen victim to a sharp onset of Stubbsitis. Double-edged swords are always only a swish away. Duck, suckers! Too late – report to the managers' office for the midweek movie matinee. Two and a half hours later we emerge shell-shocked and footballed to death. It was nearly as bad as a Michael Winner film. But it was a message movie. If we want to be winners again we've got to get back to basics. We've got to remember how to be a team again.

Friday 20 January

Whoopee! Holiday time! But sadly not for Carole or me. The 'don't know how lucky you two are' kids are off for a week's skiing with Grandad Ron and Nana Pam in the French Alps.

For all that I'm bound for the lower slopes as well – of the Pennines. A chill wind and leaden skies promised our northbound coach we might discover ideal skiing conditions on arrival outside Bolton.

Saturday 21 January

No snow business this morning but bucketfuls of rain. Still, no one said it was going to be easy. The last time I started for the first team was back on 26 November against a very strong Middlesbrough side. Today, two months later, I could look forward to all the joys of playing against an arguably still stronger side.

So it proved. Today Charlton were run over by a 32-tonne truck powered by an engine firing on all cylinders. It left us buried face down in the Burnden Park mud. The final score was 1–5. We were beaten by an all-round superior team heading, I still believe, for promotion.

In spite of which, I have to say that – up to a certain point – I rather enjoyed myself. I wasn't that bad. I can claim a part in Whytie's superb seventeenth goal of the season (briefly equalising the score) and during our best spell of the match, the fifteen minutes before half time, I was asking enough questions of the Bolton defence to justify my selection. Then, in the forty-third minute, my satisfaction with my afternoon's work was radically altered.

I had just succeeded in nicking the ball away from Bolton defender Simon Coleman. Gaining a bit of space on him I turned sharply to drive a low cross into the box. But he was coming in on me hard to compensate for his initial sloppiness. The ball cannoned off his incoming boot for a corner – and a split second later my instep, following through, had all but impaled itself full force on his long defenders' studs. Agony. Sheer bloody agony. Before I hit the ground I knew instinctively it was one of those knocks you don't run off. As Jimmy Hendry worked on me, we both wondered whether the foot was broken. It certainly felt like it.

I struggled upright again – only a minute to go, sort it out at half time – to have the pain instantly compounded. In the injury time now added on, Bolton scored a soft (where were you, Morts?) but psychologically murderous goal. It came from a free kick given against me for being offside as I was hobbling back. It must have been obvious to all but the fool of a linesman that, whatever his own propensities, at that moment I couldn't even have interfered with myself.

Limping in late, I fortunately had no tunnel vision of the subsequently well-reported passage of arms between a furious Curbs and an incensed Walshie. Not that I'd have made any sort of a referee. Pain was still blurring my vision as I scanned the changing room for the ice bucket. It wasn't so hard to spot. It was the one item in Jimmy's medical bag that hadn't been volleyed. Once my boot and sock – *Jesus!* – were removed it was obvious at a glance that my afternoon frolics were over and it was send for Kim Grant time. In between a visit from the Bolton club doctor and – *I don't believe this!* – being scalded by the changing room attendant who, forgetting I was in the shower, turned off the cold water supply, I was left to the dubious pleasures of translating the consistent eruption of glee from overhead into awareness of Charlton's wholesale destruction.

Drained of every emotion other than dejection, my team-mates re-entered the changing room like a chain gang at quitting time. To their great credit in my book, Curbs and Gritty resisted any temptation to embark on another tongue-lashing and took a mature – because realistic – view of events. They praised us for our commitment – which on this occasion had been total – and frankly acknowledged that we had been beaten by a far better team.

Bolton have not had to sell class players over the past few years. We have. Guess which club now has to face up to a relegation battle?

Wednesday 25 January

'It's too quiet. I don't like it,' they say in bad films. And they're right. Just when I was thinking it's safe to go to parties again and say that I'm a footballer, along comes another scandalous flashpoint that will fill tomorrow's tabloids, front to back, with still more 'it's a game of villains' indignation. This time, though, the jackals are going to be battening on already proven gamey prey. And this time the tabloids are going to have the clear-cut right of it. The painful truth is that there's no justifiable in-depth defence. The player deserves everything he's going to get.

A month or so ago I mentioned in connection with David Whyte throwing a 'moody' that it's so often the flair players who give their managers headaches. Score a few for me because not long afterwards Eric Cantona had me leaping out of my own chair to applaud an example of flair at the highest level – a delicate chip against Sheffield United that was inch-perfect over perhaps thirty yards. Yet even in that game we'd already seen the other side of the man. A mean little kick executed on the lee side of a camouflaging player had provoked a young Blades midfielder into the stupid act of retaliation that earned him marching orders. Along with his prodigious ability, Cantona has always taken out on to the field the calculating repertoire of a small-minded man.

Tonight his performance on a late-night soccer show had an

impact on me which I know millions of others must have experienced. OK, it was well past the watershed and a time when you expect some violence but this left me gobsmacked. I sat in disbelief of what I'd just seen that took minutes – and several replays to diminish down to the acceptance that, yes, it had happened, this is real.

The simple facts were that, having received his fifth red card while wearing one of the United Colours of Commercialisation, Cantona had been induced to half vault a barrier and launch a flying double kick and several well-aimed punches at a particularly provoking Palace fan.

That was as much as I could take in or, indeed, wanted to right then. I went to bed wishing that tomorrow was scheduled to be a holiday for the national press rather than, as it now would be, a field day. The scribes would go to town over the Frenchman's knee-jerk (and how!) reaction. The match had ended in a draw but there had been a very obvious loser: the game of football.

Thursday 26 January

The treatment to my foot is now 'localised' in more than one way. The discomfort has shrunk to a relatively small area – just where you side-foot from – on the inside of the instep. The therapy I'm now receiving for this comes courtesy of Brighton and Hove Albion. Not that it would make the slightest difference today, frankly, where I was being treated. In all the treatment joints in all the towns in all the country just one identical conversation will be taking place.

The super-obvious flip summary of the incident is that it is the ultimate instance of the shit hitting the fan. I think that's wrong for a start. At the very least it's a case of the shit hitting another shit. Ignoring his 'previous', the 'victim' was clearly no innocent bystander. Anyone who descends ten or fifteen rows to the front of the stands the better to hurl obscenities is arguably spoiling for what this character got. A fight. The *Guardian* suggests, this morning, that he may have thrown something more tangible than a comment on M. Cantona's Gallic ancestry.

Cantona's demonstration, however, that he's not just one to

kick a man when he's down (unless at Carrow Road) but when he's up as well, was, for all its athleticism, inexcusable. The truth is that at Cantona's age you can't go on being an *enfant terrible*.

There was one saddest note of all about *l'affaire Cantona*. Today is the fiftieth anniversary of the liberation – if that's the word – of Auschwitz. It would take some twenty Wembleys filled to capacity to contain the people done to death there for being what they were. Only on Channel Four's News did reports of today's memorial service take precedence over Eric's antics. So great is the box-office appeal of the trivial pursuit called soccer.

Friday 27 January

While the kids are away, the mum and dad can play. After my treatment we're heading for a hotel weekend break in Tunbridge Wells. The town is a handy halfway house between the training ground and Dover where, first thing on Sunday, we'll be meeting Carly and Christopher in what will doubtless be an emotional reunion – 'Hi, Dad, did you mend my bike, yet?'

My past week of, in effect, R and R has me mounting the scales with some trepidation. I am, it emerges, a tad heavier but it's not enough to earn me a financial penalty. Which has not been the case up north. The Manchester United Board have suspended their Monsieur Hyde until the end of the season (sixteen weeks) and hit him with the double whammy not of two Nike boots but a fine of two weeks' wages. Commendable stuff, you start to think. And then your cynical side starts whispering 'Damage limitation' in your inner ear. By going in so hard they're probably trying to pre-empt as much as possible the most rigorous penalties the FA might impose. Not to mention the courts.

Cantona, of course, earns more in a month than I do in a year. Carole is perhaps the one other person in the UK blind to the logic of this. For her the whole incident boils down to a lesson to be taken to heart.

'If you ever get fined two weeks' wages,' she sweetly informs me, 'I'll volley you with two feet at once. But I won't be aiming at the chest.'

So much for the romantic break.

Monday 30 January

Let off the invalid leash at last to rejoin my team-mates. The fit ones, anyway, of whom, looking around, there aren't many. Is it purely coincidence that it's always when teams are struggling that you find it's 'standing room only' in the treatment room? Is there an over-compensating factor at physiological work here? Does the extra mental stress of living with failure generate a tightening of the muscles leading in inevitable turn to strains and pulls? I wonder if any medico has ever done some kind of a paper on this.

It could be that it's all in the mind. Today the management execute a master-stroke that presents a strong *prima facie* case for believing it may be. A decree goes out that all players needing treatment must report at 9.30 a.m. and remain on the training ground premises for vetting at 4.30 p.m. The threat of having to put in nearly a full working day acts like a laying on of faith healer's hands. It's far more efficacious than the thousands of pounds-worth of state-of-the-art equipment Jimmy and Garry Moss drive. In no time at all 'standing room only' becomes 'was it something we said?' You have to hope that players with niggles aren't being fools to themselves and putting a quick get-away above sensible repair work.

Injuries are a player's way of life. Ten minutes into training there's a new and nasty one. A misdirected shot by Alan Pardew – he should have been easing the keeper into the day by aiming at his midriff – has Mike Ammann diving full length with All-American gung-hoism. The ball arrows straight downwards off the under-side of the crossbar in '66 World Cup fashion and Mike effectively traps it for a second underneath his body. Twisting round he lands with all of his fourteen and a half stone ('Hey, Nelse, what's that in real numbers?') momentarily supported by his right hand. He's rushed off at once to the nearest hospital for investigatory X-rays.

On his way in he may well have been able to wave – with his left hand – to Colin Walsh. They could have passed in a corridor as Walshie was being wheeled in for his second knee operation of the season. He's been playing despite the painful handicap of frag-ments of bone floating about his knee joint. Although he's had nothing to be ashamed of on the field – his performances have been well above our collective average – this has been getting to him off it. As a rule he's as cheerful as anyone you're likely to meet. But the past couple of weeks a marked shadow has fallen across this usually sunny disposition. 'How bad is it?' he must have been thinking. He's almost my age, after all. Let's hope that this time the surgeon gets it right and allows Colin to resume his classic normal service.

Tuesday 31 January

Sometimes it goes right. The first person to meet me at New Eltham this morning is a beaming Walshie. He's every reason, he says, to believe this time the consultant has cracked it. Sometimes it doesn't. Mike Ammann is on the wrong end of a different crack. The damage is as bad as first feared. His wrist is broken and his hand now looks like one of those joke jobs spectators bring in sometimes. His season could well be over. There's one not negligible consolation for him now, though. Whistling 'California Dreaming' he wanders off to look up the flights going up, up and away to LA and away from the English winter.

One door closes and another one – shuts. The implications of the injury are not lost on Andy Petterson. The chances of him having his brief, unhappy marriage with Charlton annulled are themselves now dissolved. He's a wanted man again and no one else can have him, so there. We've got a contract that says so.

I'm also a wanted man. By Keith Peacock. For a Reserve fixture against Luton tomorrow. Dilemma time again. In the last two training sessions I've performed like a footballing nerd. There's been a reason. The best way to protect the left foot has been not to use it. But putting my worse foot forward has put me right in the running for the yellow jersey. If I'd been a trialist, I'd be writing this at the bus stop on the way back home.

To play tomorrow will mean using my bad good foot. In an ideal world I should still rest it for a few more days but when was my world ever ideal? Not since 1961. This is Reading re-visited. There's three months of the season left. The last three months have been nothing short of a bloody disaster. During them I clocked up just three full first team appearances, two full reserve

207

games, countless late arrivals on to the pitch as a sub and nearly as many troublesome knocks.

The thing is that, from a fitness point of view, I need some games under my belt. I need to show people I can still cut the mustard, still turn it on. If I don't play tomorrow, I rule myself out for Sunday. That's another week gone by and then, maybe, another and another . . .

'No problem, Keith, I'm fit for tomorrow.'

'Nice one, Nelse, 12.45 at the Valley.'

'I'll be there.'

As if I had a choice.

FEBRUARY

Wednesday 1 February

Nature is welcoming the new month by orchestrating another of its dirty tricks campaigns. Torrential overnight rain continuing non-stop into the morning has meant the inevitable postponement of another Reserve game. It's good news for my still aching, still healing left foot but bad news for my overall match fitness. As they say in racing circles: 'He could do with an outing.'

I only wish I had a similar engine to the model powering Sir Stanley Matthews. Fitness was never a problem for him and he was comfortably able to play at top level all the incredible way up to his fiftieth birthday. Thirty years ago. He still looks and sounds incredibly chipper today, his eightieth birthday.

To make mention of Sir Stanley is instantly to revive that perennial cluster of 'how would he stack up today/what would he be worth/was the game better in his day/do they still make them like that' questions. I myself find these attempts at comparing personalities and eras intensely irritating. Because irrelevant. The game has changed so much in a relatively short passage of years that to put 'then' alongside 'now' is like comparing apples and pears.

There's no doubt either that the difference between what he actually earned and what he could have earned now is immense going on the infinite. Throughout his time in the old English game he exercised his mesmerising skills for a pittance, all the more derisory when you take into account the numbers of spectators who flocked to see him and roar him on. But I doubt if that irks him. I shouldn't think for a minute that Sir Stanley is the sort of person who would measure out his lifetime achievement in terms of bank account deposits. He will be well aware that he enjoys a reward beyond that sort of calculation in the affection and admiration entertained for him not only in the UK but right around the footballing globe. Respect, sir! Happy birthday!

And a happy return of a sort today for a latter-day player. His rehabilitation hasn't yet climbed to Sir Paul status but this evening marked the comeback appearance for 'The Merse' as a sub for Arsenal during their Freight Rover Trophy tie (or some such thing) against AC Milan. He looked leaner, fitter and, dare we hope, happier. He got into the game well too. Let's hope he continues to stay on song in all keys.

Friday 3 February

Having experimented with several permutations in training yesterday, Curbs and Gritty decided to name their team for Sunday's game before this morning's session. I reckon this is good planning on their part. It now gives us two days in which to work on our game plan so as to ensure that by Sunday everybody understands exactly what role they are required to fulfil. To an outsider it might seem little short of shocking that with the arrival of the first week in February we should still be addressing such an elementary issue. But there's a need for us, as allegedly for others, to go back to basics. It has to be collectively acknowledged that a root cause of our problems has been the lack of co-ordination in our overall play. We've been guilty of far too much ad-libbing. Don't mistake me. I'm not knocking spur-of-the-moment improvisation. But it has to be the right moment. Off-the-cuff, instinctive play works so much better when you are 3–0 up and relaxed than a goal down and tensely chasing the game.

Today is certainly the right moment for one of our number. Jamie Stuart of Watford Gap fish and chip fame has been given not only a definite place in the starting line-up on Sunday but also a grown-up professional contract. The full league debut for the youngest member of the squad thus coincides with a recall to the colours for the oldest. Carl is injured once again and Steve and

Alan have opted for my experience rather than promoting the listed Kim Grant in television's shop window.

Saturday 4 February

The game's little cruelties never stop coming. Subject to intense transfer speculation a few days ago, Kim Grant reports in today barely able to walk. Quick diagnosis ensues and it becomes clear he has got fragments of floating bone gungeing up his knee. The only place he'll be going over the next few days is the OR for a spot of key-hole surgery.

Around 4.50 p.m. this disappointing news is followed by considerably more. As the day's results come through we hear how, one after the other, the teams below us in the league have picked up one or three points. By the time they are displaying the latest league tables we are separated from the condemned bottom four positions by only one point. Our notional 'Serie B' Premiership status is borderline. More than ever tomorrow's game, live on TV (Jinx time again! Twelve outings on the box and we've never won) assumes crisis dimensions. It's vital for the club. It's vital for the management now under pressure as open as it is intense. It's vital for me. If we all emerge further losers tomorrow, it's hard to imagine where the consequences might end.

One course of emergency action might well be to sign a forward on loan. Not good news for me. A more drastic, but by no means impossible, option might be to go for a change of management. Not good news for me either. What is the new broom going to see when he looks in my direction? A veteran of thirty-four who's almost at the end of his contract and not played in the first team on a regular basis for three months. He won't have too much hesitation in deciding where he'll start sweeping clean. OK, I'm in the side tomorrow, but even that's as much a liability as an advantage. Yes, unlike Kim, I'm on the box tomorrow. But as potentially interested managers of minnows sit in their armchairs window-shopping what are they going to be looking at in my case? A striker whose foot is still giving him gyp if knocked in the wrong way and who knows not so deep down he's not tuned to proper match fitness. I'm being given prime-time opportunity to play like a donkey in front of millions.

Sunday 5 February

Sometimes, just once in a precious while, you do get the feeling that somebody up there likes you after all. Sunday 5 February, let the record show, was something of a historic day in the annals of Garry Nelson. By its close I was warmed and lifted from within by that satisfied glow we all get from knowing that when the chips were down, the pressure really on, we managed to respond. My little moment of personal history certainly began inauspiciously enough. About fifty minutes before kick-off Steve Gritt abruptly materialised in front of me as, stripped to the waist, I sat in the crowded, backchat-filled Hawthorns Away changing room.

'Nelse,' he said, 'you're coming with me.'

Age has its uses. As I stumbled after him down the corridor, it slowly sank in that for the first time in some 670 first-team games I was being given the captain's armband. Gritty was arguably a little late in the day letting me in on it. Then again, surprising me in this way, he pulled off a master-stroke of psychological warfare. I went in to the obligatory teamsheet exchange meeting with the referee and opposing manager and skipper rather lacking sartorial finesse. I had one sock on and one in my hand. The shirt I'd had to hastily tug on was back to front. If Gritty had wanted to lull West Brom into a sense of false security by persuading them they were up against a disorganised bunch of country boys, I was doing a bang-up job for him.

I'd pulled myself together by the time we trotted out for the real confrontation and when the whistle went so did the team. That's the operative word. Making things hugely easy for me on my debut as skipper that's exactly what they suddenly were – a *team*, a cohesive unit. The more important debutant, Jamie Stuart, excelled; Salmsy was at his brilliant best when called upon; Stuart Balmer was now ice-cool on the field where he and Richard Rufus, our new centre-back pairing, were close to impregnable in defence; Pards and Keith Jones dominated the midfield.

We went in at half time with the score 0–0 but a pleasing sense of having had the better of it. I saw no reason to change a (potentially) winning game.

Then the moment of grace. In the thirteenth minute of the second half I went on yet another run down the right-hand channel. The ball found me. I was one on one with the defender. It was the Derby situation all over again.

If I could just have it to do once more!

Well, that was exactly what was happening. As before I was dummying the full-back off balance and cutting inside. This time I got it right – except, on the heavy pitch, I half slipped-cum-stumbled. So did the recovering defender. I'm sure that for an instant he considered tying my bootlaces together. But we were on the edge of the area. While he was undecided and inhibited, I was the quicker to regain full balance and control. I had a couple of yards of space and a clear view on goal. Now! I hit the ball hard and true. The keeper dived, got a hand on the ball and – failed to stop it.

If I could just have it to do once more!

OK, Nelse. Just this once. Why not?

We held on to our lead. It took a first-class save from Salmsy to ensure as much and, my stamina ebbing fast, I was down to the reserve tank for the last quarter of an hour but – we did it!

During the coach ride back we could at last afford to admit out loud to one another what a crucial result it had been. The three points had eased us up the table. The win on our thirteenth live appearance had finally nailed our television hoodoo. And we'd found a collective rhythm.

On a personal level, the game had been no less crucial for me. A duff performance and it might literally have been my last appearance in a Charlton first-team shirt. But my fitness had – just! – held up and not only had I been honoured (as I genuinely feel it) by the club with the skipper's armband, I hadn't squandered my moment in the televised shop window. It had doubtless done less for the cause of Yellow Pages, but my goal had been an infinite improvement on my last major contribution to live TV.

And, beyond all that, I'd been enormously lucky myself. Perhaps even blessed. I'd been able to nail an incipient personal jinx – the ghost that had been haunting me since my Derby miss. Football had granted me what it very seldom allows – an instant second 'take'.

Somebody up there loves me.

Today.

Monday 6 February

A day off. And as a direct consequence of yesterday's brief appearance in the spotlight not the slightest chance of getting on with anything useful. The phone never stopped ringing. Probably the response wasn't quite up to the volume I generated by earning an early bath at Wolves. People identify more with villains than heroes, I suppose.

Certainly the number of calls fell well short of the number I will be getting non-stop during the second week in May. Three things are certain in this life for a footballer. Death, taxes and people phoning you up just to wonder if you'd happen to have access to any odd FA Cup final tickets. Ah, the comfort of having so many sincere and caring and annual friends.

Tuesday 7 February

I was met at the training ground, this morning, by the beaming smile of our security man, John Yarnton. Charlton Athletic runs through his veins. He's typical of the invaluable group of loyal people all football clubs can call on through thick and thin. Sadly, John lost his wife Barbara a couple of years ago – someone we all knew because she was the training ground cook – and the pain of that loss is still there to be seen, sometimes, etched on his face. It was quite obvious from the warmth of his greeting today my goal had made his week. There must be a lot of sad, lonely weeks for a lot of retired widowers. And it's no doubt true that for nearly all of the time we players completely lose sight of how much pleasure (and, all right, pain) we give to people like John. This morning, though, you couldn't miss it and I got a big lift myself from seeing him so 'up'.

Buoyed by this as well as Sunday's events, I went in to the start of training full of the joys of spring. When given the responsibility of warming up the rest of the squad I opted to take them on a twenty-minute stroll in the late winter sun. I don't think it was exactly what the management had in mind but the rest of us enjoyed it nevertheless. After the doom and gloom of the past few weeks, it was great to hear the jokes, the tales of alleged daring-do, the piss-takes, flashing around. Go and ask any ex-pro what he most misses about the game and I'm sure that without a moment's hesitation he'll answer 'the changing-room banter'. What our stroll was all about wasn't improving fitness but morale.

Wednesday 8 February

Back to everyday trials and lifelong tribulations. Today a distressed YTS lad came up to me after being told by the club he's not going to make it and they're letting him go. I spelt out his immediate options. The PFA can give him general careers guidance; can try to interest a (minor) club abroad in giving him a contract; can set up a trial game for him in front of spectating representatives from American colleges handing out soccer scholarships. There's not much hope in that lot. Virtually none, to be frank. He's one of so many that the odds are massively stacked against him. He looked at me looking at him and, without a word being spoken, we both knew the dream had died.

This career deadend seems a million miles away from the events of this day one year ago. Today is the anniversary of our then much-heralded FA Cup fourth round replay win away against Blackburn Rovers. It's strange to discover now which elements of that seemingly unforgettable achievement have in practice slipped away and which have lodged firmly in the mind.

I can effortlessly recall, for instance, the pre-match meeting in our Bolton hotel. As ever, Gritty was taking ballsaching pains to go through every conceivable set-piece option Blackburn might choose to work on us. Finally, unbelievably, he had finished. At this moment a wee Scottish voice was given sarcastic utterance.

'Gritty, would you mind just running over those few points again?'

Stuart Balmer. I believe to this day that he was doing no more than trying to relieve the tension but I'll never know for sure. The words were no sooner out of his mouth than they were backed up by a distinctly audible and peculiarly malodorous fart. This too was attributed to Stuart but actually the gas man was a ventriloquial Mark Robson who had polluted the environment without moving his lips – whatever else. We were instantly reduced to smirking schoolboys tee-heeing behind our hands. And earning thereby an appropriately blistering schoolmasterly rebuke from Alan Curbishley. Central to his lecture was our unprofessional fecklessness in not taking Blackburn seriously. God help us if we let him and Gritty down.

It did the trick. On the night we gave our managers the best result of their twinned careers. The team was magnificent – each and every one of us. When that delayed and delayed last whistle finally sounded, it was as if my blood had been converted into wine. I may just have set a world record for human vertical take-off as I punched the air. Our fans were ecstatic and, be it said, the Rovers faithful and their team thoroughly generous in defeat. Coming off to their applause we were ten feet tall. Not even the fiddly logistics of having to wait in a holding room for the minibus that would return us to the temporary changing room down the road from the rebuilding Ewood Park could puncture our hundred per cent pure elation.

And yet from that point on, our mood began to be qualified. What should have been a night of unrelieved celebration developed into a progressively damper and damper squib. Curbs and Gritty must hold their hands up for starting us on this downward spiral. Low-key in the moment of glory and hence their congratulations, they swiftly focused our attentions back to the three points we'd dropped at Grimsby the previous Saturday ('I'd rather have had a win there than here tonight,' Curbs actually said) and the forthcoming league game against Oxford.

Taking the long view they were right. We were well in the hunt for the Division One title and promotion would have been better than the FA Cup. But what they surely failed to see was that here was an occasion where they could have had their cake and eaten it.

If they'd let us off the leash for twenty-four gloriously riotous hours, we'd have gone out and died for them the next Saturday. Had I been manager that night I would, if necessary, have stumped up a couple of hundred quid out of my own pocket to set the champagne corks popping.

Which is exactly what I would have had to do. If afterwards the champagne flowed like beer, that's because that's exactly what it was. Beer. Nothing had been anticipated. Nothing was improvised. The directors bought us a drink but not even in person. They sent a bar steward to take down the order. All of the magic of an hour ago was now leaking fast out of our pumped-up spirits. On reflection it may not have been Manchester United teaching us a lesson that sent our season into terminal decline but the savage, unthinking, unnecessary let-down of that post-victory evening.

With each succeeding mile down the motorway on the way home the sense of anti-climax further obliterated the satisfaction of having achieved one of the greatest results in Charlton's history. The stops and starts. The impossibility of sleeping. The greasy, everyday fish and chips. The arrival back at the training ground in the small hours.

I got home at five in the morning along with the night shift workers knocking off and passing the still-yawning milkmen and the airport staff on their way in to work. But just eight hours earlier I had been a hero and, instead of crawling into bed sick at disillusioned heart, I would have liked to have been able to hold on to the glow for just a day or two longer. It's not true it's only a game.

A year on and the Division One ecstasy belongs to Wolves and Millwall, both of whom have beaten Premier sides in penalty shoot-outs. I watched the games on television while, ironically, drinking champagne courtesy of Steve Gritt. No, he wasn't feeling retrospectively guilty about (non-)events of a year ago. He was caught on television last Sunday promising to buy me a drink should I score the winner. True to his word, he delivered. So raise your glass, Nelse. Absent friends. An anniversary toast to the victors of Ewood Park.

Better late than never, they say. I'm not sure they're right.

Friday 10 February

Carly's *eleventh* birthday. I can hardly believe it. No replica kit for her, no shiny new boots. To her eternal credit she finds football a total bore. She's monumentally underwhelmed by the manner in which her father earns a living. If she ever had any burgeoning interest in the game, it has long since been nipped in the bud through having to spend countless hours sitting in a car before transferring to a freezing cold stand to watch those twenty-two idiots chasing around after a ball while being urged on by several thousand footballers. She's had to learn to ignore her dad being rubbished one minute and acclaimed a super-hero the next. And she's learned the lesson well. She fully recognises that Triumph and Disaster are imposters who will get in the way of her re-reading *Little Women*.

There's one enormous benefit. I'm not going to have any worries about her transmuting into a teenage football groupie when boys take on a little more importance in her life. The antics of some of our younger pros would make even the most liberal father – well, draw the veil.

Footballers are often described (mistakenly) as being lucky in that they get paid for doing what other people would do for nothing: but for me the most fortunate aspect of my professional life has been the opportunity it gave me to involve myself very directly in my children's growing up and watch them learn and develop at first hand. Carly may have learned to dislike football intensely these days, but she does have the stupid game to thank for the close relationship she and I have always enjoyed.

Saturday 11 February

Wet and windy. The need to concentrate on the motorway drive allows only the most obvious thoughts about the afternoon's business. Today's opposition are once-mighty Sunderland, now currently floundering among the division's bottom four stragglers. For all that, they have the meanest record of conceding away goals in the league. They're racing certainties to get everybody

218

behind the ball and work at guaranteeing themselves a point – a win through a breakaway goal then being a sneaked bonus. It's not going to be pretty.

At 2.15 Gritty confirms that I'm still skipper and I thus join him, Mick Buxton and Kevin Ball (Sunderland's manager and captain respectively) to exchange teamsheets in the referee's room. These formalities actually induce a bit of split focused vision in me. On the one hand there's the present: my privileged first glance at the Sunderland line-up confirms their defensive attitude to the game. The sheet bears the names of three centre-halves. Space will definitely be at a premium today.

On the other hand, seeing Mick Buxton again immediately takes me back four years. In August 1991 he served as the managerial representative on the FA's transfer tribunal committee when it met to decide the fee Charlton should pay Brighton for securing my services. This was actually my third appearance before this body and I really ought to get on to Mr McWhirter to confirm what I think may well be the case: that this represents a record for an individual player.

Transfer tribunals were the logical and inevitable consequence of the PFA gaining 'freedom of contract' rights for players. Their coming into being arose from the need for an independent body to reconcile the 'legal rights' of the parties – existing employer club, employee player, would-be employer club – involved in negotiations/dispute as an existing contract comes to its end. A player's current club have two options. They can dispense with a player – i.e., give him a 'free' – or retain him. Crucially, to retain him they must offer him a new contract that is at least as favourable as the one just ending. This does create problems for Boards. With players who are doing the business well enough to justify the original outlay on them and justify their first team selection, the club will not want the contract to expire. Every attempt will usually be made to offer a new one that is sufficiently attractive for the player to want to sign. But he (and certainly, where applicable, his agent!) will appreciate that he is negotiating from a position of strength. What he now considers 'attractive' may be a considerable escalation on his previous terms.

219

But the player may not be such an obvious asset. He may be getting long in the tooth, no longer performing at his former level. This may not weaken his bargaining position as much as might appear at first glance. Initially, he may have been signed for a large transfer fee plus a huge signing-on fee and very substantial wages. The common sense move now may be to sell him. But in order to be able to command a transfer fee (as opposed to giving him the free and writing off all their past investment), the club must have him on their books. That's to say, they must renew his contract on at least the same terms. Knowing a good thing when he sees it, the player is almost certain to re-sign at once. The club are now paying the same high level of monies as before to a player they don't really want but whom, if they want to balance their books at all, they need to sell at the same top end of the market they bought him in.

'Freedom of contract' has made it possible for players to let their contracts expire and yet put themselves in an enhanced bargaining position. Consistently good form should clearly earn appropriate reward – no problem, you would think. But in many cases clubs offer even on-song players the legal limit they are obliged to – the same terms the players are already on. The Board's hope in such instances is that, not attracting any interest from other clubs, the player will be forced to re-sign on the old terms. But if there is outside interest and the player has more than one option, the club's gamble is more than likely to misfire. The player has leverage. He can wait to see what is the best offer on the table; even play both ends against the middle.

If, finally, a player refuses to re-sign with his existing club and signs for another, a transfer fee still has to be agreed between the two clubs. If they don't agree – and usually they don't – by now there's likely to be a lot of acrimony flying about and the transfer tribunal enters the equation. It will arbitrate and decide the fee.

My own first appearance before it was at Highbury in 1983. My contract at Southend had expired as had manager Dave Smith's employment. When we reconvened for pre-season training, Southend had nine senior pros, no manager and a boardroom power struggle. I had already agreed to sign for Keith Peacock at Gillingham but there were problems over agreeing my fee.

Southend were asking £40,000; the 'Gills' could go only to £10,000. Lurking in the wings were Swindon, also interested in me, who were prepared to go to the tribunal. When Southend appointed a new manager, Peter Morris, his first duty was to try to get me to re-sign for the Shrimpers.

I walked into his office and found myself facing two men: Morris and, the plot thickening by the second, Anton Johnson, chairman of Rotherham United. It became immediately evident that he was in *de facto* control at Southend too. He gave me an ultimatum. Politely expressed it went: sign this contract or piss off.

It was totally the wrong way to handle me. On principle, whatever the terms in the small print, I won't cave in to this sort of pressure. Aged twenty-two, I said I'd exercise the second option. As a result I then travelled to Swindon, discussed terms with Ken Beamish and agreed to sign for him the following week.

Things thus resolved, I went back to my home in Southend and spent the entire weekend decorating it to put a few bob on its re-sale value. I then went back to Swindon and signed.

A few days later, Ken Beamish received a letter from Southend. It stated that over the course of that same previous weekend Bournemouth had come in with an offer of £45,000 for me. The letter stated that Southend officials had consistently tried to contact me by phone over the weekend but, there being no reply from my home number, they had not been able to update me about this latest twist in my transfer tale. It was on the basis of this Bournemouth 'offer' that Southend were now intent on extracting a well over-the-odds fee for me out of Swindon.

Ken Beamish, putting it mildly, was extremely concerned by this development. He certainly didn't want to pick up that kind of a tab to get me. But I was concerned too. I pointed out that the letter he'd received was cobblers. I'd spent the entire weekend in. There was no problem with my phone. This needed a bit of investigation.

It was as I'd suspected. As well as at Rotherham and Southend, Anton Johnson was financially involved with AFC Bournemouth.

This is the scenario I unfolded to the tribunal. The extent of their surprise greatly influenced, I'm sure, their setting of my transfer fee at £10,000. Ken Beamish was absolutely delighted with my performance (about the only one ever!), as it had probably saved the Robins around another £10,000. The FA asked me to put my account in writing and their further consideration of it actually prompted a rule change in Football Association regulations, namely that a Football League chairman could have no form of financial involvement with any other club.

Though not by popular request, my return appearance before the crowned heads of the tribunal – this time at Lancaster Gate – was two years later, my contract having expired. When Swindon's written re-engagement offer came through it seemed obvious to me that they had offered me terms that were less favourable than my previous contract's. At £210 per week, the basic wage was the same. My appearance money had been raised from £10 a game to £50. But a signing-on fee was nowhere mentioned. I immediately contacted the PFA.

My argument was that appearance money is not guaranteed money. To get it you had to be picked. To play. Once the signing-on fee was eliminated I was fundamentally worse off, I argued. The PFA agreed. The Football League, bless their little cotton socks, didn't. With oracular power they pre-ordained that I would definitely figure in more than twenty-six first-team matches (the break even point) in the coming season and so arrive at more favourable term status.

Win some, lose some. Lou got his £15,000. And although, refusing to stump up for a pre-train journey meal at Paddington, chairman Peter Bloom sulked all the long way back to Plymouth, Dave Smith got his man. When Swindon were later found guilty of dirty tricks in respect of, among other irregularities, transfer tribunal dealings, the irony was not altogether lost on me.

My third and, let us hope, last appearance before the tribunal arose over my move to Charlton from Brighton. My last year at the Goldstone had been a personal nightmare. Treated shabbily by Barry Lloyd throughout its greater part, I suddenly found myself back in the first team during the club's exciting push for the end-of-season play-offs. Although I positively added to the momentum

222

by scoring three goals in five games, Lloydie couldn't wait to stick me back on the bench. He did concede that I had performed well and that I shouldn't worry too much about my contract nearing its end: a new two-year deal was in the offing. A couple of months later, sure enough, the new deal slithered across the table. For one year. And no financial improvements. I exercised my rights under Football League regulations and took freedom of contract. Messrs Curbishley and Gritt, newly appointed as Charlton's co-managers responded swiftly. They signed me on a two-year contract and began the process of agreeing a fee with Barry Lloyd, among many other things Curbs' old boss.

I'd gone up in the world, it seemed, even allowing for inflation. Charlton offered £40,000. Lloydie asked £125,000. Poles apart. Hence my third appointment with tribunal destiny. The process was exactly as on the other occasions.

First I appeared alone to give my side of the story. Then I was asked to step outside while the two clubs put their cases. Of my three appearances this seemed the most cut and dried and I was privately reckoning that the committee would settle at somewhere around £75,000. I was rather surprised, therefore, and Brighton mightily disappointed, when the verdict handed down emerged as £50,000. As the Brighton contingent raced away from the scene of the mugging, I expressed my surprise to my two new owners who were hugging themselves with glee. They told me that in their estimation, admitting straight out that he had over-inflated the Brighton asking price to give himself a bit of manoeuvring room, Lloydie had given a nightmare performance shooting himself in the foot on several further occasions.

Now, close to four years on, here was Mick Buxton trying to de-psyche me for the immediate game by saying what good value for money I'd proved at the level he'd helped set. Gritty seconded the motion saying I'd more than justified the fee. Far too much sweetness and light for preparation for the dour battle lying immediately ahead.

Both teams, all in all, gave value-for-money performances. Hard fought, the game was basically clean and always going to be

223

close. But for one moment of extreme skill separating the truly gifted from the run of the mill, it could well have finished scoreless. In the second half who else but David Whyte was in the right place with the right answer to the demands of the moment? The cross was going behind him, but with the sweetest of acrobatic overhead kicks he despatched the ball unerringly into the net for his eighteenth goal of the season. This time it was Sunderland who had had their chips. I may even have detected several of our players joining in the Valley's thunderous chants of: 'David Whyte, Whyte! Whyte!'

Tuesday 14 February

Valentine's Day. I decided to leave home a little earlier than usual in order to allow myself time the other end to deal with the inevitable pile-up of mail-bags bearing 'Garry Nelson' labels around their necks. I should have grabbed an extra hour's beauty sleep. That's the obvious priority. Not a single envelope to open from any single – or married – star-struck admirer. Either there's a postal strike or the vans have all gone off to Stamford Bridge in search of Scott Minto.

Training was no love affair either. The extremely heavy conditions were not deemed reason enough to lighten our full-bore flat-out programme and most of us ended the morning looking like members of 'Bugs' Moran's gang after Al Capone had paid them the compliments of the season.

Wednesday 15 February

Another day off. Another chance to erase all footballing thoughts from the memory banks and recharge the enthusiasm batteries. In theory. We all know life is more of a merry prankster than that. The reality has been another run on my reserves of affection for the beautiful game. Today, it has shown us two too many of its seemingly inexhaustible supply of unacceptable faces. The one was totally stomach-turning. The other, well, a mite less than handsome I would argue.

The lesser matter first – lesser but still eyebrow-raising in the pre-meditated cynicism of its timing. Ron Atkinson started the week by becoming the beneficiary of a huge settlement on his Villa contract. Yesterday, Coventry sacked Phil Neal in what can only be described as a case of synchronised backstabbing. Today, the gears meshed to complete the opportunism with the naming of Big Ron as the new Coventry manager. His current chairman is an old mucker from West Brom days and I've small doubt that, deploying the loadsamoney denied to Phil Neal but granted him, the Premiership's now oldest manager will steer the Sky Blues away from the relegation whirlpool. When he does, nobody will give a damn about the business ethics surrounding his appointment.

The second soccer eyesore to fester into view today won't be so readily forgotten. This evening in Dublin, twenty-five minutes into a Republic of Ireland v England international, a group of saboteurs masquerading as English supporters staged a riot of sufficient violence to cause the almost immediate (and correct) abandonment of this 'friendly'.

Flash-point for the rioting was the Republic's going ahead through a David Kelly goal. It was a lead their greater appetite for the game fully merited, but it triggered an instant throw-back to those many – too many; *one* is too many – dark days of English mobs on the rampage in Copenhagen, Berne, Luxembourg, Gothenberg, Brussels, etc. when, during the eighties the trail of soccer hooligan slime oozed across most of the non-police states of Western Europe.

As at Lansdowne Road, the ignition points of many of these riots have been carefully preplanned and orchestrated on the ground as the football occasion has been turned into a backdrop for the 'look at me' ego trips these losers indulge in. Losers, of course, is what they are. Some may wear Pringle sweaters, tote mobile phones, hold down well-paid jobs but what each and every one has in common is their inherent lack of any positive talent. None of them can come anywhere near playing football as well as the opponents they obscenely and racially badmouth. Whereas patriotism used to be the last refuge of a scoundrel, it is now the first excuse of the soccer braindead.

Short-term, of course, and as always, it was the overwhelming majority of the innocent bystanders, the spectators, who were the losers. Many will feel aggrieved and already knee-jerk reaction has started to criticise inadequate policing of the ground. I think that, although this proved to be the case, such a line of criticism is too harsh. A lot of people were daring to hope that football had largely rid itself of these walking cancer growths. Better policing techniques, closed circuit video surveillance, more considerate stewards, more sophisticated ticketing arrangements and the general education upwards to more grown-up crowd attitudes were all combining to promise that a corner had been turned. Now, on the occasion of the first away fixture of Terry Venables' reign, this couple of hundred losers have shown that the chemo-therapy has not been a hundred per cent successful. Stopping this game in its tracks, the mobile malignancies have called into question England's staging of the European Championships next year.

I would be very surprised if, the dust settling, England does lose the tournament. Too many big Euro-bucks have already gone into its being staged here and the lead times for its being relocated are already tight. But you have to wonder what punitive action will follow as a result of Lansdowne Road. Other than from Graham Kelly who, while present, didn't seem to want to trust himself to comment prior to a vigorous and wide-ranging enquiry, condemnation was instant and universal. But what will actually be *done*? Not a lot, I suspect. Parliament will silence its own hooliganistic exchanges for a moment to criticise the FA for lack of planning. The FA will say they don't have the legal power to punish those responsible, but that the courts should impose stiffer penalties. Saying that, they would be right. The courts should visit upon these criminals – and that is the word – the full force of their sentencing potential.

Simultaneously the press, as well as revelling in another juicy 'Soccer Violence' story should report the trial and sentencing of all found guilty with commensurate prominence.

If. In practice, the courts will impose fines that are nominal rather than stiff and help out our beleaguered prison service by playing the community service card. Please don't do it again, lads.

226

Let's not give them that chance. Let's ensure that next year those who can't will not interrupt the performances of those who can and the pleasure of those who appreciate.

Thursday 16 February

Further conversations with Baltimore today. Thankfully last night's sickening and disheartening scenes didn't seep into the Maryland television network to turn all the locals off the idea of involvement with what the English curiously choose to call 'the beautiful game'.

I've got my coaching team in place now and, as I thought, drawing up a short(!) list was anything but a problem. It's quite amazing how word spreads once the phrase 'freebie holiday' passes your lips. I was all but trampled to death in the rush.

Suddenly thrust into the role of a selector, I found it a thoroughly difficult job. I'm sure that the major consideration influencing my choice – wanting to work with people I know and get along with – has resulted in my settling on what to an outsider would seem a right motley crew.

As a specialist and qualified goalkeeping coach, I've managed to secure Bob Bolder on loan from retirement. He's not only a bumper bundle of laughs, but should we ever stare danger in the face down some mean Baltimore street, his formidable presence should see us through.

My former team-mate and, indeed, founder member of the Gatwick Express, Steve Gatting, was always going to be in the frame. He's been doing a lot of coaching since leaving the full-time ranks. What's more, he'll come in very useful if our former colonists wish to turn to a strike-free game and, reviving their Victorian sporting heritage, take up cricket again.

The last two places are filled by two of my former team-mates from Brighton – Russel Bromage and Mark Barham. Russel was my room-mate on the FA Full Coaching Licence course at Lilleshall. As the course lasted two weeks and there was never an opening when Russ was short of a wisecrack, he books his passage on entertainment value alone.

Mark has been a good mate for a few years now. The latter part of this time has not seen luck running his way. OK, this coaching expedition may not be a long-term position, but a couple of weeks in the sun with his mates can only lift his spirits and – who knows? – maybe signal a change of fortune.

Yes, I know. Not a bunch of household names. Not the cream of PFA Award-winning soccerdom. But every one of them has had a long and honourable career in the game. Everyone will coach his socks off and represent their profession and the English game admirably. I know I'm biased but take my word for it anyway – they're hand-picked diamonds.

Friday 17 February

A crack-of-dawn farewell this morning to a Carole flying out to Tenerife for a well-earned break in the sun with her sister and parents. For me a less glamorous destination and mode of transportation: Ayresome Park in a glorified bus. The prospect of five hours in the latter was not improved for me by a stomach bubbling away like a mad scientist's laboratory. My quickest sprint of the day was dedicated not to Gritty's warm-up but to effecting the earliest entry possible to one of the two traps in the training ground lavatory. All the way north the interminable journey was a fitful juggling of trying to sleep, fighting off bouts of nausea and making sure that in case of diar(rhetic) emergency I could make it to the coach's solitary loo. The road to hell is sign-posted 'A1'.

Our arrival at the hotel saw the squad heading straight to the dining room and me straight to bed. Much as I love my food, spaghetti carbonara was not what the doctor was ordering. As I drifted into gurgling sleep my last thoughts were that my chances of trotting out – that had to be the operative word! – on the morrow looked distinctly dodgy.

Saturday 18 February

What a difference a day makes! The fourteen hours of my sleepathon seem to have worked something of a cure. Despite, or because of, not having eaten for twenty-four hours I felt a good deal better when I finally woke up. Drained, certainly – but my

228

head had lost that woolly feeling and my temperature was now back down to normal. The engine will run today, I think, albeit missing a bit at higher revs.

Which will probably be needed. Call it Awesome Park. Middlesbrough are going to be a very stiff test. They may lack Bolton's flamboyance, but what they have going for them is what I currently lack – a very well organised solidity. Hard not to have it when your game is marshalled around the massive influence of Bryan Robson. Any chance we might have may come less from the improvement we've shown in the last two games than from Boro's sense of guilt about sliding downwards from the table-topping pinnacle of last November and their awareness of being under intense pressure from their own fans to reverse this decline.

I wish! Instead, cue the perfect cock-up. Fifteen minutes into the game and, relapsing into our carefree habits of yore, we gift Uwe Fuchs all the space he needs to break his goalscoring virginity in English football: 0–1 already and it's 'Oh, look! We've got a mountain to climb' time once again. Despite an honourable assault we never made it. There were moments when we had hopes because, as we got going enough to put them under pressure, Boro clearly did start to come apart at the seams and, yes, their own fans did get on their backs to a perceptibly negative effect. Talking of negatives, it was disappointing to see their manager, now deep into the twilight of his career, playing the man almost as regularly as the ball. When a great footballer dies does he have to become a clogger?

A play-off spot for Boro would be my prediction. As for us – we're likely to fall just a bit short. By several million pounds.

Monday 20 February

Fit and able to train. Not so Colin Walsh. He really should have known better. Not content, though, with picking up my cold earlier in the season, he's now come back for more and purloined my twenty-four-hour gastric bug.

Colin's sick leave means he's missing out on today's holding of the annual ballot of PFA members (the men who know!) to determine this season's Player and Young Player of the Year and the make-up of the Endsleigh League Division One Select Eleven. The forms were sent out today and I have to collect them in again by Thursday so that they can be scrutinised in Manchester prior to April's PFA Awards dinner.

A snap exit poll from the Charlton constituency gave Alan Shearer prominence in the main event and Robbie Fowler the nod as leading young player. Although my reservations about his surly attitude to the game and those around him came close to him losing my vote, I still finally chose Paul Ince in the main category. Nor did my being an Evertonian in any way influence my choice of David Unsworth as the Young Turk. He won my support entirely on merit – and anyway Robbie Fowler plays for that other Premier Merseyside team whose name escapes me for the minute so there's no way that jammy little genius putter-away of brilliant goals is going to get my unbiased vote.

Tuesday 21 February

The prime time hits just keep on coming. Today Eric Cantona was at Number One as he finally made his South London appearance at the Old Bill and Beaks. Represented by a mouthpiece who also handles the legal ins and outs of an outfit whose Board he's on, Manchester United (I expect he was grateful for the extra few bob and it keeps it in the family), Eric the Too Ready was formally charged with common assault. Sources close to him suggest that he was desolated by the choice of adjective but the scale of the potential fine won't be any noticeable skin off his considerable nose. He was bailed to appear before Croydon magistrates around the Ides of March.

This, mind you, was only the warm-up. The main event is three days on from now when he's got an appointment with the FA's disciplinary committee.

From one falling idol to another. Across London, George Graham no longer finds himself an employee of Arsenal FC. Having been apprised of the Premier League commission's findings on transfer irregularities, the Arsenal Board have terminated his eight-year reign. Poetic justice. He who lives and flourishes by the contract must die by the contract.

My coach for a year at Plymouth, Stewart Houston, now finds himself in the Highbury hot seat. 'Whitney', as he was inescapably known, was fired by boundless enthusiasm and is an excellent coach. As the Scot is stereotyped, however, he definitely came within the 'dour' category. I would unhesitatingly nominate him as best man for the permanent Arsenal post. He's typecast for boring, boring Arsenal.

Not many laughs this evening either, it has to be said, in the Charlton changing room after our game with Tranmere. Arguably our best performance of the season had been rewarded with total territorial domination and a 0–1 final scoreline. The three stolen points left a very far from impressive Tranmere sitting proudly on top of the table. For us, my four games as skipper had seen us advance two steps and go back two more to re-occupy that position only a couple more ahead of the big trap door. Alan Curbishley led our community thinking by letting us know quite uncategorically that as far as he was concerned we had let four points go blowing in the wind in our last two games – three tonight, one against Boro. Quite right, too.

One grassroots consolation came in the shape of our 11,500 gate. In spite of our indifferent-to-rubbishy home form, attendances are now beginning to break the five-figure barrier. The seeds sown by our various community schemes encouraging youngsters and ethnic minorities to visit the Valley are starting to bear fruit. Our customer base is growing again. It only remains to make SE7 once more a perceived centre of footballing excellence.

Wednesday 22 February

Fat chance of a lie-in this morning even though it's my one rest day of the week. It's the half-term week and my sole-parent-in-residence status guaranteed that the ringing of the alarm clock had scarcely faded away before it was replaced by the stereophonic chorus of 'Dad! We're *bored!*' blasting from two loud little speakers.

'Come on, Carly. Come on, Chris. I did have a game last night,' fell on ears gone unsympathetically deaf. Swimming costumes, towels and goggles were thrust under my nose. Off we went, me stiff of limb, bleary-eyed and envying all the single players still abed.

Thursday 23 February

A day of commuting and training in which to recuperate from yesterday. Today's press coverage of the sacking of George Graham contained full and detailed accounts of the 'yet to be announced' Premier League commission of enquiry's report. These now reveal that the former Chief Gunner had no less than £425,000 temporarily stuffed down his personal barrel – the additional load coming along with his acquisition of Pal Lydersen. Our collective paupers' opinion was largely that, being in the club's long-term interest, Arsenal's sanitising operation was justified. Any sympathy towards George Graham seemed to be diluted to extinction by the scale of the amounts involved. There was a general consensus he should not have cut out the fiscal midfield to go Route One.

Speculation going more rife, as they say, the word 'scapegoat' entered more and more into our conversations as did its first cousin not so very far removed 'tip of the iceberg'. You have to think both expressions were relevant. We've all heard rumours about other managers and Rune Hauge was, after all, an honest broker – I believe that's the expression – in well over twenty other deals bringing players to this country. It's stretching probability to be confident George Graham was the only UK manager acquiring (unsolicited) gifts.

Another topic – one with perhaps even wider ranging long-term implications – also helped to distract us from training. According to a low-profile item in yesterday's *Sports Night*, a Belgian player, Jean Marc Bosman, is taking a test case to the European Court of Justice for the legal right to seek employment as a professional footballer at the end of a contract without having the ball and chain of a transfer fee shackled to his leg by his current club. This is already the system in neighbouring Holland.

The Dutch could be the pioneers in this regard. If the European Court turns Jean Marc's plea into a benchmark decision, the transfer market across the entire European Union could be altered beyond recognition. Indeed, it could become obsolete.

Should this happen, it would further divide professional soccer into 'Haves' and 'Have Nots'. The small clubs would almost certainly be reduced to 'part-timer' status or, propagating talent for later harvesting, act very much as nursery clubs for big boys. You just have to ask yourself how much would Andy Cole have received if he had been available on a free instead of tagged by Newcastle at £7,000,000. The wealthy, arguably power-mad, Premier clubs will cream off the pick of the crop and monopolise the five-star players. They in return will receive rewards and contracts rivalling the wildest dreams of avarice. Yes, a small, throw-away *Sports Night* item. A cloud, you might say, currently no bigger than a goalkeeper's glove.

And just for me twinned with another one. I hadn't heard a word, my subconscious suddenly threw into my mind's foreground, about my CIM exam. You're supposed to hear towards the end of February. And they let those who've passed know first. The longer there's no word, the more it's a case of no news is bad news. February is a short month.

Friday 24 February

Training was on the light side today. After an enjoyable piggy-in-the-middle and a few sprints we expended most of our energy on discussing how we are going to overcome Vicarage Road's passable imitation of a ploughing competition arena tomorrow.

Concurrently Eric Cantona was coming to Lancaster Gate, seeing the FA's disciplinary synod and partially conquering. Seeing the good in everybody, Graham Kelly broke off from polishing up the knocker on the big brass door long enough to announce that Eric would be forgiven and English football prepared to forget once another week's wages had been surrendered and a playing ban running up to the end of next September served out.

At the other end of the celeb scale, the FA faced the further problem of a demonstration by young footballers and their (organising) parents to protest against the ruling forbidding kids under ten participating in recognised eleven-a-side games. The news will probably shake Lancaster Gate to its foundations, but on this issue the FA enjoy my whole-hearted backing. I'm all for encouraging the real tinies to play in small-sided games on smaller pitches on a friendly basis.

'Foul!' goes up the cry. 'It's not real!' But the cry, significantly goes up not from the kids but from the adults. It's the parents who, desperate to project their own egos on to the field, are not interested in gently nurturing talent and not over-stretching childish physiques, but impatiently insistent on reproducing the 'real thing'.

I had to bear the distasteful cross of witnessing these parents' antics when, during my Southend days, I coached a young boys' team. Week after week I became increasingly disenchanted with the 'real' abusing of the referee, the non-stop touchline rows that seem endemic to under-tens football. Worse: it was utterly dismaying that all the emerging technical skills my lads were able to demonstrate in midweek gym sessions sank without trace on Sundays in the sea of anxiety and pressure generated by the parents.

The final straw for me came one freezing morning on Canvey Island. We had come up against a side fielding several boys who had plainly not even been taught how to kick a ball properly. They nevertheless deployed with ruthlessly boring maturity one of the most efficient offside traps I've ever seen. My lads, their coach naively thinking that at their age playing positively and creatively was the object of the exercise, were scarcely aware of the concept of 'offside'. A half-time chat put that right and once we'd taken the lead there was never any question of the other team equalising. Not that the result in the circumstances was relevant one way or the other. Steam pouring from my ears, I sought out my opposite number when the whistle went and started to berate him. He was not best pleased. There's a corner of a Canvey Island field that not too long ago came quite close to becoming forever Nelson.

But it would have been to die in a good cause. Purists persistently wonder why so many British players are technically bereft. Being obliged to play 'real' matches from the tenderest age

234

goes a long way to supplying the answer. Guaranteeing a ratio of one football to each kid at evening training sessions and ensuring that once in a while they benefit from the services of a qualified coach would help much more than blowing the lion's share of any funds on meaningless trophies.

Sabotaging our national game at grassroots and infant level is a variant of the mentality that you hear voiced in all of our Saturday afternoon stands. I have one question for the likes of that Canvey Island ignoramus: whose interest do you really have at heart, your kid's or your own?

Saturday 25 February

Two early morning calls. One announcing the safe return home of a sun-kissed wife; the other from a frustrated Steve Gritt announcing yet another gap in my Saturday afternoon scheduling. Not in the least sun-kissed, Watford's ploughman's pitch has succumbed to the elements. At least it hasn't required a trip this time to learn of the postponement.

March

Thursday 2 March

Into March and still no letter on the mat with my CIM result, but if you believe in omens I earned a first fine of the year today for late arrival at the training ground. No justice in it, mind you, as the cause of the Gatwick Express's delay was the aftermath of a particularly nasty incident (a suicide leap, as we suspected) under a high bridge crossing the M23.

By the time 'Old Faithful' rolled through the gates the rest of the squad were well into their warm-up and, Sod's Law never missing a trick, going through their stretches right in front of the staff car park. Before you could say 'piss take' the Tempra was surrounded and all possibility of exiting it denied until three crisp tenners had been dispensed through a slot in the temporary ATM.

Brownie, who watches the pennies very carefully, was rendered close to distraught by such a loss. Robbo, a twenty-three-year-old Victor Meldrew if ever I heard one moan, was pushed all the way there. The tenner was being divvied up on top of a thirty per cent docking of his basic pay for the week after his third booking for dissent ('I don't f——ing believe it!') in last night's 6–0 Combination triumph over Southampton.

Fines are part and parcel of a footballer's life. They vary from the relatively token, as today's for our lateness, to the genuinely punitive – since very few of us are on Cantona's income level. The small ones aren't regarded as being so demeaning as some out-siders imagine. They do, after all, stake out the parameters of our professional environment and, in any case, are almost invariably

237

set aside in a kitty dedicated to a Christmas or end-of-season knees-up. Being sent off for dissent commands a going rate of losing a week's wages. As I can confirm from my dismissal at Molineux (where I was but echoing the running touchline commentary of my managers), that's a level of loss that hurts. It's a lot less clear where *those* monies go, by the way.

I underwent further economic deprivation for a breach of regulations while abroad with the team in Spain (as Shaun Newton perceives it) to play Brescia in the Anglo-Italian Cup. To be honest, we were treating the whole expedition as a mini-break but, with our hotel turning out to be in the middle of nowhere, boredom Italian-style was soon beginning to take its toll. Skipper Alan McLeary accordingly petitioned the management for a relaxation in their strict anti-drinking rules. Alan and Steve replied, 'Yes, fine, no problem so long as it's just a couple.'

As the Peronis started to flow, it emerged that this very day was Darren Pitcher's birthday. Cause for celebration. A 'Gang of Five' of us at once set about extruding the inch we had been given to a length of several miles – a process pursued with all the more festive fervour when we were joined by two directors totally willing to aid and abet our liquid diversion therapy. When, well into the small hours, I finally called it quits, a hard core were just getting their sights adjusted.

Now – the hotel bar was adorned by a wonderful collection of 'Serie A' pennants. One of our original five was finding them increasingly irresistible. I shall not cite his name here, but his initials are Alan Pardew. Surely, Alan mused as he scratched his grey locks, in Italy such things are so easy to replace. The hotel staff would never miss the overnight absence of their Sampdoria and AC Milan prize exhibits.

Oh wouldn't they! Mamma mia! A rapid game of Italian Whispers ensued. Barman to hotel manager to Charlton chairman to the two co-managers. One question soon needed no translation in either direction: where were the pennants?

A meeting was hastily convened. The infamous Brescia Five were isolated and grilled. In the cold light of early morning, enthusiasm for the pennants flagged. The two absentees miraculously reappeared and in pristine condition at that. No lasting harm done. Except to our pockets. Each member of the Italian job was informed that his next pay pocket would be lighter by a pristine hundred quid. We should regard it as our penance.

We lost the next evening's game. I put it down to home advantage.

Friday 3 March

Now I know what it feels like to be taking your side's fifth penalty in a shoot-out to decide the European Cup final. Not that I ever have or will but . . .

I was just tucking into my second bowl of Frosties when Carole plonked it down on the table in front of me. Between two beats my heart went into overdrive. I picked up the envelope on reflex and then got stuck as a sour apprehension made the printed initials on its front wobble and dance. 'CIM' my dazzled eyes could still make out and I knew this was a second fluffed take. I'd been down this dead-ending road before. Into March now. '*Your paper was given extra scrutiny . . . we regret to inform you . . . an award of "D", a marginal failure . . .*' Well, when the ball is on the spot, all that is left to do is run up and kick it. I opened the envelope.

The print still danced on the page as I scanned it too rapidly. It told me what I already knew. I was re-reading the marks of the three exam elements I'd already passed. The result for the vital one I'd just re-taken must be on the other . . . Abruptly the house was shaken to its foundations by a war-whoop that would have stampeded a Panzer division. A pass! I'd passed! I'd put the ball past the despairing keeper and we'd won the European Cup! I was Garry Nelson, Dip M! The next time the phone rang it would be Saatchi and Saatchi begging me to come in and rescue them. A measure of reality, of humour, started to creep into my awareness. I'd got through with a 'C', the lowest passing grade. But what the hell! I'd gone into the exam with a lot of distractions on my mind. And, as I keep trying to get across to David Whyte, a pass is a pass is a pass.

Mine wasn't the only heart to thump at an unnatural rate today.

239

By the end of training Keith Aubrey Jones, a footballer of no fixed position, had been reduced to a white-lipped – so to speak – and trembling wreck. With good reason. He had been summoned to appear before the Charlton Athletic kangaroo court accused of the heinous crime of bringing the piggy-in-the-middle circle into disrepute. There are few graver charges.

The case for the prosecution was cogent and overwhelming: that having been unable to prevent twenty passes being strung together around him, Jones had wilfully played another man rather than the ball, fraudulently claiming nonetheless to have intended to make and, indeed, to have made *de facto* contact with said spherical object. Further, the error of his ways having been pointed out to him in a formal warning, Jones had proceeded to flout the authority of one Keith 'You said what!' Peacock by withdrawing his labour from the said porcinely centric exercise.

Apprised of the weight of hostile evidence – 'We've got more witnesses against you, Jonesy, than Cantona's up against' – the accused made desperate efforts to secure the services of George Carman, QC. Having failed, it became apparent to all that he now only too clearly appreciated that he faced a dilemma no less serious than that of Charlton FC prior to Christmas – the total absence of any viable defence. Standing in the dock, the pitiable miscreant could do no more than throw himself on the mercy of the court.

A battery of the Valley's keenest legal brains occupied the bench. Sitting in awful (*really* awful) judgement, Mr 'Rough Justice' Peacock presiding, were Mike Salmon ('Mickey the Fish' to those he's banged up); Mick Bennett, no mean practitioner himself of the noble art of banging up; Alan Pardew, already sporting his black capped wig (he thinks it makes him look younger); Mike Ammann, bestowing a cool air of *LA Law* to the proceedings; and Kim Grant, who proceeded to combine the administration of justice with a self-administered pedicure.

The verdict was never in doubt. The penalty, however (and as always), was hotly disputed. Its suggested severity ranged from 'yellow jersey' to 'ten per cent of salary'. Finally, in a judgement worthy of Solomon Grundy, Mr Justice Peacock determined that the penalty should be set at 'twenty quid and the yellow jersey for the morning'. In a bench-mark summing up, he revealed that he had resisted the firing squad option on the grounds that Charlton's shooting ability would have led to the bankrupting of the club through an excess expenditure on ammunition.

Mr Jones accepted the verdict with a commendable brevity that never deviated into words of five letters.

Side by side with this distinctly CAFCaesque trial, an exercise with rather more serious legal import was being conducted. We had the drug testing squad in our midst. Just routine. Five players, selected totally at random, were asked to give a urine sample. This practice of training-ground testing is a recent development. It's been introduced partly on account of the length of delay encountered by away teams, desperate to get back on the road after a game, having to wait and wait for their two players to pass enough urine to satisfy requirements. Which gives a pretty good indication of the degree of dehydration we undergo. My solitary experience of being tested was after a Cup tie at the Goldstone against Leeds. It was well after six o'clock before the four of us could deliver enough liquid gold by way of evidence – this despite our all having consumed several cans of lager whereby to prime the pump. I cite the occasion as a shining example of piss-artistry for the greater good of the game.

Occasionally the testers do come up with a positive reading. Chris Armstrong appears to be the latest high-profile player to register on the dope scale. And even the FA has conceded that there are a handful of other such idiots among our ranks.

Saturday 4 March

A chance of close-range hero-worship today for a true blue Evertonian. Garry Nelson shakes hands with one of the Goodison greats. Alongside Ball and Harvey, Howard Kendall completed a very special midfield. Later, of course, in the eighties he managed Everton to the old-style Division One Championship. But times change and the mighty are comparatively fallen. He now finds himself managing a different team at the foot of a very different Division One. After our rather unconvincing win condemned

Notts County to further misery on their way back to the East Midlands and beyond into the rest of the season, he looks to have an enormous job on his hands.

Ironically, this very low-level encounter attracted the largest crowd at the Valley since our return. The reason isn't far to seek. Some 13,500 were enticed away from their tellies and video-games by the slashing of admission prices to a fiver for an adult and a quid for a kid. Breaking in my newly acquired marketing hat, I can't help but get up on my soap box for a minute to argue that a priority for many clubs should be a major review of pricing strategy.

Public demand for First Division soccer is undoubtedly there, only, for too many too often, it's a latent demand. It needs prodding into positive action – up from its couch-potato apathy through aggressive marketing and pricing strategies. If, in the midst of a very mediocre season, Charlton can attract a full house against the bottom club by slashing prices, surely there is every good reason to believe that the established ticket price is seen as being too high by Dads and Mums and offspring.

The flexibility the Charlton Board is beginning to bring to its pricing policy will not please season-ticket holders locked in to a pre-paid admission. But the higher priority has to be converting potential spectators into actual. As a player, I can say that it's a genuine pleasure to play in front of a capacity crowd. But it's not just a question of atmosphere. There's more buzz, sure, coming off a 12,000 crowd paying five pounds a head than a 6,000 crowd paying ten. But there's also more profit. Programme sales, hot dogs, hamburgers, the club shop – sales in all these areas will be up. And, above all, the customer base will have been extended. Seeds will have been planted with every first-time visitor. Not all will have fallen on stony ground.

No chance of prices being slashed at Old Trafford. Because no need. Market forces enable the Board to charge pretty much what it likes. The product is that good. People want it regardless. Whatever they paid, they'll have reckoned they got value today. The Reds banged in nine. Somewhat erasing my question marks about whether *he* was value for money, the seven million man grabbed five of them. Mind you, given Ipswich's out-to-lunch defence and the level of support he got, I reckon I would have got four of them. Well, three . . . well, when I say three . . .

Tuesday 7 March

More commotion involving the high and the mighty. The FA have now formally charged George Graham with bringing the game into disrepute; the police have charged Paul Ince with common assault over his 'I'm with you, Eric, *mon vieux*' action at Selhurst Park; Graeme Souness is suing *Today* for libel. Very interesting.

Less enthralling for the tabloid-fixated masses is that Charlton now have a real chance of distancing themselves from those tap dancing on the relegation trap door. A win tonight from our away fixture at fourth-from-bottom Bristol City will see us ten points clear of the drop zone. Last Saturday wasn't pretty, but it did consolidate our reputation for becoming more solid. We go into this game pretty confident of being able to beat the other 'Robins'.

Ashton Gate is another ground to benefit from the Football Trust's generosity. It now has new, spotless changing facilities to go with an attractive covered stand behind the goal. It was in these shiny surroundings that I met up again with Buster Footman (what a name for a physio!) who was our sponge-man in my very early days at Southend.

It came to seem quite appropriate that he should have witnessed the first strides I made in professional football, because by the end of tonight's game he was watching what could well have been my very last steps. We were into injury time and (such are the hopes of mortal men) 0–2 down with no hope of salvaging anything. I had the ball but, like the team, I was going nowhere down a blind alley. Abruptly – Aaaargh! This is why it's called injury time! – I was poleaxed from behind. As the assailant's two legs wrapped around my straight, weight-bearing right one, I began to fall. My body kept on going. My leg stayed where it was. I finally hit the deck as the highest order of pain I've experienced in my long career started to hit me. Over the next few minutes/centuries, I was as close to fainting from sheer physical anguish as I've ever come. Maybe the urge to lose consciousness was abetted by the thought that had zapped me even as I was still on the way down: '*That's it, your career's finished.*' The stretcher took forever to arrive. The trip back to the brand new – who cares! – medical suite even longer. But there was diversion for me on the way. As I was being carried along the touchline, a City fan leaned out from the crowd.

'That's your career over, you bastard!' he crowed. 'You'll never play again!'

Nice guy. I thought back to the City fans I'd met on the London train after the home game and reflected what terrible things an unwise perseverance with cider can do to the personality. It was no doubt a novel and refreshing change for him to be abusing someone other than himself, but it was no help to me at all that he was giving moronic voice to exactly what was going through my own mind. Now my thoughts turned on the instant to Eric Cantona. If only he'd been there carrying the stretcher, I'd have paid all his fines for him if, dropping me like a hot potato, he'd vaulted the hoardings and, at the risk of losing his boot in the scum-bag's mouth, delivered a studied reply. Well, no. Not the way. But let the record show that in those few tortured seconds I distinctly felt that Eric of the Red Mist had a very justifiable attitude towards *agents provocateurs*.

Not that you can judge everyone on the strength of one mental pygmy's behaviour. Totally sympathetic locals saw to my every need in the medical room. City's club doctor opened the door on hope by being confident there was no bone fracture and that none of the knee's ligaments had been ruptured. Severe strains to the knee and ankle was the diagnosis. I would live to play the violin again. Once again I had been lucky. Comparatively. I wasn't, after all, dancing up and down for joy. The pain was still intense and I had to be looking at a long lay-off.

The patient had visitors. Joe Jordan popped in and enquired as to my well being – a nice touch. Then, yet again, I was shaking hands with Joe's recently appointed assistant, the concerned and truly apologetic John Gorman. There's not a more decent man in the game. One person was conspicuous by his non-appearance. The perpetrator of the foul (for which the colour-blind referee had shown him the yellow card), I had learned, was Martin Kuhl. I was expecting him to appear to explain why, with the game won and me in no threatening position, he had done his earnest best to terminate my means of earning a living. But he never showed. Well, you've either got it or you haven't. Class.

Wednesday 8 March

By the time Jimmy Hendry was pulling up in the car park of the Blackheath Hospital, it was already 1.45 in the morning. He'd had to fight the elements every inch of the way to get us there. A snow blizzard had done its best to have us overnighting on the hard, cold shoulder of the M25, leg agony thrown in for nothing. By 3.00 a.m. the formalities had been completed and Jimmy was very belatedly heading home as I began to lose myself in sleep. At 6.30 a.m.: rise and shine! Oh what a beautiful morning! I must have at last drifted into some kind of a sleep but that was as much as I was going to be allowed. No shortage of staff in this private hospital and all attentive, friendly and very inquisitive about my footballing life. In spite of the abbreviated shut-eye and the now nagging ache, I found myself playing to the crowd. It's hard not to, you'll find, when three very attractive nurses – all female – are at your bedside.

All over too quickly. I was wheeled away for yet another close encounter with an X-ray machine. I may be a player who has remained relatively injury-free, but my radioactive snapshots must fill several albums. If Yellow Pages give me the elbow, I can always look an the bright side and glow orange for Ready Brek. No breaks, the X-rays confirm. The specialist's examination corroborates the immediate diagnosis of Bristol City's doctor. Not only no need for surgery but no need for further hospitalisation, either. Discharged on crutches, I'm told that with the wind in my direction I can expect to play again in about five weeks.

Sorry about that, Big Mouth of Avon.

Thursday 9 March

The phone rang so frequently today it might have been Cup final week. But this barrage came courtesy of genuine friends.

'How is it?'

'Not too bad. I've been lucky.'

'Good.'

One of the first to call was Chris Carter who'd been at Ashton Gate and actually grabbed a quick chat with me as I lay drugged with pain in the away changing room. His status as my lucky charm has taken a severe dent.

Saturday 11 March

My dad's sixtieth birthday – and the occasion of an ever-thickening and twisting plot. Scheduled highlight, planned well in advance down to the last, brilliant detail, was a surprise party attended by no less than twenty of the extended Nelson clan. As hugs and kisses were being exchanged, there soon wasn't a dry eye in the hotel where we met. The day passed in even more wonderful a fashion than we had dared to hope – a special day for someone who holds a very special place in my heart. Happy birthday, Dad.

Meanwhile, Charlton were beating Portsmouth 1–0. My replacement, somebody called Leaburn, scored the goal.

Sunday 12 March

The hotel breakfast was again a family affair although our spirits were not quite so high now due to the lingering hangovers engendered by the, er, spirits of the previous evening. And we knew we'd soon be saying goodbye. All too suddenly it was time to go our separate ways. There was method in the timing of our various departures. Everyone was firmly intent on being back in time to take a seat for the afternoon's televised FA Cup quarter-final tie at Goodison.

I myself made it back just down the road to catch the earlier Manchester United v QPR game. I had a sort of vested sentimental reason for watching it. Today is the anniversary of our own attempt to knock the Untouchables off their FA Cup perch.

It's not a difficult occasion to recall. A rather large print of a photograph taken during that game stares at me from my office wall. It shows me waltzing around Roy Keane as I successfully avoid both his lunging tackle and his bulging wallet. Open-mouthed in the background at this utterly unexpected reversal of the natural order of things are Andrei Kanchelskis and, captured in a rare moment of having both feet on the ground, E. Cantona.

All right, if you take the ninety-minute view, the camera can lie. But the photo is still my souvenir of the highest pinnacle I shall ever reach in the game. Our 1–3 defeat has been forgotten by all but the Charlton faithful and diehard statisticians, but for me it remains vivid as the biggest, most important, game of my career. I was out on the park at Old Trafford – that perfectly focused ground where all you can do is play football – competing against the best in the land. More. For forty-five minutes we gave it our best shot and delivered a performance worthy of the eruption of delight and encouragement our fans had given us when we ran out. Almost matching United stride for stride, we held them to a goalless first half.

Enter Mark Hughes. In the elapsing of two seconds, a lifetime's dream of reaching Wembley was shattered against the reality of being up against players able to reproduce on the actual pitch those things the rest of us can only do in our heads. We weren't dishonoured. We nicked a very neat consolation goal. It had been a privilege to come second.

Dreams of Wembley. Back in the present, a perfect finale to the weekend was vouchsafed the Nelsons. Everton dispensed with Newcastle to move into the Cup semi-final. Could it be that I'll have the stage-managing of another clan invasion on my hands come the back end of May?

Tuesday 14 March

After two days with my foot up allowing Nature to take its course with the swelling and bruising, business as usual. No transport of delights, Brownie and car constitute a fifth emergency service delivering me once more to the healing hands of Jimmy Hendry. As I'm being awkwardly and uncomfortably assisted towards the treatment room, our snail's pace is stopped in its tracks by a radio news bulletin. In classic dawn-raid fashion, Bruce Grobbelaar, Wimbledon keeper Hans Segers and John Fashanu's girlfriend

have all been arrested in connection with the match-fixing allegations of last November.

One thing strikes me as very odd – dodgy, even. Bruce's
arrest was attended by TV cameramen whirring away, tabloid
reporters and the media world and its wife. How? The case
against Bruce is that money passed hands to ensure a result
nobody could have known about for sure in advance. This
massive media presence at the scene of the arrest – could it be
that money passed hands in the direction of officialdom to
ensure on-the-spot coverage of an event nobody should have
known about in advance?

It seems that the profession I so naively entered into sixteen
years ago has entirely capitulated to greed. Big money now calls
the shots. The characters – no, the *personalities* – in the game now
achieve celebrity status more from their off-field antics than their
achievements on it. Scarcely able to believe their luck, the press
have their snouts in a never-emptying trough of kung-fu kicking,
nose-biting, drug-taking, match-rigging, bung-taking, crowd-
rioting footy.

And I don't think I'm being that paranoid when I say you can't
help feeling that the mud and worse is flying off in all directions
and sticking. We're all in danger of being tarred by the same sleazy
brush. A footballer? Then he must be bent, mate. Not so. This
growing, I fear, public reaction is totally unfair on the decent,
hard-working, vast majority of contemporary pros.

Conversation soon turns to a topic much closer to home and the
mortgage. It is driven by the players whose contracts are about to
expire this coming June. Although the transfer deadline is only ten
days away, the club have so far started negotiations with only a
couple of the younger professionals. Some fourteen players are
still very much in the dark as to their career prospects for next
year. And beyond. Hardly surprisingly, doubt and insecurity are
becoming almost visible presences haunting the training ground.
With good reason. We all know Charlton are over-stocked on
playing staff. After next Thursday no more offers can be made
until the end of the season. There's a grim irony in this for me. As
the PFA delegate I've already had players coming up for what help

and advice I can give. But after Mr Kuhl's intervention, my own career prospects are more than ever uncertain. If the days off have helped my leg a little, they've done nothing but harm to my peace of mind.

OK, I know now that, thankfully, the injury is not, of itself, going to end my career. But it's touch and go whether I'll play again this season. Not too many people are going to be interested in a thirty-four-year-old, apparently injury-prone pro with as many miles on the clock as his car. In my case, the balance could have been tipped in the 'Go' direction.

The truth is that this season I've been mentally up and down more often than a manic depressive on a pogo stick. I went into the season convinced that this was it – curtains. I'd be playing out my last contract in the anonymity of the stiffs. Then injuries to others saw me starting for the first team and my form kept me in it. I was playing with some sparkle and vision, scoring and making goals. By October I was convinced I was a racing certainty to be offered another contract – so much so that like an idiot I never went ahead and bombarded the world with my CV. Then a reversal of fortune. Injury and a positional change interrupted my personal winning streak. I was dropped, back on the bench – in no way an automatic cert for anything. Then a mini-revival. An injury-assisted recall to the team, the captaincy (largely by default – the senior citizen getting the nod), some wins. Then, wallop! Life sidelined me again. That tackle has perhaps done me more lasting harm than could have been expected. As I sat on the sun-lit pavilion watching my fit and younger team-mates strutting their training stuff, I felt my anxiety level shooting up into the stratosphere. They all looked so skilful. Suddenly, so capable. Who would need . . .

'Nelse! Get your arse in here!'

It's Jimmy Hendry rescuing me from my dark day-dreaming and shortly bringing me bolt upright by inserting an acupuncture needle into an energy line commencing in my toe and proceeding on up out through the top of my head. Then he strikes another nerve. The managers want to see me as soon as training is over.

In the circumstances, this takes two centuries. At last, though, I'm hobbling up the stairs to knock as nervously on their office door as a schoolboy on his headmaster's. Come on now, Nelse, you're supposed to be a grown-up!

Inside I substitute the unpleasantness of standing on one and a half legs for that of sitting in the hot seat. We run through a bit of token small talk about the state of my leg and last Saturday's positive result. Then Curbs comes right out with it. 'We want to sort you out, Nelse. You've done it for us over the past four years and we'd like to offer you another year's contract. The terms'll be the same as the last one. If you tell us that's all right by you, we'll get right on with having the contract drawn up.'

A cocktail of emotions swirl through me. I'm both shaken and stirred. Relief. Gratitude. A sense of foolishness. How could I ever have doubted! I was always in the frame to be re-engaged! Like hell I was!

Now it's relief that's bubbling to the top. I feel lighter all over as the anxieties of the past few days drain magically away. Hence my gratitude. Steve and Alan must have had a very good idea of what was going on in my head as I lay around at home. It speaks volumes for their perception that on my first trip back to the training ground they've made an immediate point of putting my mind at ease. I'll never think of them as Tweedledum and Tweedledee again!

'Well, I'll have to talk to Carole,' I say. 'There's a lot to consider.'

'Sure.'

'But I don't think there'll be any problems. In principle, fine and thanks very much.'

'Good. Got to be done before next Thursday, though.'

I nod. I'm by no means the best-paid player on the club's books, but the fact that there's another signing-on fee built on to this new contract is going to make it an offer very difficult to refuse. That's generous. There was no legal obligation for Charlton to throw that in. What's more, another year under contract will carry me beyond my thirty-fifth birthday. That's the age the IRS accept as the official retirement milestone for us short-careered footballers. Worst coming to worst it'll give me a breathing space in which to punt out all those CVs.

'Well, nice one. Thanks.' I remember my good manners just in time.

I hobble back down the stairs a different man. It's a great morale booster to know that Curbs and Gritty have made this positive effort to look after me. Almost a novel feeling. Too many times with my former clubs, it's seemed that my efforts have gone unrewarded; that certain people were only too anxious to cash in on me rather than pay me my dues. I'd have considerably more respect now for Peter Bloom at Plymouth and buckets more for Barry Lloyd at Brighton if they'd been big enough to acknowledge I was a labourer worthy of his re-hire – as I'm convinced I was.

God! I suddenly think. I owe the man! From now on I really must take in all Gritty's set-piece briefings!

It's not difficult to keep my secret to myself during the trip back south in Brownie's car. The radio is now full of the news that, along with a Malaysian entrepreneur, the gladiatorial John Fashanu, currently with Villa but possibly self-crippled out of the game by a mistimed tackle, has also been arrested.

The evening of this eventful day Chelsea found enough to overhaul FC Bruges at the Bridge and put themselves in the semis of the European Cup-Winners' Cup.

Wednesday 15 March

Curiouser and curiouser. Is it wonderland or blunderland? There seems to be a lot of slack malice about. All five alleged 'fixture fixers' have been released from custody on police bail without any charges being brought. They've apparently got to make themselves available for further proceedings in July. The FA, quite rightly, are saying 'innocent until proven guilty'.

With my ankle ligaments showing no great desire to heal quickly, the most appropriate therapy is old-fashioned rest. There's no need, consequently, for my daily attendance at training and I can lie back and enjoy putting my foot up at home. Partially, at any rate, I'm off the commuting hook. This is a state of affairs I'll have little difficulty in adjusting to.

Not all decisions are so obvious and acceptable. With what seems like complete abruptness, Carole and I now realise that we are confronting a major, even a vital, one. Initially totally welcome – they still want me! I'm not on the scrap heap yet! – the new contract threatens to pose nearly as many problems as it solves. The Nelsons have got some hard thinking to get through and commuting is close to the heart of our dilemma. Accepting Charlton's offer will stick me with another year of it. Three hours a day of strictly non-quality time trudging up and down the same roads I've covered every inch of these past three to four years. I've simply had enough of it.

The only alternative, clearly, is to move closer to London. That's not to be lightly undertaken. I think it has been established by sociologists or their like that moving house is next in line in the human stress stakes to death, divorce and losing in the last minute to Millwall. From my own experience that seems dead right. Even to open the door on the thought just tentatively is to find a worrying flock of basic questions come crowding over the threshold.

The property market, taking the obvious first, is stagnant at present, awash with would-be sellers. Can we expect to shift our present home? Where precisely will we go anyway? What schools are available where? What's the local crime rate going to be? Most eyebrow-raising of all is the scale of property values closer to London. A quick scan of a local Kent paper suggests that to end up with the same amount of 'living room' in an unfashionable area that's within reasonable striking distance of the training ground will cost us about £40,000 more than the going rate in Worthing.

Jobs are at a premium across the whole spectrum of our present-day society. But for footballers and their wives moving house has long been a career fact of life; a natural by-product of changing clubs. It's cost me many a sleepless night and looks set to do so again now.

It was my transfer from Plymouth to Brighton that brought us to the home in which I now sit writing and which I'm now considering leaving. It won't be easy. We've been here longer than the time spent in all the others added together. Seven and a half years. That's a pretty sustained stretch by the nomadic standards of the footballing lifestyle and, no question, we've been very happy here. It's here that the children have attained full consciousness of their surroundings. We've put down some pretty deep roots.

A lot hangs on Carly and Christopher's ages. Naturally, they've got their friends whom it will grieve them to move away from. But change is being thrust upon them anyway. As it happens, Christopher is due to change school this coming academic year and, while Carly must do another year in her middle school if we stay in West Sussex, in inner Kent, say, she would go straight into senior school – a move she's certainly ready for. If we are going to shake up the kids one more time, this would seem to be the optimum moment to choose.

As for myself – that's not so cut and dried. But whatever happens, I'm a long way from conventional retirement on the South Coast. Most of my business contacts are – or are likely to be – in the London area. Getting closer to the action is less a matter of temptation than of necessity.

As many things taken into account as Carole and I can think of, the 'ayes' seem to have it. The scales have come down on the side of making a move. It's going to inflict a workaholic's summer on us. On top of the Baltimore clinic, it'll be a case of every man to the paint brushes and the hedge clippers.

The major dramas and minor traumas of the Nelson family moving from pillar to post won't be essentially different, give or take, from those of millions of other people in hundreds of other walks of life, but they point up a hidden stress that dozens of footballers at any given time will be enduring. Only the Chris Suttons of this world get lobbed the odd extra quarter of a million with which to buy a few sticks of furniture and a roof over their heads. Most players are left in the same boat as everyone else – trying to contrive and improvise as best we can somewhere between the nappy pail and the Halifax Building Society. It's something fans might bear in mind. When you're up against a Peter Shirtliff or an Alan Stubbs on a Saturday afternoon, the last thing you want to see on the Friday night is the rejection of your mortgage application lying on the ironing board next to the cot in your one-room flat.

Thursday 16 March

Got off and running in one sense today. An appointment at the training ground with the club doctor. After thoroughly examining my lower right leg, he declared that it might be the moment to set up my deck-chair. His verdict is that it will be another six weeks before the ligaments are fully recovered. I received this diagnosis with infinitely more composure than I would have done had my contractual status still been up in the iffy air.

It was thus with a clear conscience that I adopted a couch potato position from which to watch Arsenal overcome Auxerre 1–0 in France. No danger of aggravating the injury through leaping to my feet in ecstasy. Ian Wright's very tasty goal apart, the game was largely forgettable.

Friday 17 March

A further temporary departure from the bunched ranks of Charlton's squad. Joining Wycombe Wanderers *pro tem*, Peter Garland is following in the outward-bound footsteps of Scott McGleish who signed for 'Matchroom' Orient under a similar arrangement a few weeks ago. The loan system is a useful practice that allows clubs to plug gaps and try players on for size on the one hand and, on the other, lighten the wage bill burden.

Saturday 18 March

Via the phone I heard that Charlton's 1–2 defeat at the hands of Sheffield United was no classic. It wasn't just that we lost, it was the manner of it too. The Blades scored from two set pieces. This must really have cut Gritty up. He worked overtime this past week anticipating Bassett's all sorts of variations.

Monday 20 March

No possibility yet of any call on my footballing skills; but my negotiating experience is in considerable demand. Not on my own behalf. My time in the treatment room coincided exactly with the squad training session and I thus had no chance of speaking to either of the co-managers. I, by contrast, was a sitting duck. Several of the younger players came up to pick my brains over the contractual discussions in which they are currently embroiled.

Five o'clock, Thursday the 23rd – the deadline time and date loom steadily larger through the mists of indecision and a rogues' gallery of poker faces on all sides bears witness to the 'call my bluff' tactics being brought to the negotiating table. If new contracts are not signed before the deadline everything goes on hold. Thenceforward, no contract can be signed until the season has ended – hence the anxiety of our younger members. No one likes to slip into non-wage-earning limbo.

My own instinct is that, come quitting time Thursday, all will be swell. Charlton is not the moneybags club we would like it to be, but it is a fundamentally fair and decent one. Within its unavoidable financial limitations it will give its squad members a fair reward.

Who says the grass is always greener? Just a fence separates our training ground from Millwall's. On its further side a very different scenario is unfolding. Economic pressures – the New London Stadium is proving an Old Kent Road white elephant – are forcing the Lions to sell Mark Kennedy to Liverpool for £1.5 million. I know he's got almost the ultimate Anfield name but if he's worth this much at eighteen, what's the market value for a twenty-year-old veteran like Richard Rufus?

Tuesday 21 March

A rare solo trip in this morning and, on arrival, the depressing vista of an all but deserted training ground car park. With the active members of the squad on countdown for tonight's very important game against Grimsby (a win and we're all but safe, a defeat and we're back in the relegation penumbra), the only people on view are the lame, the sick and their carers. I'm joined in my personal fitness fight by David Whyte who turned his ankle last Saturday. We may have made up quite an effective early season partnership, but we couldn't have looked anything like as threatening as we both visibly cowered in the face of Jimmy's acupuncture onslaught.

In the evening, one of my main customers for my picture-framing business, Bellegrove Ceramics, had very courteously invited me to join them in their hospitality box at the back of the imposing, steeply raked East Stand. The view from there is excellent but, come the kick-off, I'm pleased to clock that, to a man, my hosts are football supporters enough to get the right side of the double-glazed patio doors and the artificial ambience they create.

The game was well worth savouring unfiltered. It unfolded as a contest between a team executing a series of beautiful one-touch, feet-to-feet passes that time and again built up into imaginatively fluid movements and another team huffing and puffing to no good purpose in their wake and to even less discernible shape. Unfortunately – and as the increasingly disgruntled home fans began to make clear – it was the latter description that applied to Charlton. Grimsby proved as attractive a side as has visited the Valley this season. To the legacy of Alan Buckley has been added, I suspect, a Brian Laws-engendered dash of Nottingham Forest. The visitors were soon a goal up. It was greeted with an earsplitting silence from three sides of the ground indicative of one of the most regrettable characteristics of today's fans – an away team flowingly on song is largely going to perform before an audience stubbornly damned if it'll show any appreciation. As a card-carrying *football* fan (and, of course, under no personal pressure to produce a result), I attracted a clutch of undisguisedly belligerent stares when I was spontaneous enough to applaud some of the Mariners' more defence-splitting moves. I was just preparing to re-enter the comparative safety of the box for a half-time cuppa when – uproar! Spectators on three sides of the ground were on their feet acclaiming a last-gasp equaliser against the run of first half play from John Robinson.

The pattern of play after the turn-around was a carbon copy of the first half. Grimsby's one fatal flaw was their extravagant spurning of scoring opportunities. Charlton's best asset was Mike Salmon's sharpness in goal. Grimsby blew chance after chance.

We had just one. Fortunately it fell to a totally thawed out but still ice-cool Stuart Balmer. The former Eskimo finished in style to give us a crucial, extremely lucky, win. I suppose we were due one against the run of play and all reasonable justice. Our loss to Tranmere, for instance, was just as big a travesty. Over what sometimes seems a very long period, these things even out and a result is a result. We'll just have to learn to live with it.

The end of my long day brought a personal result as well. After a quick visit to the changing room to congratulate the lads, I finally contrived an even quicker word with the increasingly relaxed co-managers. Upshot was a green light all round for my new contract. I'll be signing tomorrow morning. Two satisfactory outcomes in one night. Was that an extra spring in my step? Or just a mite less pain?

Wednesday 22 March

D-day minus one. But not for me. At 10.30 this morning and at the Valley I duly signed my new contract. For another year I'm a Charlton Athletic FC employee.

I suppose I should have gone on feeling elated and relieved by this extension to my playing career and earning capacity; but, at the death, it had all seemed so simple. Too simple, maybe. The deed done, I felt curiously confused. Mainly by myself.

I'm suddenly suspicious about how easy it's proved for me to commit myself to this further year. This time last year I was convinced that I was going in to my final season – probably with the stiffs. I'd convinced myself the time was right to move on in a new direction. All those CVs were going to be despatched to carefully targeted companies and football would drop down to a secondary role in my life.

OK, I've had a few good weeks this season and I've got a degree of longer-term security in the form of my marketing diploma – this year's CV is that marginal little bit better – but is that enough to justify postponing my move sideways for another year and obliging the whole family to uproot and start afresh?

I suppose the positive way to look at it is to say nothing permanent is being lost. Short-term, the money is good – certainly

257

compared to the average national wage and what I would probably be earning in another occupation. And, at present, we're nowhere near financially secure. It would take, face it, a very brave man to throw up a good income derived from what, after everything, he still enjoys as a cracking good job that he believes he still performs as well as most. When I *do* make a move, it's likely to be either into a speculative crack at self-employment or into an office (at whatever level) in which I'm bound to go through a shake-down, teething trouble period of adjustment. Am I just putting off the evil hour?

I don't, on balance, think so. I haven't lost my stuff down there on the park yet. I'm still in the comfort zone of sticking with what I know best. Above all, like millions of other wage earners, I'm not single and acting solely on my own behalf. I'm a bread-winner. At the moment a loaf in the hand seems a better option than half-a-loaf in the long-term bush. It was driven by this thought more than any other that my pen glided so easily over the blue document of my latest Football League contract.

Thursday 23 March

Deadline day (always the Thursday of the third complete week in March) is always one of a mad panic that only begins to subside come five in the afternoon, the ultimate 'your last orders, gentlemen' moment for all transfers and contract extensions for the current season.

As the Charlton injured sat around sipping their tea and taking in the television round-up of last-minute moves it became clear that our own club was not involved either as a buyer or seller. But then came a piece of news that starkly rendered all these reports of the merry-go-round's spasms utterly trivial. Davie Cooper, the thirty-nine-year-old former Rangers and Scotland international – a winger fairly to be mentioned in the same breath as those yesteryear maestros Matthews, Finney and Mitchell – died today. He never regained consciousness after collapsing yesterday with a massive brain haemorrhage. Just too much. When somebody of this stature, fitness and talent dies so unexpectedly at such an age, you cannot but wonder what it's all about. Why such savage arbitrariness? Why him? And why not me? Why not me next time? The traditional consolations of religion and philosophy and drinking yourself into a stupor all wear pretty thin in the face of such a randomly grim and, surely, *undeserved* happening. It makes fussing on about the pros and cons of signing another contract look very shabby.

Certainly today's television coverage was shabby. Davie Cooper's passing, in England anyway, was relegated to an afterthought item in the wake of the headline story. Pride (not that that's the word) of place was accorded the Eric and Paul show at Croydon Magistrates Court. For the record, and adding to his, Eric Cantona got two weeks in the slammer (subject to immediate appeal and release on bail), while, pleading 'Not Guilty' to a Common Assault charge, Paul Ince now faces trial in May.

From where I sit, the most interesting aspect of the day's proceedings was the written testimony of Cantona's victim/provoker asserting that he was so far from his assigned seat because he was on the way to the loo when the French striker was given leave to quit the game early. Despite this pressing need (and right after half time at that), he still had time enough (and control over his bladder) to pause awhile, shouting, as he claims, 'Off! Off! Off! It's time you had an early shower!' Hmnnn! You would have thought that all his hours spent on the terraces would have given him the chance to get the words right. I'm no legal expert, but I do have a working knowledge of the lore and language of football abuse. If that is a verbatim quote I'll happily eat George Carman's syrup. I can only assume young Mr Simmons has every intention of appearing in the dock wearing a bright yellow jersey.

Mind you, the Swindon Board may have cornered the market in them. Staring a second consecutive relegation in the face, they chose today to (under)sell their main man, Jan-Aage Fjørtoft, for a giveaway £1.3 million. Chris Carter is just one of the very hot-under-the-collar home town supporters in Swindon tonight.

Saturday 25 March
A return to the familiar landscapes of Carly's birthplace to take in the pulsating clash between the rival Robins. Chris Carter has

259

calmed down, fractionally, about the loss of Fjørtoft. At the County Ground there's many a hand for me to shake and quite a few sympathisers. In these parts, any foul by a Bristol City player is an automatic hanging offence.

After quickly looking in to wish the lads well and successfully side-stepping any appraisal from Alan Pardew of my wardrobe, I join the non-playing members of the Swindon and Charlton squads in the Town players' bar. It's not a centre of hearty good cheer. The mood of both contingents is nearly as sombre as the Addick tracksuits. The Swindon lads are down because that's where their team seems to be going. The Charlton non-combatants are depressed because they can find small comfort in having made the trip for the sake of doing absolutely nothing. Fed up and far from home sums them up exactly. As the season ebbs away and the prospect of contract renewal with it, they would much rather be somewhere else, anywhere, so long as they're getting a game and a chance to make a top-up impression. The Becks isn't that much of a consolation.

A couple of hours later and the Swindon players and fans are even more doom and gloom-laden. They had just seen a truly appalling game settled in the worst possible way for them by a sharp piece of opportunism from Kim Grant midway through the second half. Watching this stuttering, ham-footed non-event, I found the sale of Fjørtoft even more inexplicable. Swindon now have only two recognised strikers on their books – and one of these is currently out with injury! It's the scoring of goals that wins games and Swindon's need to do both without further delay is now critical. As an old boy I hope they avoid the drop but to sum up the signs today as ominous is to make light of them.

Monday 27 March

The drive was unexceptional, the treatment attentive and my ankle responding. Just another day at the soccer factory.

So we all thought. Come the evening, I flick casually to Ceefax to catch up on the day's news and – what's that on page 311?!! *'Charlton youngsters fail drug test.'*

I sit dumbfounded as the news unfolds that our England Youth (and briefly first team) midfielder Lee Bowyer and Dean Chandler, a very promising centre back, have both been found to have traces of marijuana in their urine. I sit and try to assess the situation they're now in.

Both lads are eighteen. Both have – or had – excellent career opportunities ahead of them. Now, no question, they'll have the entire tabloid press focused on their every move. As will Charlton. Two positive out of the five randomly tested the other week. How many more might we have at the Valley right under our noses – sorry, in our midst?

Their mistake, they may be feeling, was to have been caught. Wrong. To my mind they're idiots – guilty of gross stupidity. Yes, almost certainly they were doing just what most of their mates do as a matter of casual course. But these two do not exist in everyday circumstances. One short, sharp lesson they will have to take on board as a result of this incident is that as professional footballers they are obliged to operate to a stricter set of rules than the man on the terrace. The realisation that self-discipline has to be central to their sustaining a worthwhile career has to become second nature to them. Perhaps that's the very heavily disguised blessing in all of this. The adverse publicity and inevitable disciplining from club and FA must surely hammer home that, any repetition of this so easily avoidable offence, and their careers could be terminated in the promising bud.

Tuesday 28 March

Sure enough, faced with a 'slow day', the tabloid hacks have claimed the two eighteen-year-olds as their next victims. The cheap jibing references to the 'two Addicts' (get it!) and Charlton's 'joint managers' (nudge, nudge) have been fired from the indiscriminate blunderbuss. With Cantona on the back burner and Graham on hold, *The Sun* pictures the two teenagers under the back-page banner headline of 'NEW FACES OF SHAME'. This is breaking a butterfly upon a wheel. The lads' crime *today* is not that they smoked pot, but that they are fledgling professionals in a high-profile sport on a day when all the superstars are behaving themselves. They constituted the best raw material to hand for hacks given standing orders to sensationalise and seeking to do so while raising a minimum of investigative sweat.

I'd like to raise something myself: the question of whether the footballing authorities should ever have made the youngsters' names public. You also have to ask how squeaky-clean Wapping or Fleet Street would emerge from a series of random drug tests.

Wednesday 29 March

The pleasantest change of pace from yesterday's naffness. A very enjoyable lunch spent in the company of the Charlton Athletic Supporters Club, Bexhill and Hastings branch. A committed branch, they can really relate to one of my own central circumstances. To get their partisan kicks from professional football they too have to face a ninety-minute journey up from the South Coast.

The questions they put to me are mainly predictable – 'How's the injury? What'll happen next season? What's your opinion of "The Valley Two"?' As with all good PR exercises, the chief objective is to accentuate the positive and eliminate (or at least minimise) the negative. No great problem with these chaps. I'm preaching to the converted – Addicks of the best order.

Steve McCall seems to have found himself a square peg in a deep, deep, round, relegation hole. After just three months at Plymouth Argyle he has resigned. He might have good reason, for all I know. There's a strong rumour spreading from a source not a million miles away from Home Park that my old mate Dave Smith might be the father figure Argyle turn to in seeking to avoid descending into the bottom Division for the first time in their history.

Thursday 30 March

Positive news from the treatment room. The Hans Krankel is on the mend. I might be able to start jogging next week. Meanwhile, the word from Plymouth is that Steve McCall resigned yesterday rather than function as a *de facto* number two for the rest of the season to Dave Smith. Plymouth didn't want to lose him – but neither had they made an approach to Dave! When, belatedly, managerless now, they did, Dave drew on all his vast experience to turn down their offer of taking up the reins again. At sixty-something, Dave prefers, I suspect, to sit back with his feet up basking in the glow born of a very successful reign in the 1980s that brought him hero status in Devon. He clearly doesn't want to jeopardise that through a quick return not only to the limelight but to a probable lost cause too. As for the Plymouth Board – if the rumour is true, I'm speechless. What a cart-before-the-horse way of sorting out who's going to run your team!

One role of any manager is delivering his lads from temptation. Particularly, these days, temptation coming in the form of chemical substances. This sermon was preached with very sensible effectiveness today by our co-managers and Keith Peacock. Their approach was thoroughly grown-up without any head-master–pupil overtones to defeat the object of the exercise. Understandably, given my earlier train of thought, it was the words of Dave Smith when I first became one of his charges that now came back to me.

'As a professional,' he said, 'always remember who you are, what you are and who you represent.'

It's so simple. And it says everything.

Friday 31 March

A lovely, sun-filled morning. Spring at its most optimistic. And all utterly at odds with the black clouds of despair thickening in the Youth Team changing room. The second-year YTS lads have just learned their fate. As is invariably and inevitably the case, the majority of these young gladiators have just been given the imperial thumbs down. This particular crop has yielded three professionals and two others whose careers are going to be extended a whole further three probationary months. As for the other eight, it's back to the cold outside. Welcome to the real world. Any moment now and they'll be walking out the gates for the last time. I hope character-building was an integral part of their learning curve. They're going to need all the practical and psychological help they can find out there. I do what I can in this last regard, but my PFA delegate role at this crunch time is embarrassingly meagre – a few words of advice and (hollow) encouragement, a few possibly useful contact numbers and addresses. They don't really take in even this small attempt at help. I sense my words going unheeded. It's the negative replay of their attitude when I spoke to them at the time of their starting with us. 'Not me! I'm going to make it! You go talk to the others!'

At a much more established level, my quasi-diplomatic skills are required by the player known to one and all as 'Cloughie'. This is not due to his emulation of the father's drinking feats but to his striking resemblance to the son. Having been an outstanding linchpin in the Reserves' drive to the top of the Combination League, Paul Linger has just signed a very well deserved new contract. But there's an immediate fly in his ointment. In a recent game he was red-carded off (a touch capriciously, most felt) for a second bookable offence. As this was his second dismissal this season, Keith Peacock feels that a wrist-slapping fine is in order. But what level of fiscal punishment best fits the crime?

My fear (and Paul's!) is that it could be a week's wages. No laughing matter: I find myself plea-bargaining with Keith for something a touch less severe. Always approachable and willing to listen to rational argument, Keith begins to incline to my suggestion that a Brescia-like amount – a hundred quid – would be appropriate while still doing a deterrent job. However, all must be referred to the Supreme Court. The proposed sentence must be sanctioned by Curbs and Gritty.

Justice prevails, of course, the length and breadth of our green and pleasant land. And in Croydon too. Today saw Eric the Red appealing. If not to me, to the judge who converted the Frenchman's two weeks inside to 120 hours of community service. Given the length of time the FA have already put the block on his playing, I think this is a fairer public penalty. The judge gave as his opinion that the magistrates had been technically wrong in terms of the Law (well, that must be an all-time first!) and Cantona should not be awarded a severer than normal sentence simply on the grounds that he is a role model with a high media profile. This has to be right. Whenever I hear a judge speaking about 'being obliged to set a sentence that will deter others', I feel there has to be grounds for appeal right then and there. The sentence has not been solely assessed on the interior merits of the case.

Cantona's subsequent press conference was a triumph of wilfully witty upyoursism. He left immediately after throwing the scribes a contemptuously obscure crumb.

'When the seagulls follow the trawler, it is because they think the sardines will be thrown into the sea.'

He's dead wrong there, of course. Horses, yes, dogs, birds, whatever took our fancy, – but when I was at Brighton we never wasted our time on trawlers.

Eric is going to have to coach 700 kids. I can only smile. He's going to be compelled to do in Manchester what I'm volunteering to do in Baltimore. Perhaps we can arrange a match between our respective star pupils. Cantona's Kids versus Nelson's Nippers.

It was once Busby's Babes, of course. In the days when Sir Matt guided United with iron gentlemanliness, Cantona would have been out of the Old Trafford door the day after his Selhurst assault. Assuming he could have made the team.

APRIL

Saturday 1 April

Thank God it has fallen on a Saturday, this year. When it's on a normal training day the strain of being on your toes non-stop becomes almost insupportable. Salt in the teapot, mentholatum smeared around the toilet seat, knotted together shoelaces, toes cut out of your socks, underwear up on the roof. Alan Bennett would be totally out of his depth.

Lou Macari was a merry prankster too. Not just on April Fool's Day. Quite often in the course of a road run the wee man would order us to do just what he was doing. Then – ho! ho! ho! ho! – he would dart into a phone box. It used to tickle him enormously seeing his entire first team squad cram itself into such tightly constricted, injury-encouraging confines. Well, little things . . .

The date proved completely appropriate for the visit to the Valley of Stoke City. Both teams, it was to transpire, had combined in misleading the spectators that they were going to see a footballing entertainment. What they got was a bummer worse than last Wednesday's Wembley. They'd have been better off following trawlers.

The harsh truth was that the Potters' league position left them no margin for indulging in fun and games. And Charlton were devoid of wit all afternoon. The goalless bore of a draw was probably as cruel a hoax as was perpetuated all day across the country. By its end nobody was laughing.

Not even smiling today was Howard Kendall who – 'April Fool!' – became the third sacked victim this season of Derek 'Hitman' Pavis, the Notts County chairman.

Monday 3 April

There was a real 'up' feeling as we trained this morning. Richard Murray, our recently installed managing director, caught the mood as, emerging from his top-of-the-range Merc, he drew in a deep breath.

'What a wonderful day to be a footballer!' he exclaimed.

'And a bloody sight better one for being a millionaire!' Alan Pardew instantly retorted. It was by some way his best strike of the season.

Amid all this euphoria my own gentle jog in the sun lasted no more than 200 yards. A stabbing pain every time my right foot hit the now hardening ground made it discouragingly clear that I'm going to have to spend a few more days walking before I run.

I headed back to the medical room with my own spirits no longer in tune with the rustle of spring around me. I was just starting to work up a really enjoyable case of feeling sorry for myself when my self-centredness was punctuated by Colin Walsh and Alan McLeary coming up to say good-bye as they set off for a Reserve game at Portman Road. At once I felt better.

There's always someone worse off. My two veteran and vastly experienced team-mates must really be sweating on whether they'll get to experience the luxury of another year's contract. Walshie needs just one more season under his belt to qualify for a testimonial year and it would be a very hard-nosed club, indeed, that denied him this richly deserved bonus.

Macca's position – shades of our respective fortunes when we met in Orlando last summer – is looking far more fragile. Until recently our automatic skipper and a tremendous reader of the game, he now finds himself a regular in the Reserves with no immediate prospect of a recall to the senior side at the expense of the younger central defenders now going from strength to strength. His Reserve team partner, Phil Chapple, is in an identical position. But one important distinction separates them which could strongly influence the 'Will he stay or will he go' decisions made in their respective cases. Macca arrived from Millwall on a free. Phil was bought from Cambridge at a cost of £125,000. If squad-trimming and cost-cutting are pressing needs, one of them will have to go. It may not be the best criterion to base a decision on, but I don't think Charlton will write off that amount of outlay over just two years.

With most of the youngsters having signed new contracts, the Reserve team bus is not the vehicle to be travelling on if you're a veteran on the point of running out of contract. Equally, one or two on the first team bus won't be sitting very comfortably either as they trek off on the 'Take two!' journey to Turf Moor. Sole topic of discussion around the hotel dining room table tonight will be who's going to be breaking bread with whom come the autumn.

On reflection, having to be patient for a few more days is no big thing to get worked up about.

Tuesday 4 April

As throughout the season, it's a case yet again of one step forward, and another one back. Tonight the first team lay down at Turf Moor and died 0–2. I gained this information from one of yesterday's three very big winners – the trio who started to earn their corn by heading off for Portman Road to play against Ipswich in a Reserve game and then, after a lightning shower, by hightailing it all the way across country to Lancashire for a strictly non-romantic midnight rendezvous with the first team.

At tonight's game one got to sit on the bench, two got to watch. Sometimes it's a privilege to be injured.

Wednesday 5 April

There will be a grim management dialogue today. My scout's report that the team's performance against Burnley was abysmal has been corroborated not only by all innocent bystanders, but by all culpable participants as well.

It could be that the 52 points we've now scraped together have given us a false sense of security and an actual dose of complacency. It was Burnley, down among the dead men, fighting for

Division One survival who supplied what fire and sense of purpose was to be seen at Turf Moor last night.

Personally I doubt if our sense of security is that false. It would certainly be due to one of the worst ever losing runs in Charlton's history if we failed to take a single point from our last remaining seven games, but, even if we plumbed such depths, I still think 52 points will see us safe. Too many sides below us have to play each other and there just aren't enough points in the pot.

A former Liverpool favourite went all the way back to Anfield today to be anything but red-carded. In what has to be called a highly emotional reunion, Bruce Grobbelaar received, as opposed to a morning visit from the cops, a standing ovation from the Kop – a gesture made all the more obvious in its generosity by the fact that the Kop is now all-seater.

It could be interesting to read tomorrow's newspapers.

Thursday 6 April

After Tuesday's woefully token effort, the managers have given the guilty both barrels from close range, perhaps with too full a load. A close-encounter, keep-ball session did not achieve its usual therapeutic function of easing frustrations. On the contrary, with everyone trying too hard to compensate, tempers rapidly boiled over. In no time at all, too much over-reaction had led to a couple of minor injuries and the exercise being tersely – to put it politely – aborted. The decision made sense. With Steve Brown and Keith Jones suspended, our own twin towers of strength can ill afford any further cry-offs for Saturday's ambiguously anticipated local derby against our training ground neighbours.

Saturday 8 April

'Whatever you do this season, make sure you beat Millwall.' Or Liverpool/Everton. Rangers/Celtic. Lazio/Roma. United/City. Real/Atlético. Wherever two teams are gathered into one space, there you will find a local derby and the inescapable fact of life that the workplace, playground, pub or, indeed, home becomes a miserable, all but no-go area when your lads are on the wrong end of that all important result. In terms of this form of neighbourhood watch, Charlton fans have long had their problems. In close to sixty meetings, the reds have only beaten the blues nine times.

This is only Charlton's second visit to the pompously, OTT-named New London Stadium. On the first, I gave our makeshift, injury-hit team an early lead but the game ended sickeningly for us with an injury-time Millwall winner. It gave me one further reason for disliking the Lions' computer-designed, state-of-the-art and, hence, characterless New Den.

In its hi-tech, brutalist way Millwall's new ground is a lot more impressive at first glance than the Valley – not least on account of its sheer scale. But for me, its undeviating four-square symmetry lacks a human dimension, that sense of the past. Impersonal, it's a stadium people can forget themselves in: a stadium, be it noted, therefore waiting on an incident to occur. From a fan's (impeded) point of view, the original Den with its stewards exuding intimations of imminent GBH may have been a tip of a ground in comparison. But I always quite enjoyed playing there. The hostility of the home fans may have been total – but at least they were creating an atmosphere you could react to and play off.

Perhaps it is the New Den's lack of character as much as the geographical inconvenience of its site that is responsible for the disastrously low gates Millwall have experienced this season. Their ground is twice the size of Charlton's: their current crowds are half as big. I had to pinch myself as I took my lofty perch in the directors' box today as a reminder that the game I was about to see was supposed to be all about local derby passion. The spectators were so thinly spread out and separated that not only were they diminished but the occasion was too.

The game opened with a quick exchange of goals. Millwall were up after three minutes, but captain for the day Stuart Balmer (the remarkable turn-around in his Valley fortunes thus given official recognition) equalised after nine. Parity was not preserved for long. A long-range bolt from the blues, goal of the season volley from, in my opinion, the prospect of the season, restored Millwall's lead. It hadn't escaped my notice that several Premier clubs had

271

watchers at today's game. The name they were suddenly all simultaneously jotting down was that of Ben Thatcher. (No relation, he insists.) Given the recent record of the Lions' Board, this outstanding full back will not have to put up with playing in front of such sparse support much longer.

He had the scouts putting pen to paper again in the second half. It was his inch-perfect cross that set up Kerry Dixon's crisp finish: 3–1. There won't be too many more Charlton fans abroad on the streets of South-East London tonight than on the streets of Raith.

Sunday 9 April

The sabbath – but again no peace for the wicked. It's a big day in the soccer calendar. In the afternoon there are two FA Cup semi-final ties moved to the Sunday and arranged with off-set commercial artifice around the television schedules of the Beeb and Sky. In the evening, for the players, there is the annual pilgrimage to Park Lane for the PFA Awards Dinner. With Everton appearing in their record twenty-third semi-final against 'they shouldn't be there' Tottenham, I had a keen interest in both the sporting and the social encounter.

Lacking not only the toweringly influential Duncan Ferguson but, as the experts had been telling us all week, the basic class, Everton had long since been written off. The pundits had already used up a deal of ink anticipating the delights of the dream final, Spurs v United. Everton simply hadn't read the script. As is so often the case, the underdogs made all prediction a mockery.

Spurs were never allowed to establish their own rhythm. Everton's work-rate saw to that. But, additionally, the quality of their passing and finishing was a revelation. The completeness of their game tore the heart out of Tottenham.

Contemptuously consigned by so many to oblivion after his fanfared arrival at the club, Daniel Amokachi used this game to apply for the 'most unlikely Goodison cult hero of the year' award by arriving late for the game (and arguably the season) and scoring two goals in the last ten minutes.

Everton, be it admitted, did have one huge advantage going for

272

them – the choice of venue. In general terms I would applaud the FA's decision to ignore current commercial pressures and return the two semi-final ties to neutral, club grounds. Wembley, for me, should be held back for the big one, the final. For fan and player alike, the final should be characterised by that extra, indefinable, 'holy of holies' mystique. That said, the decision to use Elland Road this year did Everton a very big favour indeed and Tottenham absolutely none.

But 4–1 is 4–1. It's the Blues who will be going. And the Nelson phone will soon be glowing red.

Revved up by my ear-splitting, air-punching reaction to my team winning the game, our dinner party set off in buoyant mood. Our immediate destination was the Plaza on the Park Hotel, hard by the FA's Lancaster Gate headquarters. But we're not proud. For several years the Plaza on the Park has been our rendezvous watering hole, a convenient pit stop wherein to climb into our penguin suits prior to waddling on to the Grosvenor and its Great Room.

Our first priority was to dump our excess baggage in the ninth-floor room booked for the night. We summoned the lift. As its doors juddered open all hell was let loose. Not from its interior but from alarms and klaxons sounding on all sides. Either World War III had started or someone had pressed an illicit button. The latter hypothesis came to take on greater plausibility. As we withdrew from the now automatically non-elevating lift, we were struck – well, soaked, actually – by a certain Yorkshire club's distinguished custodian showing off his excellent handling and distribution skills. Medium of his demonstration was a powerful fire extinguisher. Ah, if only he could handle his liquor as well as deep crosses. As we gathered to drip-dry on the pavement outside, it was only too clear that what he had most distinguishedly extinguished was any chance of our getting a bevvy at the hotel bar.

Maps were scrutinised, natives closely cross-examined. A nearby wine-bar was delighted to have its usually dead Sunday afternoon turned into a money-spinner as it off-loaded on us the 'probably the worst lager in the world' Lapland speciality of the house.

But soon, the main event. Duly resplendent in our DJs, sober as judges at their claret, we proceeded thither. Only, alas, also to proceed further and further into anti-climax. The players attending the PFA Dinner, for a start, were in the minority. They were distinctly outnumbered by guests, bringing with them a faint but perceptible aura of soccer-groupie gawping. This has been an escalating tendency over the past few stagings of the Awards and it threatens to distort the core purpose of the evening. The cuisine was no splendid compensation. With the Great Room filled to capacity, you have to expect mass-catering and being chiefly served up with a sense of being under-fed and over-charged. This was much the impression – along with a distinct flavour of reheated left-overs – generated by Jimmy Tarbuck, the main guest speaker.

The result of the formal awards – Alan Shearer getting Player of the Year; Robbie Fowler, Young Player – came as no surprise whatsoever. As goeth Charlton, so goeth the PFA. In a brief acceptance speech, Alan Shearer had the twin good graces to thank his team-mates for providing a launch-pad, and to remind his fellow pros (and their multitude of guests) that if soccer was to be seen to have cleaned up its act, everyone still had a way to go. Having missed out on Young Player of the Year, Gordon Strachan gained compensation in the form of a Special Merit Award. Richly deserved. A split second of his on-the-pitch wizardry shown on the closed-circuit TV monitors was the gem of the evening and worth a dozen cabarets.

The event was basically a disappointment. On the Nelson Awards scale only 5 out of 10 – a judgement confirmed for me by my having the good fortune to run across Greg Stanley, chairman of Brighton and Hove Albion, as we were leaving.

This is the man who, during my four-year stay at Brighton, made a point of always seeing that the PFA Dinner was one hell of a do. Door-to-door transport was standard, as was a hotel suite, clothes-changing and bar-raiding for the use of. At the dinner itself, all drinks were on Greg's tab. The year I myself was honoured by selection for the Divisional Team, several bottles of Moët et Chandon appeared on our table precisely on un-announced, miraculous cue.

I've seen a lot of directors come and go. Many have been extremely wealthy – not least the tightwads among them. Greg, however, has never been tainted with charges of well-heeled stinginess because when it came to looking after his players out of hours he would always put his hand in his pocket.

Monday 10 April

Other people, other lives. And deaths. Focused on the Everton game and the later social whirligig, I was unaware until this morning that English football had been guilty of yet another – and a particularly nasty – own goal.

The United–Palace game ended in a 2–2 draw. That's but a trifle, though. Black centrepiece of the tie was that, in the car park of a Walsall pub, the still simmering animosity engendered between the two sets of fans by the Cantona affair boiled over into fighting. Caught up in the rolling brawl a thirty-five-year-old Palace fan was sent sprawling to his death under the moving wheels of one of the supporters' coaches.

What can you say? How can you react? Already there are rumours that the encounter was by prior mutual arrangement. We talk about 'the beautiful game'. But how can we dare to describe it as such when behaviour like this goes on and on and on? Was it ever a 'beautiful game?' Well, yes, the record seems to show it was. Crowds of 80,000 watched over by just a handful of policemen, would stand unsegregated and do nothing other than watch and enjoy the game. The game was the end in itself. It was not the starter for it all going 'off' somewhere round the corner. 'Beauty' is taken out of the game whenever supporters lack the generosity of spirit to give credit where credit is due, credit justly earned by those they don't support.

Wednesday 12 April

All eyes on Villa Park but not so many pairs evident inside the ground. The boycott by Palace fans was largely honoured. The disdain that Palace feel over the unseemly haste the FA are insisting on has led to a very thin spread in the seats assigned to the Eagles.

It was a good one to miss, anyway. Before the kick-off both managers appeared on the pitch to ask for calm and measured behaviour. Both evidently neglected to repeat their exhortations in the changing room. Forget the stands: on the field we got anything but calm and, instead, two players sent off – Roy Keane for a Twickenham-style stamping and Darren Patterson for rushing forward to shove him in the face. Viewed against the dark prelude to this game, such thuggishness stretches beyond belief and understanding. For the record, United won 2–0 but, given the events of the evening, who was counting?

Thursday 13 April

The pink forms arrived this morning along with all the explanatory information which any player whose contract is up at the end of the season needs to know.

This form is to an unsettled player what an UCCA form is to a would-be student. Sent out by the PFA, duly completed and returned to them, it lists the complete career details of every player being given a free transfer or opting for freedom of contract status. Not just for the record. In each case, copies are circulated to every professional club in Britain and to the Football Associations of most of the world's other countries.

A player failing to complete his form in time is held to be guilty of one of the biggest own goals it is possible to score – as bad as not fully understanding his contractual rights.

Most definitive of these is that an offer of re-engagement in all ways financially equal to the existing contract must be extended to him in writing by the third Saturday in May. The non-receipt of such a document automatically allows the player the bolt-hole of a free transfer.

It is scarcely surprising, therefore, that letters renewing terms always arrive well in advance of the deadline and always, but always, arrive in the form of recorded deliveries. The scenario of a player worth millions pleading for a 'free' because, honest guv, he never received his re-engagement offer in time simply doesn't happen.

Once in receipt of an offer from your club, you are legally

obliged to reply within four weeks. Neglecting to respond within this period means you will stay on under the terms of your existing contract and not have the right to approach other clubs. In working reality you reply in good time in one of two ways: you accept the new offer and re-sign, or you turn it down and hope for something better. The latter policy is just great if you can attract someone else's eye. It's absolutely awful if you can't. If you've signed nothing by 1 July you automatically go on a dreaded week-to-week contract.

The feature of this variation is that, so long as they go on paying you week by single week, the club retains ownership of your registration. (Technically, it is the registration that is bought and sold when a player is transferred.) If they think that they will get an eventually reasonable return for you in the transfer market, or if they think that sooner or later the insecurity of your position will drive you into re-signing, they will be comparatively happy to keep you on this week-to-week string. After all, the longer it goes on, the longer they can hang on to any repeat signing-on fee lump sum.

For your part, should events have taken you into this short-term limbo, you will find that your nerves have become very taut and your stomach very liquid. If they should decide to cut their losses and give up on you, the club now only needs to give you two weeks' notice in order to be able, quite legally, to terminate your contract. Equally, injury in training or a pre-season friendly could be a career terminator.

The only insurance that you can take against this latter contingency is not to train at all. It's also perfectly legal and you still get your money. It doesn't do a whole hell of a lot for your goodwill quotient or your bargaining position, though.

At Charlton there are now only nine players out of the sixteen coming to the end of their contracts this summer who do not as yet know their mid-term fate. All will be sent pink forms in the course of the next week or so. I would like to think these documents will be surplus to requirements but I know for certain that five or six will find their way back to Gordon Taylor in Manchester.

Friday 14 April

A Good Friday this ain't, as the rabbi remarked. My mood darkened when I took on board the lack of improvement in my right ankle. On Monday I was able to run without untoward discomfort. The intervening days have seen the pain, albeit localised, return with interest. An appointment with the doctor was arranged on my behalf today. Or as I would put it, appointment with fear. It means only one thing. A cortisone injection.

Not such a good Friday, either, for my tip for the top. Surprisingly Tranmere have beaten Bolton 1–0 and it is they who are now closing in on Middlesbrough. At the other end of the Mersey Tunnel, Ammo's cult status is confirmed. He scored two more goals for Everton today.

Saturday 15 April

Agony! Via a hypodermic needle it seemed you could blow up a football with, the doctor delivers his mighty potion straight to the heart of my fleshless ankle's injury. The only consoling benefit I can derive from this great prick (check one) is the clinical necessity of resting for three days so as to allow the concoction to work its magic.

Curbs and Gritty didn't have to wait quite so long for a magical response to the kick up the backside they had delivered to last week's gutless wonders. Ninety minutes of pulsating, technically high-class action gave today's spectators the kind of game their tongues have been hanging out for all season. The visitors were Wolverhampton, arriving all fired up to consolidate the play-off spot they currently hold. The challenge of denting these prospects brought out the very best in the Addicks.

Magnificently marshalled by a fully fit, all batteries recharged and imminently out-of-contract Colin Walsh, they rose to the occasion to win 3–2.

The Board must have been rubbing their hands in glee – the best game of the season was coinciding with the inclusion in the programme of the annual season-ticket application form – until the inescapable, unanswerable question came to qualify their rapture. If we can turn it on like this, why haven't we been putting it together all the way through the season? Don't ask me, I just play to orders.

Sunday 16 April

A very quiet Easter Sunday with the kids completely taken up by their private duel to see who, through the non-stop devouring of Easter eggs could first be sick. For the second day not running, I got the needle. The little angels saved me not so much as a single crumb from their stockpile.

Tuesday 18 April

Flashback time. A return to where, in a sense, it all began. A return to my Roots Hall roots. An away visit to the nearest I've got to a home town club. I don't expect, though, there will be any choruses of '... it's so nice to have you back where you belong.' Over the years I've played down here against the Shrimpers plenty of times and, it has to be squarely acknowledged, more often than not come away with my pride battered and bruised. It's not merely that I have to contend with such subtly original chants as 'Southend reject' or 'Garry Nelson is a winger, is a winger, is a winger' (I *think* that's what they're saying). I've also conspicuously failed to retaliate by registering that all-important 'you don't like it up you, do you?' revenge-is-sweet goal.

The one stand-out exception to this dolorous chronicle was the day two seasons ago when, as rare coincidence was pleased to arrange it, I made my 500th league appearance on the very ground where fourteen years earlier I had run out for my first. It was a heartwarming moment made all the happier by a 2–0 win.

Flip the coin over, though. My last game at Roots Hall became the source of unrelieved humiliation when, much to the delight of my fellow burghers (as I like to think of them), I was subbed early in the second half.

Such up and down memories of one ground are really just the swings and roundabouts of my entire career writ small. Take, for instance, the peaks and troughs of just the first four years of my professional experience. Elation came with my first full league debut, my first league goal (ironically against future team-mate, Baltimore-bound Bob Bolder) and winning my only tangible honour, a mighty Fourth Division Championship medal. Offset against these pluses, however, have to be the slings and arrows of involvement in relegation to the Fourth Division in my first full season, an unacceptable inconsistency in my personal performance and the consequent rough ride I got from the home supporters.

It's a strange but true aspect of the game that, more often than not, the fans don't care to see a local lad making good on the park. I suppose it tends to generate 'that could've been me' feelings which cut a little too close to the quick. When I moved on from Southend, fans for whom I was at first a stranger and an unknown quantity immediately extended me a much warmer and, when necessary, forgiving relationship.

No chance to obliterate the negative associations tonight. I'm still a non-runner. My dad alongside, I take my seat – a strangely novel experience, this, for several reasons – in the North Stand and think back to the early seventies when this was where the densely massed ranks of us ever-present blues fans (there were at least twenty of us) congregated to sing the praises of Billy Best, Bill Garner, Spud Taylor and Co. In those days it was always the North Stand that generated whatever you could detect in the way of atmosphere at Roots Hall.

Now as a Charlton player, I'm surrounded by Charlton fans singing the praises of, er, David Whyte. Once again with good reason. With his twentieth goal of the season, Whytie shot us into the lead of a game otherwise so scrappy I felt certain the single strike would settle the issue.

Was I right or was I right? This time completely wrong. With more to play for – a need to edge further from the relegation trap-door – Southend found the will to dig deeper into themselves and, with two goals in three minutes, turn the game.

The Charlton fans were no longer praising anyone and my saga of Roots Hall woe had acquired another drearily familiar chapter. Next year, though, now the Shrimpers are also safe, the story's going to take a different twist. Maybe.

Wednesday 19 April

A day of jogging for yesterday's non-runner. The ankle stood up well. Could be, come Friday, I'll be putting boot to ball again.

Thursday 20 April

With no adverse reaction to yesterday's hard workout I stepped things up a notch today. Inevitably, my stamina has suffered from six weeks of relative inactivity. I'm determined to play one full game before the season's end. I need to psychologically. I need to dispel any doubts lingering in the back of my mind and spreading their false counsellor whispers that I'm bound to be giving it less than my best shot after suffering – and suffering from – so damaging a tackle.

I'll feel far easier in my mind if I can well and truly resolve all doubts before the summer break. To have them come ghosting back pre-season will do me no favours whatsoever.

Saturday 22 April

Three points for a win is a meaningless statistic today. Relegation has been avoided. Qualifying for the play-offs is a lost cause. Both Charlton and our opponents today, Luton, have only one marginal reason to get at all worked up over this game: a win should avoid the possible ignominy of going out in the first round of the Coca-Cola Cup next year at the hands of lower-leagued opposition. Big deal. The first half-hour of this mediocre, end-of-season match could only have conveyed to fans that frankly, my dear, neither side gave a damn.

The game badly needed a goal or a flash of individual genius. What it got instead was a sending off. Rock steadily reliable and virtually ever-present Steve Brown demonstrated his innate sense of theatre by choosing this low-level non-event as the backdrop to his and Charlton's first red card of the season. Two latish, despairing rather than vicious, tackles combined to earn him this distinction.

It did the trick. We suddenly had a great game on our hands as Charlton chose to combat numerical inferiority by attacking. The

281

second half was played with three Charlton men constantly pushed forward. It was the Wolves game over as we bobbed and weaved, passed, ran and received back. Poetry in motion – not least when yet another Mark Robson assist set up yet another Whytie finish: 1–0 at the end and deservedly so. Food for thought over the hols, let us fondly imagine, for the two managers.

I am, be it acknowledged, human. Consequently, I can't resist feeling that by end of play this evening a degree of poetic justice had gone towards balancing the Nelson books a little. Bristol City are definitely relegated. I don't direct this at the lads on the train, but I shan't lose any sleep over the disappointment of one specific player and, most definitely, one particular supporter.

Tonight the Charlton species of supporter had the opportunity of honouring the player they themselves had chosen via a phone-in vote as Player of the Year. And were I a betting man I could now easily be minus my house, my wife, my kids and my Alan Ball fan club membership card. The odds-on favourite and, in my opinion, surely the deservedly certain winner-to-be was David Whyte. But no. Whytie was pipped on the post by a young pretender. Not merely content with walking off with the Young Player award, Richard Rufus scooped the senior prize as well. I won't carp. Since forcing his way into the team, he's had a quite excellent season and, already selected for the England Under-21 squad, he's an outstanding prospect for the future.

Still, as a paid-up member of the Forwards' Union, I would like to demonstrate my solidarity with twenty-plus goals brother Whyte by suggesting that Richard's speech was the stuff of which yellow jerseys are made. I quote verbatim: 'Thanks for voting me . . . Thanks.'

His agent had better steel himself. He'll be inundated by bookings for his protégé on the after-dinner speech circuit.

Sunday 23 April

When you're a lad spending more time playing down the local park than those looking after you think good for your school work, you always have a private dream: one day you'll be scoring a Cup

282

final hat trick for the team you stick up for. But there is only one Geoff Hurst. Every recreational player wakes up one morning and there, staring him in the eyes like an unwelcome stranger on the doorstep, is the final, certain awareness that the only way he'll get to Wembley is by buying a ticket. The dreams of glory finally die.

In my case, after a fashion, they lived on. Once I'd turned pro, after all, I was operating in an environment that fostered them. Pretty soon, though, I was dreaming on in a muted minor key. It wasn't going to be a Cup final. It wouldn't be at Wembley. But, for game after frustrating game, season after indifferent season, diminishing in force though they might be, I never quite let go of the striker's great expectations of standing there amid the cheers to receive the match ball saluting my hat trick.

Dream never became reality. Then, when scarcely any longer expected, it all happened.

Today marks the anniversary of my first hat trick. First and only.

Peterborough United, our opposition a year ago, arrived at the Valley knowing defeat would condemn them to relegation. Neither their cause nor their morale could have been aided by the knowledge they possessed the worst defensive record in the division and were having to field a rookie goalkeeper making his league debut.

There for the taking, then. But, surely, Seaman, Shilton, Southall – the sheer quality of my strikes would have done the business against no matter what calibre of opposition. A thunderous left-boot drive, an inch-perfect, right-foot curler and a header tucked away to sweetly judged perfection.

The second, true, was a candidate for the thunderbolt category and a strike any forward would be proud of. But those framing it were absolutely the slapstick stuff of silent movie. The first was an attempt to slot the ball precisely past the keeper's feet. I utterly mishit it. The ball bobbled onwards so feebly that if it wasn't the keeper's first-night nerves that allowed it, on the third bounce, to trickle over his hands, it could only have been compassion for my embarrassment. There wasn't even enough pace on the ball for it to reach the back of the net.

Still, it counted. When, by half time, I had a brace to my name and Charlton a 3–0 lead, the name of my game was reduced to a matter of simple monosyllables: shoot when you see the whites of their posts. From anywhere and with either foot. As my team-mates were left in no doubt, I was a man with a mission. Now – it was almost a unique career experience – I became the only passing option. They force-fed me like a pre-Christmas turkey. One ball found me too far out and with an impossible angle on goal. Nevertheless, with my better foot I gave it my best shot. Sweetly struck the ball powered into – the stretching-out shin of a Posh defender. No intervention, intended or accidental, was ever better timed. Its new, now perfect trajectory took the ball over the keeper's desperately upward lunge and, quite beautifully, into the top corner of the net, where, I swear it on a stack of Bibles, I had all along intended it to finish.

My reward at long last was a match ball; Peterborough's was residency in Division Two.

A year later that ball lies out of sight and out of mind, un-loved and as deflated as Charlton's current season. Anticipation is always superior to fulfilment, the philosophers tell us; or, as I have come to learn and express it, the trouble is if you want something that much for so long, when it finally does come, you're left wondering what all the fuss was about to begin with. All the same, we need a new Geoff Hurst or two. Dream on lads.

Monday 24 April

My impatience got the better of me today. Not contenting myself with the rare pleasure of jogging round and round the training ground, I decided that the time might be right for tentatively taking part in some real training. The Youth Team were on the point of starting a five-a-side. I therefore casually strolled over and, lying about my age, fooled no one. All the same I was allowed to come on board as a mature student going back to school to bone up on the art of sweeping.

It was great to be involved. Using my geriatric's experience, I managed to avoid any significant physical contact. Although the ankle, truth to tell, was barely strong enough, no one noticed. After all, it is my right one and nobody has paid any attention to it for sixteen years.

Alas, my comeback performance did not win me call-up for Bob Bolder's testimonial game against Sheffield Wednesday. All credit to the Owls. They flew the Sheffield coop with a full-strength side that ensured the game would be meaningful. Hugely entertaining, it was better than that. Charlton fielded two promising trialists – a Robert Lee and a Gordon Watson – and Wednesday's manager gave a run-out to a former Serie A striker who gave occasional indication of genius but seemed prevented by the language problem from communicating with his team-mates. As always, Bob Bolder never stopped smiling. This, like everything else in his make-up, was big of him because, to my mind, the attendance of just under 3,500 was disappointing. As so much else in soccer, the testimonial is a litmus paper clearly separating the 'haves' from the 'have nots'.

The giants of the game can actuarially guarantee that they will be banking hundreds of thousands of tax-free pounds the day after. The overwhelming majority of players, however, know, no less certainly, that they may be lucky to clear a five figure sum. The reward for ten years of devoted hard labour, the compensation for a career-shortening injury, can be offset and eroded by such random factors as the weather, an undue congestion in the home fixture programme or the quality of the opposition it proved possible to secure. The sad, unpalatable truth is that the big-shots will probably pay more in VAT than Bob (a keeper who probably double-handedly gave Charlton one more season in the old First Division than they had the right to expect) will receive in total from tonight's game.

Tuesday 25 April

With Charlton's place in next year's First Division assured, Curbs and Gritty can now take a longer view of how they orchestrate their human resources deployment options – i.e. who's going to stay and who's going to go. They're no longer feeling obliged to cover all contingencies by hanging on to everyone. They have already taken the unusual but helpful step (it normally doesn't happen until after the last game of the season) of putting those players whose contracts are up for renewal out of their suspense-ridden misery.

Definitely out is Alan McLeary, who began the season as club captain but significantly – his going won't appear like a blooper in the Profit and Loss columns – came to Charlton on a free. Since the two macho men met in the Orlando shopping mall last summer a lot of water has flowed under their respective bridges, but the currents have been travelling in opposite directions. Along with Macca will go Mickey Bennett (who's played well when in the first team but has mega-competition in his position), young Scott McGleish who could do, I think, with gaining steady first team experience at a lower level and Alan Pardew. Pards' wages make not entirely negligible inroads into the weekly Charlton payroll but, rather than trying to recoup, the club are handsomely rewarding the service he's put in on first team park and training ground by giving him a 'free'.

A clutch of players are now up for new deals – Stuart Balmer (current captain and now batting very much on the front foot), John Robinson, Phil Chapple, Colin Walsh and Dean Chandler. Which of these will agree new terms – let alone sign happily – is anybody's guess at present but my own is that, come our pre-season reunion, two, at the very least, will be operating on week-to-week contracts.

The timing and pacing of their delivery will vary, but in every club across the country the same messages are working their way through the system. 'You're retained . . . you're being let go.' Last season the league clubs showed the door to some 900 players. Just one third of these were lucky enough – if that's the appropriate expression – to secure new playing contracts. The trend in our cost-cutting age has to be towards squad-trimming and another summer of heavy job losses. The average career-span of a profes-sional footballer in the UK now stands at no more than eight years. I've had twice my ration.

Yup, better to be a lucky player than a good one.

Thursday 27 April

The sun is out, the temperature is up into the breeze-blessed sixties and the pressure is all the way off. Training was light-weight – and immensely enjoyable. Every manager and coach should have a framed maxim hanging over his mantelpiece: improved performance is directly proportional to increased relaxation.

It's not all comfort and joy, however. The inexperienced players who have just been given the good, good news that they are being let go keep seeking me out in their anxious need for information. Who should they talk to? What letters should they be writing to whom? They're being pushed out of the nest into frighteningly unfamiliar territory. The most pressing short-term concern is to establish when exactly their money will dry up. The answer is: the end of July. Although contracts terminate at the end of June, the clubs are obliged to pay all players to whom they are giving a 'free' an additional month's salary.

The prospect of redundancy and the morale-sapping tedium of the dole queue is a certainty for some of these lads. I feel somewhat guilty that, sympathetic and helpful though I try to be, the foreground of my mind is mainly taken up by the state of my bloody ankle. My determination to race back to a level of fitness good enough to allow me to take part in a couple of serious games seems to have misfired. By the end of today's five-a-side the nagging aches and pains had returned and the ankle was angrily swollen in protest. Apart from anything else, it's becoming a bore.

Friday 28 April

My instructions were to work with those pros not considered yet ready for the grown-up squad. They go through their young paces under the astute eye of Keith Peacock, the man in the Charlton camp with most left to play for this season.

Keith's Reserves have done splendidly well in the Combination League. With just three games to play and despite being up against such monied clubs as Arsenal, Chelsea, Spurs and

287

Norwich, they are right there at the top of the league with a distinct chance of winning it.

It's now utterly apparent that I won't be contributing anything to their run-in. So as to clinch the championship, Keith would very much like to field as strong a side as possible; but renewed pain today tells me that my chances of playing a part are receding faster than Steve Gritt's hairline. My week-long involvement in active exercise has served to establish only one thing: for me, it's all over for this year. Fitting. The anti-climax to my own season is all of a piece with the club's.

Saturday 29 April

The last home game of the season and a chance, perhaps, to round off in style what has otherwise been an undistinguished eight months. We're not blessed, to be frank, with what seems at first glance the most attractive opposition. Port Vale are not a glamour club and, although John Rudge certainly knows how to make his teams play a bit, this year they have put together a season very similar to our own. Hearteningly, the prospect of a clash between also-rans did not act as a disincentive to our supporters. A crowd of over 12,000 (many of them youngsters lured by an admission of £1) rolled up prepared to enjoy the champagne spring weather and maybe even the game. This final gate ensured that attendances at the Valley this season averaged comfortably over 10,000 – cause for real congratulation to the Board and the administrative staff.

Contrary to what the respective league positions might have indicated, today's game was much more enjoyable than not. Charlton certainly shaded it territorially but the game ended in a diplomatic draw with Steve Brown's first goal in open play equalising veteran Martin Foyle's cannily taken opener.

A few of the lads trotted out a fairly token lap of honour and then, abruptly, it was all over at the Valley for another year. But not elsewhere. As the supporters filed from the ground many were tuning to Radio 5. Their team might have done no better than run on the spot this year, but the destinies of other favourites and of deadly rivals still hung in the balance. My own attention was focused first and foremost on Goodison Park where Everton are

288

still very much in need of the five or six more points that will guarantee their safety. The news was less than all good. A 0–0 draw against the perennial party-poopers Wimbledon means a fair amount of nail-biting remains to be done. The Endsleigh scores filtered through to the changing room and it was confirmed that Chris Carter will be wearing a black armband tonight in mourning for Swindon's second successive relegation.

I was delighted to learn that on the strength of an excellent 2–1 win at Wycombe, one of my former teams, Plymouth, have gained themselves a stay of execution. The reason for my delight is simple – and personal. Today, 29 April, will always be associated in my mind with the happiest night of my career. Plymouth had beaten Bristol City and so clinched promotion to the Second Division. It was hardly, I admit, an event to shake the world, but for me it was the sweetest of results. I would have hated the same date to also mark their first-ever relegation to the Football League's basement.

We'd been there or thereabouts all season long. By December we were in second place and flying. Then crashing. We visited table-topping Reading and lost 4–3 after being 3–0 up. Our morale drained from us, we were like a boxer out on his feet. But Dave Smith helped us to re-group tactically and mentally for our remaining sixteen games. We then put ourselves right back in the promotion frame with a run of nine consecutive wins.

I was now struck down by the ME bug (as it was belatedly discovered to be) which instantly destroyed my peace of mind and made it impossible to train. I had to miss five games and seemed likely to be excluded from any direct involvement in all the excitement building up in the West Country. Then, though well aware of my less than total fitness, Smithy gambled on sticking me back in for the final eight games. It was, many felt, a mistake. Eventually, it came down to a win for us against Bristol City, and, if was our nearest rivals Wigan failed to win, promotion was ours.

On the day, such was the demand to see the game, its kick-off had to be delayed by twenty-five minutes. To comply with safety regulations, the gate was officially recorded as 19,900. The pay-out on the players' crowd bonus, however, was based on a figure of

289

24,000. None of us was inclined to disagree with this estimate either in terms of economics or decibels.

A huge roar greeted our first goal. It was scored by that wonderful striker, Tommy Tynan who had taken the ball off my toe to nudge it home when I was about to shoot.

But Tommy was so much more than the best finisher outside the First Division. He could really play. Early in the second half he redeemed his debt with a through ball that put me clear from just inside the Bristol half.

It was, I now see, a watershed moment in my life. It was the button on six years of hard work in the game that all added up to my getting nowhere much, to my being on the point of giving up, to my missing out on a promotion push through illness. And yet, with devastating literalness, the ball was at my feet. I'd been granted a chance to wipe all of that out. If I could put this one away I'd start tomorrow with a clean slate.

A City defender bearing down on me, the mystery bug seeming to weigh down on my shoulders, I made for goal in the eerie silence of the whole ground holding its collective breath. I was worried the defender on my heels might bring me down. Instinct told me to shoot from way out. I primed the trigger. And got lucky. Just as I shot the ball bobbled on the bone-hard ground. It met my left instep beautifully. On countless other nights the shot would have cleared the stand but this night was mine. I delivered the best strike of my career. The keeper never moved as the ball rocketed into the roof of the net. I don't think he even saw it.

The ground – the whole West Country, it seemed – erupted. I sank to my knees and discovered I was crying. Then I was engulfed by team-mates not only in rapture over the goal but genuinely thrilled that, after all I'd been going through, it had been me that scored it. If there was one moment in my career I could buy, this would be it. I can still vividly recall the sense of disbelieving elation that rose up through me. The memory of that burst of pure ecstasy I suddenly knew I'd won for myself still makes my throat go dry, still makes the hair on the back of my neck stand up. OK, it's a game only a few now remember. But it brought me one perfect moment.

Wigan had only drawn. We knew we were up and we were celebrating already. The next week was the stuff of Roy of the Rovers dreams. No, it was a not a cap or the Cup or the First Division title. But for us and all the Pilgrims' supporters it might just as well have been. Everywhere we went we were heroes – drinks on the house, slaps on the back, handshakes and kisses. And we had our open-top bus ride around Plymouth. It poured down that day. No one minded. Thousands turned out to cheer and the rain couldn't dampen a thing.

Nelse, if you could have one moment . . . ?

I don't have to stop and think.

Sunday 30 April

Glorious memories . . . and bitterly sad ones. Somewhere up there is a malign joker, an artist at constructing black, ironic connections. The events were separated by seven years and a day. The dates are consecutive. As of two years ago the still vital thrill yesterday's memories bring is always going to fade into the dark shadow of one of the deepest bruises the game has dealt me. Today is the anniversary of Tommy Caton's death.

In his early days, when he was a teenage god bestriding the old First Division and being hailed as the natural successor to Bobby Moore, Tommy must have known many moments matching my one golden Home Park memory. He had, it seemed, the footballing world at his talented feet.

As fate would cruelly have it though, Tommy was like a climber defeated just a paltry few feet below the summit of Everest. Entering the game so early, he became a veteran ahead of his time. By the time I was his team-mate at Charlton, he knew very well the true glory days had gone for ever.

I am left with an indelible picture that is bordered in black. It is of the open grave, surrounded by player after player from Arsenal and Manchester City and Charlton and who knows how many other clubs. At the centre of the mourners, Tommy's brother stands right over the grave. In his hand is the Manchester City shirt Tommy wore in the memorable Cup final against Spurs. Such is his grief, his unwillingness to admit by the gesture the

291

acknowledgement that Tommy has gone for ever, there is a moment when he seems physically unable to drop the shirt on the already lowered coffin.

April 30th 1993. I wonder how many fans remain aware of its black significance.

MAY

Monday 1 May

You can absolutely bank on it. In the muddy depths of winter as you trudge off the field to the boos a heavy home defeat has earned you, as at the end of a murderous running session your legs turn to water, some bright spark will dredge up from the depths of his shattered being the oldest of all the straws footballers clutch at: 'Roll on May.'

Well, here we are at last. The season is all but over. Soon it will be holiday time, when the living is not only easy but high. Everyone is in the best of spirits.

Except me. There's nothing festive about my day. It began with a futile thirty-minute wait at Pease Pottage for a no-show Kim Grant, followed by a hell-for-leather sprint up the motorway by a three-quarter-filled Gatwick Express. We arrived slap bang on 10.15. No fines were levied but Jimmy Hendry was not best pleased that two of his patients were half an hour late for their treatment.

Two can play at that game. His surly mood and my own exasperation at the non-progress of my ankle were suddenly escalating us into an ugly off-the-ball confrontation. To the vast amusement of six or seven little wise-arse eavesdroppers (as they seemed at the time), one veteran striker was despatching a free, frank and unfettered volley straight back at the unprepared and slightly out of position physio.

Within moments I was regretting my behaviour. In four years Jimmy and I have never had a previous cross word. Now I could see that my out-of-character (I hope) tirade had left him

293

shell-shocked. What really caused me to blow my stack is the essential pointlessness at this stage of the season of being obliged to commute to London every day.

Jimmy, of course, has seen it all before. A few deep breaths and some intervening activities later, we had a second, more diplomatic dialogue and, as we should have done in the first place, looked at things from each other's point of view. The upshot was that there were no hard feelings and I now had only to report to the training ground for a once-a-week assessment.

In the midst of all this kerfuffle, a far more serious injury put my irritation into perspective and had Jimmy sprinting on to the training pitch. A low-key, nothing on it, five-a-side in the last full week of the season had been the Sod's Law setting for Paul Mortimore rupturing his Achilles' tendon. Roll on May and the holidays, indeed! It's a certain six months out of action and, the worst, not entirely impossible, scenario is that the injury could be career-ending. The one ray of consolation we were immediately able to point to was that Paul is at least covered by another year in his contract. If it had been one of the squad currently in contractual no-man's land – Stuart Balmer or Walshie, say – or just released on a free ... Well, I shudder to think.

Tuesday 2 May

Blue skies and a blazing sun warm on my back. For the next three days, as training becomes a DIY job, I'm off the motorway treadmill. Pedal power rules! In T-shirt and shorts I headed the mountain bike in the direction of the Sussex Downs. I didn't let myself off lightly. I backed up two and a half arduous hours of up hill and down dale with a swim and plenty of ankle exercises. And enjoyed every moment. Variety, let it be proclaimed, is the spice of training schedules.

Come the evening, however, there was scant enjoyment for my fully fit team-mates. They went down away to Watford 0–2. The (yet another) disappointing result can only reinforce everyone's gut feeling that for Charlton the end of the season can't come too soon.

It's come – and with smiles all round – for Bournemouth. The town's seaside status militating against their playing at home over Bank Holiday weekends, their last fixture was accordingly brought forward to tonight. The Cherries' 3–0 win earned them Second Division salvation and, to my mind, their manager Mel Machin exclusive rights to all Manager of the Year awards for turning round their season, gaining twelve victories in the last twenty-three games. Unfortunately for my own sentiments, Bournemouth's rise from the ashes was largely at the expense of poor old Plymouth. The Cherries' win administered the *coup de grâce* to Argyle, who are now relegated to the Fourth Division for the first time in their history. Argyle's chairman's investment of several million pounds has reaped only the dividend of relegation.

Wednesday 3 May

Traffic was at a standstill around the Valley, this evening. It's not only the first team who are drawing big crowds. Now, only two games away from a possible Combination championship, the Reserves are on a roll. They beat Bristol Rovers tonight in front of an almost sold-out West Stand.

As of today, the title milestones will begin to be passed. With Bolton, for instance, failing to pick up the three points tonight that they needed to maintain mathematical contact, Middlesbrough have found themselves Division One champions. Boro have an air of a big club in waiting about them. They can count on fervent mass support and this will be enhanced and focused when they move next season to their purpose-built (and long overdue) new stadium. For Bryan Robson the Premiership will scarcely constitute a whole new ball game. The immediate key to his personal ongoing success will need to fit the chairman's safety-deposit box, but if enough cheques are forthcoming, Boro should be able to sustain their upward mobility.

Friday 5 May

A day at the funny farm. Under the terms of the arrangement thrashed out in the heated atmosphere of Monday's treatment room, Friday is check-up day.

There weren't many visible signs of hard work when I reached the training ground. With May rolling on towards the ever-closer summer holidays, the playing staff poseurs were obsessed with laying the foundation to their mandatory, sexuality-enhancing, sun-tans. Tops were discarded, shorts were raised to indecently minimalist levels, no sock was above ankle height. The fierce sun was yet another reason why no one wanted to be saddled with a white bib. My assessment was over in the twinkling of an eye. I high-tailed it to the sun-deck where – doing it without their socks on – my fellow invalids were already grabbing their rays. I dispensed with my own top to reveal a torso white as the driven snow.

'Nelse,' Mike Salmon laconically asked, 'are you going to keep that bib on all morning?'

There's not a drier fish in the sea. It had been nice to linger at home. It was great to be back.

Saturday 6 May

Irrespective of the calendar date, this Saturday traditionally marks the last fixture of the season. Like the very first, it's a game for which everyone wants to be selected. Club and individual alike want to finish on a high note that says: 'we weren't really that bad/I really am the ace player to build next season's team around.' It suddenly seems vitally important to leave an impression good enough to last in people's minds over the next couple of interim months. Even with sides for whom the day's result is essentially meaningless (as for us this year), it's still a time of considerable tension, pressure, surging adrenalin, excitement, laughter and tears. For those with – seemingly – everything hanging on the result, it can be a compression of a lifetime's emotions into a ninety-minute microcosm. I think I can rightly say that my sixteen years' involvement in the game has taken me up every climb, plummeted me down every drop, in the footballer's A to Z roller-coaster of last-day emotions.

In my very first year, I started with a low. Southend were away at Hull in the Third Division. I was a non-playing squad member. Thus I copped the dire duty of relaying to my team-mates who had just trooped swearing and cursing back into the changing room after a 0–1 defeat that, yes, the other results had gone against us too. We were down . . .

The expression 'you wouldn't want to see a grown man cry' is often used in jokey contexts. When it happens, though, you don't. I had to watch the experienced, hardened players that, as a rookie, I'd come to respect, break down and weep over their failure. There and then it was borne in upon me with bitter permanence that football wasn't the romantic dream I'd hitherto imagined it to be. There's all the difference in the world between dreaming of scoring goals for England or settling Cup finals and actually getting relegated at Boothferry Park.

Eleven years on down that rockily unromantic road, no longer a rookie, a scarred and battle-hardened professional was crying tears of his own. They were streaming down my face as I came off at Twerton Park. Another 0–1 defeat had guaranteed that there would be no play-off spot, no Wembley glory, no place at long last in the Premiership for either Charlton Athletic or Garry Nelson. My distress was all the more intense for the mocking burden of knowledge I was carrying. In spite running myself into the ground week in, week out, I had failed to score in over twenty matches. But what a difference a scattering of just two or three Nelson goals into that horrific run would have made! For our league position. For my morale.

As that particular season came down the home straight, I had to endure four months of privately worrying myself sick about how and when the goal would come and why the bloody hell it hadn't. But only four years earlier had seen me being presented with the player of the year trophy before the kick-off to the season's last game at the Goldstone. It's a classic example of how cruel footballing contrasts can be. In a season in which I could do no wrong, I had found the net thirty-one times. Those goals had flown in from all angles, almost, it seemed, without effort. My confidence was so high, why, I'd given up thinking about the game. Let your mind alone and scoring was hardly more difficult than walking.

Except, perhaps, on this last day. This time we had the reverse problem – expectation. A Brighton win would mean that, after their relegation the year before, the Seagulls had earned an immediate return to the Second Division. Moreover, for me there was added pressure. It was an open secret that among the spectators was a fistful of top club scouts clocking the twenty-seven-year-old Nelson completing his first full season as a main striker.

Pressure? What pressure? For me, on this roll, it was all water off a Seagull's back. Completely unfazed I let everything fall into place around me and notched my thirty-second goal as Brighton won 2–1, the crowd went wild and the roller-coaster peaked again. The highest of highs, the lowest of lows. Come 4.45 on the first Saturday afternoon in May, men were meeting triumph and disaster in mirroring circumstances in dressing rooms across the country.

Today in the Never Never Land of the Premiership and the play-offs in other divisions, television contracts rule OK. To maximise home viewing box office, the season's conclusion is staggered. Thus the Endsleigh League season finishes tomorrow, and the Premiership runs on until a week tomorrow.

And what was the outcome of those watching the twenty-seven-year-old hot-shot? Nothing, is the short answer. At twenty-four, yes. I would have still had developable potential in me and, knowing it, been straining at the leash to move up to the top echelon. But now I was too set in my playing ways. And, those ways, for all my secondary virtues, simply weren't good or skilful enough. I might be able to bang in thirty-two goals in a Third Division season, but I couldn't do enough on or with the ball to cut it at the very top. Nor were the scouts fooled. They had another one for the road and departed.

Sunday 7 May

With nothing hanging on the result, with Meridian TV lashing out on an OB Unit for live coverage from Elm Park, my deciding not to travel to Reading for Charlton's last game didn't cost me much lost sleep. By two o'clock I felt completely vindicated. The sun was shining with benign strength as the Nelson family gently bicycled their way to a nearby pub lunch.

'Mount up, gang.'

With kick-off fast approaching, I at least felt sufficient solidarity with my Charlton comrades to want to cheer on their efforts on the end of my tube.

Macho man, I brought up the rear of our six-person caravan. I thus had a grandstand view of Carly tumbling from her bike. It seemed incredibly innocuous as, picking herself up, she calmly announced that she had broken her arm. Given the histrionics the slightest graze will provoke in her – like father, like daughter, I have to confess – her magnificent restraint lulled me into a sense of curiously false security. It lasted only a second. A single glance at the sickeningly unnatural angle of her left arm made it clear to both Carole and me it was going to take a lot to set things to rights.

Finding paternal panic a miraculous healer of trivial ankle problems, I sprinted back to the pub and its telephone. I had the easy role. Carly had to wait an excruciating twenty minutes for the ambulance to arrive. Then it was that drawn-out waiting game they always leave out of the Casualty Ward soaps. It was not until seven hours later, and after an operation to reset both ulna and radius, that I finally quitted the hospital for home, minus both daughter and wife.

So would it have made a difference? Would it, in hindsight, have made a difference if I had obeyed my professional instincts (you really ought to be there) and gone to the game? That's the trouble with decisions. You make them and they don't seem to have any relevance to most of what happens next. That, of course, goes a long way to explaining why football is so popular.

Monday 8 May

Given the traumas, literal and otherwise of yesterday, it's scarcely surprising that it was not until mid-morning today – while at the hospital waiting for Carly's release form to be issued – that I learned how Charlton got on yesterday. They had lost 1–2. That scarcely came as a surprise, either. Reading, after all, have finished the season in second place. Last year this would have automatically served to win them their second successive promotion. This year, however, with the Premiership downsizing itself, they will have to battle through the play-off system.

What specifically caught my eye was the team Curbs and Gritty had sent out at Elm Park and the name of the man scoring our last goal of the campaign. The side's average age was just twenty-two. Centre back Dean Chandler marked his debut with the goal and his 'Face of Shame' sidekick Lee Bowyer also played.

I'm pleased for both lads. Playing will have gone a long way to settling them down in the right groove after the six-week ban that followed on their brush with marijuana and with the authorities. Six weeks? Chris Armstrong drew only a four-week ban for his offence. There would seem to be some inconsistency in the, er, speed with which the Drug Squad people go about their re-testing procedures. Charlton's senior administrative staff, I know, became increasingly exasperated by the uninformative wall of officialdom that confronted them at the time of the unhappy incident and during the 'Valley Two's' subsequent 'probation' period. It was a fitting move, I believe, to rehabilitate the lads so emphatically the moment the wall was dismantled.

Tuesday 9 May

A twenty-four-hour extension in several Nelson households to the VE-Day anniversary celebrations. The Blues have ensured themselves Premiership status for another year with a somewhat fortuitous – but who's counting? – win over Ipswich.

Wednesday 10 May

For every great escaper there's a loser. Failure in football always exacts its toll. The price is now being paid as the end-of-season clear-outs begin. Swindon and Bristol City, both relegated more ignominiously than not, have between them released a dozen players on 'frees'. Seven more, though still under contract, have been put up for sale. That's just two clubs. The switchboard at PFA headquarters is about to be swamped with calls from distressed players. Manchester postmen will be building up their biceps on bulging sacks of pink forms.

There promises to be virtually a Cup final atmosphere at both Anfield and Upton Park this coming Sunday. The Premiership race is going to go the full distance. This evening United scraped past a distinctly unlucky Southampton 2–1. With eight minutes to go Blackburn were on track to regain the premier league title they last captured a mere eighty-one years ago. Then there was an incident in the Southampton penalty area which added up to more in the referee's eyes than it did in those of most other observers. Denis Irwin did the match-winning business from the spot. All to play for now. Ex-king Kenny must return to the ground where his managerial nerve cracked and try to mastermind the victory that will regain him his crown.

The last minute of extra time in the European Cup-Winners' final between Arsenal and Real Tharagotha (as the commentators insisted we come to know and love them as) produced unquestionably the most extraordinary goal senior football has seen in living memory. David Seaman, hero of the semi-final shoot-out, was a couple of yards off his line. The ball at his feet, Nayim was a couple of yards in from the touchline. And at least forty-five yards from goal. Another penalty shoot-out was seconds away as Nayim looked up and sussed the options. Nothing to lose, so go for it – he unleashed a full-bore mortar shell of a shot high into the floodlit sky. Seaman didn't do anything *that* wrong. But, descending from the steepest of angles, the net-seeking missile of a ball was under the bar before he could get his hand to it. He was understandably distraught. It was bad enough for Arsenal to lose 1–2 at the very death. But for the instrument of their despatch to be a former Spur was grief indeed.

Friday 12 May

The last official training day. With all due mock seriousness the morning got off to a suitably fun start. The vast rag-bag embarrassment, the vast rag bag of personal misdemeanours, cock-ups and foot-in-mouthery which their perpetrators had been hoping would rest in perpetual oblivion were held up to renewed scrutiny in the merciless light of day. At stake was nothing less than the prestigious 'Yellow Jersey of the Season' award. The winner will hold the coveted garment until next season's resumption of hostilities.

Among those shortlisted for the dodgy honour were Scott McGleish for a series of lacklustre displays in training; Keith Jones for his piggy-in-the-middle tantrum; Shaun Newton for both short- and long-range geographical dyslexia (he thinks Brescia is in Spain; he's been in three car shunts this season); and training ground cook Jeanette. This arraignment led immediately to a plea for mitigation. The clapped-out kitchen gear she was stuck with, she maintained, gave her no chance of trotting out her cordon bleu repertoire. Spontaneous applause was drawn from the management by this defence and all charges were at once dropped.

There could be, however, only one winner. By concerted agreement, our kit man, Ron Thomas, was scrunched into the winner's frame. The indictment? That whether the team won, lost or drew, come rain or come shine, his moaning was unremitting. But to understand all is to forgive all. As Ron duly donned 'The Shirt' his face split from ear to ear in an amazing grin. Of sorts. Not the slightest trace of calcium deposit was visible in top or bottom gum. It was a sight to behold. Once.

All teeth happily still present and correct, I was able to indulge in some uninhibited smiling of my own later in the day. My being rested from formal training has proved just what the doctor ordered for my ankle. Recovery is so far advanced that I comfortably joined in an (admittedly easy) five-a-side with no backlash in the form of nagging aches and pains. My timing for once was perfect. Put that down to the relaxation and relief. Continuing problems could well have sentenced me to the summertime blues of a weekly visit to the training ground for further assessment. Now, though, I'm not only off that hook, I can be sure of going into the next pre-season in trouble-free nick.

Sunday 14 May

'Super Sunday'. For once Sky Television's hyping seemed justified. Unlike so many of the efforts on their movie channel, the climax to the Premiership season could not have been better scripted: victory for Blackburn at Anfield and the title would be theirs. Anything less and, courtesy of a win at Upton Park, United would retain their crown for the third successive season. The satellite supremos must have been hugging their offshore wallets in glee. They could guarantee that, with Sky 1 showing live action from Anfield and Sky 2 at West Ham, remote controls would be pulling up with cramp all over the country.

With minutes to go, identical scorelines of 1–1 were stretching nerves close to breaking point. There must have been thousands unable to bring themselves to watch. If so, what they missed was Andy Cole missing. The £7 million marksman showed that he was human and not bionic. Another day, another game, he would have been the man. But today was today. United failed to grab a second and it was the new Kop that erupted in euphoria. By default – a sardonic and apt final comment on the essentially mediocre level of English football at present – Blackburn were champions.

After a wait of eighty-one years for a title, Jack Walker's money has at last bought success. Good luck to the man, anyway. He's lived to see his dream fulfilled and nobody will want to put a price on the happiness, the boost to civic morale that he's thereby brought to his home town.

Several other football communities ended the day confronted by the emotional highs and lows that football so evenhandedly dispenses. Deep despair stalked the streets of central South London tonight as Newcastle clipped the Eagles' wings and Crystal Palace, finishing in the last four of all the competitions they entered this season, were relegated.

Birkenhead, meanwhile, will seem as desolate as its once teeming shipyards. Despite (or because of) it being their third consecutive crack at the play-offs in a row, Tranmere, usually so impregnable at fortress Prenton, got the jitters. They were trounced there 1–3 by Reading, who have refused all season to listen to those saying that the bubble of their flukey run was going to burst any minute.

In the other divisional play-off game, Wolves beat my tip for the top, Bolton, 2–1. With all to play for in the return leg at Burnden Park in four days time, we can put all our money on there being a Royals versus Wanderers clash at Wembley. But which Wanderers?

Monday 15 May

One of football's gentlemen, a man who, it has to be said, has behaved under extreme pressure with great dignity, today received a recompense for his conduct that surprised no one. He lost his job. As had been universally predicted, Alan Smith has left Selhurst Park by 'mutual consent'. For which read 'mutual discontent'.

Further word is that, with Alan's going, several of the Eagles' current playing staff will also be looking to sever themselves from their palatial surroundings.

Throughout the four top English leagues no less than fifty-two clubs, well over half, have orchestrated/suffered a managerial change in the course of the past season. In the Premiership, at eleven out of twenty-two, the all-change count is exactly half – although strong rumours suggest two more dismissals, at least are in the waste-pipeline. In some instances, of course, as an incumbent manager has upped sticks of his own accord, boards have had their hands forced. But in the majority of instances it has been the board, or, more particularly, perhaps, the Chairman, who has been the initiators of the musical chairs game. Chopping and changing the 'boss' who is not really the boss has become perhaps the biggest commonplace in soccer. A wretched one. Almost invariably the move is a last toss of the dice by desperate men.

And what is the most obvious short-term stroke that at one bound will free clubs of their worries? The simplistic one. Whether through resignation, mutual consent or a boot up the bum, the manager gets the bullet.

There's always a compensation fee to be paid, of course, not to mention the new man's terms. But that's the price you have to pay for, 'hopefully', your new success. After all, it's going to work, isn't it? It *must*. It's bound to . . .

No, it isn't and, short term, certainly, it won't.

All right. These pages have borne witness to the miracle cures of two mid-season saviours, Joe Royle and Mel Machin. But they achieve their prominence through being shining exceptions proving the rule. Ron Atkinson and Brian Little survived by the skin of their teeth and, below them in the Premiership, the other three clubs relegated with Palace all swapped managers in mid-season. In Division One Swindon, Bristol City and Notts County all dropped their pilots when the going got tough. And all to no avail. County at the very bottom of the league had – unbelievably – three different names on the manager's door before their campaign was over. More than ever these days, the *prima facie* evidence has to be that, viewed as a short-term expedient, changing a manager, especially in mid-stream, is going to exacerbate your problems rather than solve them.

One answer to this unedifying merry-go-round might be to set in concrete the stipulation that every manager is offered a contract of a full year's employment. Hiring as well as firing might then be a lot less from the hip.

Tuesday 16 May

A postscript to yesterday's sermon. Brian Horton's managerial spell at Maine Road is over.

All eyes are now turned towards Sheffield Wednesday as the count continues.

Wednesday 17 May

The car's mileage is not far off 125k as I drive in for a report in to report out day. Training is a no-go area but our weights all have to be clocked. Comparisons can thus be made on our return from our holidays and, should the comparisons prove odious, fines will be levied. The going rate for vacational over-indulgence has been set at £10 per extra pound. The weight of all flesh having been itemised, it fell to Steve Gritt to wrap up the season formally. In a (necessarily) short speech he thanked us for our efforts, bade a (genuinely) fond farewell to those leaving us and confirmed the joyful tidings that, if God spares, we shall be meeting again at the outset of our pre-season on Monday 10 July.

There was also a somewhat less formal item of business to take care of. Thanks to Keith Peacock's Reserves, a celebratory drink was in order. It wasn't *the* drink they'd worked so hard for all season. Last night, alas, at the very last hurdle, they tripped and fell from first position. Needing just to draw against Spurs to clinch the Combination title, they lost and so finished third behind Tottenham and Southampton. But it was still a very gallant performance. Charlton were the only Endsleigh side to figure in a top six otherwise made up of Premiership second-stringers.

Some personal congratulations were in order as well. No less than six of our number will be losing their single status (though little else) in the course of our summer break. They may return to training at the same weight they registered today, but they'll be carrying the invisible burden of new responsibilities.

Mickey Bennett has more than his impending wedding to look forward to. Recently released on a 'free', he's promptly turned around to jump over the training ground fence and sign for Millwall. He'll do very well there. As will Scott McGleish at Peterborough, his new club. His year with Charlton has stabilised him as a full-time pro. Finally, as for once it just gets better and better, Peter Garland obviously impressed Wycombe during his loan period. They have now asked him to tie the knot more permanently.

For the other 'freebies', Macca and Pards, the future isn't so immediately defined. But, especially after a glass or two, their optimism is high. They're well aware that, in the case of players earning higher wages, interested clubs, surprise, surprise, hold back until the end of July. It's then, as Charlton stop paying them, that the overtures will begin.

The long day progressed and, as drinks were drunk, passed through a predictable series of distinct phases. After the jokes, grievances started to be aired. Criticisms began to be voiced by the not inconsiderable number who felt they had been hard done by in the course of the season. Alcohol can be a great tongue loosener for those harbouring hitherto pent-up emotions. Now we might have been any group of employees in any occupation anywhere in the world. The workers in our world were voicing their common discontent that life hadn't turned out to be what they'd been promised by their hopes. Who to blame? The bosses, naturally. Certainly not down to us, mate.

Another drink and we were through the grievance and maudlin barriers into the feel-good area. Troubles? What troubles? Onwards and – cheers! – upwards.

The respective squads of Reading and Bolton won't yet have reached our level of tipsy carefreeness. Thanks to a brace of goals from John McGinlay who demonstrated that he's one of the best strikers of a ball in the division, Bolton squeaked past Wolves in extra time while the Royals kept Tranmere at a two-goal deficit arm's length. Neither they nor their fans can yet be in the mood to paint the town white or blue. Both teams have got so near. They're both so far away. As don't I just know.

Four years ago, in the first leg of the initial play off encounter, Brighton clocked up a handsomely useful 4–1 lead over Millwall. I didn't feature in that game, but in a very in-out season with the Seagulls I had played a clearly positive part in the final run-in clinching our play-off position. We now had to hold out for ninety daunting minutes at the Old Den. Owing to an almost endless injury list and the tea-lady pulling her hamstring on the morning of the match, I did get to play in this second leg. Anxious and intimidating are understatements as descriptions of the evening, but we didn't buckle enough to surrender our lead. We were through to Wembley and before we gritted our teeth for the final assault on the summit, drinks were briefly in order. On the rebound from the tension they'd just endured, the lads went wild. In marked contrast to my own behaviour.

I knew exactly why I remained subdued. I was thirty. A lifetime's ambition to play at Wembley was now within touching distance. No, not really. True I'd scored three goals in that last-gasp push to the play-offs, but for most of the season I'd been an outcast, consistently passed over by the manager whose plans I no longer featured in. I'd become a bit player.

There were ten days between our qualifying and the decider. With the prospect of appearing at Wembley working its miracle cure, there was ample time for Brighton's lame to find they'd been made whole. With every day that passed, my own chances of making the team were increasingly marginalised. I needed a miracle of my own.

All the same, come the weekend of the game, mine was one of the sixteen names selected for travelling to the Royal Lancaster Hotel. My hopes rose fractionally. With all hands reporting fit, there was no way I'd make the starting line-up. But the subs' bench? *Just* possibly. It was Sunday and all of us were still in the dark as to Barry Lloyd's selection.

It was in this state of collective uncertainty that, sporting our all new 'play-off special' tracksuit, we climbed aboard our coach. Fans cheered and waved all along our route. My pulse began to quicken. That most famous of stadium approaches, Wembley Way, was a moving river of blue and white scarves, flags and faces. Reality started to blur. I was living in a dream but it was not a dream. It was happening. It must be real because we were entering the stadium and I'd never imagined this bit before.

The bus halted. We descended into the cavernous sanctuary of the vast players' tunnel. We might well, indeed, have been in a cathedral. We were suddenly talking in whispers or not at all.

Now dark was turning to light. Our voices went back to normal. Trying to appear as cool as if we did this every day of our working lives, we were out strolling on the pitch itself. Yes, its surface was everything we'd always been led to believe. People were cheering us. We were waving back to friends and relations. Only one and a half hours to go now. Still no teamsheet.

We had drawn the home team changing room. I was thus in the very place Bobby and his boys had returned to, sobbing and whooping in triumph in 1966.

Only an hour and a quarter to kick-off now. Still no announcement. Nerves were getting to me. No bad thing. If chosen, I could put them to use. Right now, though, I needed the loo.

What followed had never remotely featured in my Wembley day dreams. As I turned to leave the toilet, Barry Lloyd was standing there waiting for me. He gave me a look.

'You're not involved,' he said.

Never was a setting better chosen for administering a kick in the guts. Failing access to a sewer, what more unromantic place in which to hear the most disappointing words ever delivered to me in the course of my long footballing career?

'Fair enough,' I nodded. Any third, unwitting observer would have thought two colleagues had merely agreed who was going to have the parking slot nearest the door. But that wasn't it at all.

That my Wembley fantasy had been made to end in a toilet was no accident. It was one of those moments where we both knew that he knew that I knew that he knew. In our early days at Brighton, Lloydie and I had enjoyed some very good times together. But such togetherness had long since worn thin. He had been convinced that, at the start of this same season, I'd crossed him over the bonus issue. In my heart of hearts I hadn't expected to play and the betting man in me would have laid big money on my being left out. But I felt I'd done Brighton enough service over the years not to deserve having my nose rubbed in it in that way in that setting. What small residue of respect and affection I had for Barry Lloyd evaporated then and there. Permanently.

To this day I'm glad that none of this came out on the spot; that I didn't react in any outward way. I held my head high as I walked away, as I think over the past dozen years I'd earned the right to. I made a point of smiling as I went round the changing room shaking the hands of the players who would be running out to the roar of the crowd and wishing them the very best.

Then I had to get out. I had to get some air. I was feeling physically sick. It must have been the effect of holding in all that anger.

Oh yes, the game. Brighton lost 1–3. The winners were Notts County, who earlier that season had tried to sign me. Just wasn't my day, was it?

In one regard his little set piece with me did give Barry Lloyd a result. He succeeded in dropping a veil between Wembley and the way I now look at the stadium. The tarnish is faint but it's there. The place no longer holds that magical aura for me anymore. That was the last time I was there. It's not just that I haven't since had the opportunity to go back. I don't want to.

Not that I'm such a fool to myself to concede wholesale victory to Barry Lloyd, to let the nasty passage between us be the cause of

309

my throwing in the towel on football. One quality a journeyman player surviving at my level has developed, you may be sure, is enough strength of character to be able to pick himself up and keep on keeping on whenever life dumps on him. The logic of the game compels it. If you can't lose, you can't win. If there's no rough, there can't be any smooth. The trick is to realise that 'winning' and 'losing' are terms paling into insignificance beside remaining true to the standards you believe in.

If that sounds pretentious, how about 'don't get sore, get even'. Not in a cheap way but in a broader sense. A year later, I wore my 'Brighton and Hove Albion at Wembley' tracksuit while attending the FA Full Coaching course. Every time I glanced at it, my motivation was renewed and I gained my full badge at the first attempt.

These days I only very occasionally cast eyes on the tracksuit. It lies crumpled and faded at the bottom of the wardrobe. Like my Wembley hopes, you'll quickly say. But the badge isn't on it, remember. That badge may not be a medal, but it's what you might consider an honourable enough substitute. And I can wear it with pride anywhere I like.

Friday 19 May

As it was in the beginning . . . Never having done it before until a year ago, I'm once again 30,000 feet above the Atlantic on a plane heading westwards. A wheel seems to have come full circle.

But there is irritation in my mind. Although I know exactly how it came about, I still can't believe I managed to book us on a flight to Baltimore the very day before my team will be running out at Wembley. Or any two teams. Such was Everton's form when I made the reservation, I hardly expected them to make it all the way to the final of the FA Cup. But that wasn't the reason for my *faux pas*. I booked for Baltimore safe in the knowledge that the final is always played the week after the last league game.

Fool! I should have remembered that the Premiership fixture list concludes an isolated week after the Endsleigh League's – with a consequent knock-on effect upon the Wembley date. I wonder

310

how long it will be before the Cup final is punted on to 4.00 on a Sunday afternoon or, let's be realistic about viewing potential, gentlemen, 8.00 Monday evening.

My misery is compounded by the fact that, such was the lasting influence of the World Cup being staged in America last summer that I'm not even sure the game is being beamed live to the States by satellite. If that is the case I'm going to have to phone home to learn whether my prejudiced prediction that Everton can do again to Man U at Wembley what they did at Goodison is accurate.

The same applies for the play-off finals. The last round of the high-powered version of musical chairs that will establish whether Reading or Bolton are going to be stuck with playing Charlton next year will be going on while the Nelsons are trying to squeeze their 'official' family holiday in between the old man's work load.

As before, engrossed in the in-flight movie, Carole, Chris and the well-plastered Carly are sitting in the seats alongside me. For me this trip has to be primarily about scouting the locations for the coaching clinics next month, checking the facilities, and tying down all the final details. But for Carole and the kids it's a case of the Baltimore harbour front, Washington, Mount Vernon, the Orioles and all those malls with their groovy sports shoes. The dates of the actual coaching next month will butt right up against my renewed need – as it's turned out – to report back for pre-season training. For the family as a whole it's a case of grabbing a holiday while we can.

The wheel really has turned full circle. Only there's little sense of revolution. Damn all seems to have changed. Charlton, for instance, spent the last third of their season treading water to end up, at fifteenth, in a league position three places worse off than last year's. In this under-achievement we were typical of eighty per cent of the Premiership and Endsleigh League sides. No final triumph or disaster but instead a season that was much of a muchness.

'Must do better' is easily said. But how? Charlton are probably in slightly better shape than most, but the struggle to complete construction of the entirely new ground has meant that balancing the books and putting together a side capable of winning promotion are pulling in opposite directions. Let alone the initial transfer fee, we can't even afford the salaries of average Premiership players. Delving into the lower divisions is an enormous tactical and financial risk. So, like most of the clubs in Division One, we largely make do. In our case a ray or two of hope comes from the Reserves and the Youth Team. There is some talent there. Whether it's regarded as a firm foundation for the future or as an imminently realisable asset is an open question.

In terms of the performances of this year's squad, Whytie has every reason to feel proud of his year's work. Twenty-one goals in his first full season leading the line is a major achievement. Richard Rufus' form, once he'd been introduced into the team, immediately had everyone wondering why it had taken so long to give him his place; Stuart Balmer, by the season's end, had used his feet to do the talking and negotiate a series of career road blocks that he ought never to have been faced with. For the rest of us, well, let's just say it was business as usual.

For me, the season ended with more lows than otherwise. It started well, with my snapping up nine goals in pretty short order, but then turned bad with pretty much as many injuries. I've come out the far end another year older and – what else is new? – not much wiser. It's an indictment, though, of the team as a whole, that, starting only roughly half the matches we played, I still, with that nine, ended the season as our second highest goal scorer.

For me, too, nothing so very much has changed. I thought, last summer, that I was going into my final season. Now it's 'take two' on that scenario all over again and the facts of life confronting me and the Nelson family are almost identical to those of a year ago. Once again it's not just the plane that's up in the air.

This time around, though, I sense that the question marks are a little less emphatic. Or, at least, that I'm that much more relaxed about the answers. For all its ups and downs, my form last year was largely first-team level. Taking me on past thirty-five – an age threshold all professional footballers are delighted to achieve – my new one-year contract overlaps the start of my pension. That will give me something of a cushion, small but far more comfortable than the World Cup one I bought a year ago.

It's also genuinely reassuring to know that I've now got that Marketing Diploma under my belt. I've no absolutely definite idea, at present, as to how I'll put it to work but it's there and a credential that can't be all bad.

What I do very definitely have ahead of me is the coaching opportunity, the details of which I'm now flying to Baltimore to finalise. This year it's largely by way of being a pilot study, but it may develop into something more. Whatever unknowns the future holds, the credit side of the ledger has a few more entries than a year ago.

This past twelve months has also seen the strange phenomenon of this diary. It now runs to several hundred sheets of paper covered in my iffy scrawl, and, at the very least, I've brought it to an end. I've finished the marathon and, whatever my time, feel stronger for discovering that I could.

As events have unwound, it has not been a vintage year to record. It's been a mean, low year. The national game has plainly come far too close to modelling its business ethics on the national propensity to sleaze. Huge 'bung' questions hang in the air unresolved. Whatever the various outcomes, the image of soccer is going to get worse before it gets better. An essential step towards its improvement has to be the licensing of agents under very strict regulations. To do so will be to excise the source of much murky temptation.

The actual on-the-field game has to get better immediately. The charge of the heavy brigade has to be halted. Their actions inject hate into the game. Even more damagingly, as skill goes by the board and cynical, 'professional' fouling covers up inadequacy, the basic quality of English football is eroded. We aren't that good anymore. Most English and Scottish clubs in Europe made fools of themselves this year against opponents who were more versatile, imaginative and, on an individual basis, more technically gifted. In a word, classier. English football is going downhill, at present to the almost universal cry of: 'get it bloody in there!'

313

Yet, for all this gloomy analysis, I retain total confidence in the long-term future of what, because it is so simple in concept and so difficult to execute, is, indeed, 'the beautiful game' – a game unsurpassed in its ability to captivate.

On the one hand there is my son strutting his stuff on our best carpet in his first-ever kit and giving it his novice's everything among all those other Sunday morning 'tinies' gleefully and tearfully setting out to imitate and, one day, succeed their heroes.

And then you have an old warhorse like me. What has kept me coming back for more? It's so hard to put into words because, again, it is so simple. It's just, I suppose, that every now and then in a game of football, a goal is scored which, the moment the ball is in the net, takes on a sense of utter inevitability. And with the inevitability, beauty.

Millions of words, thousands of purple paragraphs have been written about how football is a streamlined version of life – life with all the boring bits taken out, though this is hardly true of most of the games I've played in. But every now and then I've been present when one player or group of players has out-performed, out-witted another group through just the right combination of technique, courage, vision and fitness. When that happens I simply feel glad. And, amazingly, whenever it happens it's always like the first time. The pleasure is never diminished by repetition. A delighted surprise always renews it.

Once, by the very meanest count, I was at the very heart of such a moment. What I experienced then unquestionably presented me with an instant, irreversible personal decision. As long as I can still pull on a pair of boots, I'm going to be *involved* kicking a football around somewhere.

It *is* a beautiful game.

Roll on July.